Escape to Prison

The publisher gratefully acknowledges the generous support of the General Endowment Fund of the University of California Press Foundation.

Escape to Prison

PENAL TOURISM AND THE PULL
OF PUNISHMENT

Michael Welch

UNIVERSITY OF CALIFORNIA PRESS

University of California Press, one of the most distinguished university presses in the United States, enriches lives around the world by advancing scholarship in the humanities, social sciences, and natural sciences. Its activities are supported by the UC Press Foundation and by philanthropic contributions from individuals and institutions. For more information, visit www.ucpress.edu.

University of California Press
Oakland, California

Library of Congress Cataloging-in-Publication Data

Welch, Michael, 1960– author.
  Escape to prison : penal tourism and the pull of punishment / Michael Welch.
    pages cm
  Includes bibliographical references and index.
  ISBN 978-0-520-28615-3 (cloth)
  ISBN 978-0-520-28616-0 (pbk. : alk. paper)
  ISBN 978-0-520-96150-0 (ebook)
  1. Prisons—Museums. 2. Dark tourism. 3. Correctional institutions—History. 4. Historical museums. I. Title.
  G156.5.d37w45 2015
  365.074—dc23
                                                    2014038704

Manufactured in the United States of America

24   23   22   21   20   19   18   17   16   15
10   9   8   7   6   5   4   3   2   1

To Madiba
(Nelson Mandela)
1918–2013

CONTENTS

ILLUSTRATIONS

PREFACE

The journey begins in Argentina, where Maximo Sozzo asked me to serve as a visiting professor in 2008 (at Universidad Nacional del Litoral, Santa Fe). While staying in the San Telmo neighborhood of Buenos Aires, Melissa Macuare and I paged through a well-worn copy of *Lonely Planet*. We noticed an entry for a nearby prison museum. As criminologists, we did not hesitate to find it. The museum spoke to the smooth nuances of penology, including the role of religion, work, and science in the transformation of prisoners. The following year we returned to Argentina, thanks to another invitation from Maximo. It seemed only natural to revisit the prison museum, document its assorted collection, and analyze its thick narrative. Borrowing ideas from Michel Foucault and Emile Durkheim, the article was published in *Theoretical Criminology*.

In 2010, the University of Sydney offered me a visiting professorship to study the controversy over the detention of the "boat people." Due to the sobering subject of human rights abuses, I frequently sought refuge in the city's museums. Again, *Lonely Planet* directed me to the Hyde Park Barracks. With camera in hand, I captured the history of English and Irish convicts banished to the antipodes. While in Melbourne, I explored the Melbourne Gaol, which also received a good review in *Lonely Planet*. Comparing the tours at the Hyde Park Barracks, the Melbourne Gaol, and the Argentine Penitentiary Museum, another article emerged—this time in *Punishment & Society*. The next year brought me to London to work on another project on the detention of asylum seekers. In my spare time, I took my growing interest in penal tourism (and *Lonely Planet*) to the Clink prison museum. The next logical step was to prepare a third in a series of articles: "Penal Tourism and a Tale of Four Cities: Reflecting on the Museum Effect in London, Sydney, Melbourne, and Buenos Aires" (in *Criminology & Criminal Justice*).

My travel itinerary for 2012 took me first to Seoul, South Korea, where one of my books *(Scapegoats of September 11th)* was translated into Korean. That "book tour" extended to Hong Kong, where I lectured at the University of Hong Kong. You guessed it. *Lonely Planet* listed prison museums in both cities. I returned home with more memories and more photographs. Later that year, I visited South Africa to give a talk at the University of Cape Town. While Robben Island was already high on my list of places to visit, *Lonely Planet* also pointed out another prison museum in Johannesburg. With eight former prisons now in my research dossier, I decided to expand what started as a past time—then a side project—into a full-blown book. Realizing that ten is a psychologically satisfying number, I added two more usual suspects—Alcatraz and Eastern State Penitentiary (in Philadelphia). Along the way, I deepened my appreciation for Foucault and Durkheim as their insights paved the way for some theoretical exploration into the history of incarceration. In the chapters to follow, I share my thoughts and observations on this intriguing phenomenon—penal tourism. But first, I should acknowledge the many people who provided me with much needed help and guidance.

In Buenos Aires, warm gratitude is extended to Melissa Macuare (for her companionship and fancy camera work), Maximo Sozzo, Richard Salvatore, Horacio Benegas, and Sheila Recino. For the Australian portion of the research, I am grateful to the University of Sydney, Faculty of Law, Institute of Criminology. Several colleagues there made my stay worthwhile, including Dean Gillian Triggs, Pat O'Malley, Gail Mason, Louisa Di Bartolomeo, and Murray Lee. Linda Weber (at State University of New York, Utica) invited me to deliver a presentation on prison museums in Argentina and Australia; that lecture prompted me to reformulate some of my early thoughts on comparative work. In Seoul, I appreciate the diligence of my editor, Kim Jung Yun, at Galmuri Publishing as well as my translator Mr. (Jinwoo) Park. Suk-woo Jung and Kyung-mok Park (at the Seodaemun Prison History Hall) were extremely courteous. Many thanks also to Maggy Lee and Michael Adorjan at the University of Hong Kong for their hospitality. At Constitution Hill in Johannesburg, Lerato Sefume and Lorraine Majola provided excellent tours and commentary. Gail Super, Clifford Shearing, and Theresa Hume at the University of Cape Town made arrangements for an enjoyable roundtable on prison museums. Likewise, I received enormous support and cooperation from the wonderful people at Robben Island: Sibongiseni Mkhize, Boniswa Kondile, Richard Whiting, Wendy Duma, and Sipho

Msomi (political prisoner, 1984–89). Altogether they brought me into the orbit of Nelson Mandela to whom this book is dedicated.

For 2014, my academic home was the London School of Economics, Department of Social Policy, Mannheim Centre for Criminology. Tim Newburn, David Lewis, Mike Shiner, Damian Roberts, Debra Ogden, and Conor Gearty (Department of Law) are mentioned for their generosity and support. Also in London, Kevin Coyne deserves special mentioning. In the San Francisco Bay area, my friends Jonathan Simon, Dario Melossi, and Alessandro De Giorgi took time to meet and encourage me to pursue this project. Rutgers University, for decades, has contributed to my steady scholarly output, especially through its sabbatical program. I am grateful to Dean Fran Mascia-Lees, Lennox Hinds, Sarah Laboy-Almodovar, Matthew Bellof, and my many colleagues in the Program of Criminal Justice. Students enrolled in my *Prisons & Prisoners* and *Torture & Human Rights* courses are commended for sitting through the seemingly endless supply of slide shows on prison museums. Their attention—and good humor—served as additional motivation to complete this work. At the University of California Press, Maura Roessner, Jack Young, Robert Demke, and Dore Brown provided excellent guidance throughout the publishing process. The manuscript was greatly improved by insightful comments by all four anonymous reviewers (thanks to whoever you are).

In my other cultural world, I am grateful to musicians Andy Burton, Steve Holley, Paul Page, and engineer extraordinaire Wayne Dorell for their amazing contributions to The Retroliners. Finally, cheers to the Welch clan who often wonder aloud "where in the world is Michael?"

M.W.
London, 2014

ONE

_____

Penal Tourism

The resurrection of former prisons as museums has caught the attention of tourists along with scholars interested in studying that particular pastime (Ross, 2012; Strange and Kempa, 2003; Welch, 2012a, 2013; Welch and Macuare, 2011; Wilson, 2008a). Unsurprisingly, due to their grim subject matter, prison museums tend to invert the "Disney" experience, becoming the antithesis of "the happiest place on earth" (Williams, 2007: 99). With that realization, it is fitting to situate penal tourism within a larger phenomenon known as dark tourism, in which people gravitate to sites associated with war, genocide, and other tragic events for purposes of remembrance, education, or even entertainment (Lennon and Foley, 2010; Rojek, 1993; Stone and Sharpley, 2008). In the realm of punishment, dark tourism has been examined from the standpoint of penal spectatorship involving bystanders who gaze at the spectacle of pain and suffering. Michelle Brown, in her insightful book *The Culture of Punishment: Prison, Society, and Spectacle,* explains that museum goers are subjected to various techniques of positioning intended to establish certain perspectives and perceptions (see Welch, 2010a). For instance, by keeping penal spectators at a safe social distance from the realities of torture and other forms of brutality, interest in dark tourism is carefully regulated (Walby and Piche, 2011; see Piche and Walby, 2010; Huey, 2011).

Consider a visit to the Clink prison museum in London, a cramped, dingy, and dimly lit cellar that from 1144 until 1780 served as a dungeon for debtors as well as religious and political dissenters (see figure 1). The brochure advertising the Clink promotes the museum as offering "gruesome stories of prisoners" and a "hands-on torture chamber," thereby inviting visitors to become participants. Toward that end, a series of subterranean galleries are

FIGURE 1. The Clink Prison Museum (London). Entry includes a free photograph. © retrowelch 2014

devoted to the virtual infliction of pain whereby penal spectators have safe contact with the various tools of the torture trade, including the stocks, pillories, cat-o'-nine-tails, and the rack. Storyboards inform tourists about the rationale of certain devices. A sign explaining "The Manacles" reads: "One of the simplest forms of 'enhanced interrogation' was to leave a person alone, hanging in manacles for hours and hours, or days; lack of food and water, accompanied by the increasing strain on the arms, and the total solitude might well be enough to induce compliance." Curators are quick to point out that the manacles were used to evade the rule of law: "Since this treatment left no grievous marks, it was not legally classed as torture and could therefore be employed without a royal warrant; the only great risk was that the victim might go mad before confessing" (see Welch, 2009a, 2009b, 2011a).

The Clink's "hands-on torture chamber" also contains a key interactive component that invites tourists to "take the role of the other." For example, visitors can literally put themselves in the shoes of prisoners by trying on "The Boot." A placard located above a replica of "The Spanish Boot (or the Scottish Boot)" explains:

The Boot was an awful device used to crush the foot, the victim's foot would be placed in the boot, wood would then be packed in around the foot. The boot would be filled with either oil or water resulting in the swelling of the wood and crushing of the foot. The Boot would then have a fire built underneath it bringing the contents to a boil resulting in the victim's foot falling off.

Things to do:
1) Try putting the boot on your foot.
(We do advise the removal of your shoes)

That technique of interactive pedagogy is used frequently in the Clink's "hands-on torture chamber." Consider "The Collar" that "would be placed around the individuals neck, the collar is lead lined and contains a number of spikes." While inflicting excruciating pain, the spiked contraption would infect the victim with lead poisoning, resulting in death. Visitors are encouraged to think about such suffering:

Things to do:
1) Feel the weight of the collar and imagine what it would
have been like locked tight around your neck.
2) Imagine how the victim would be able to swallow with such a
tight item around their neck.

At the Clink, there is no shortage of "hands-on" experiences with torture instruments, which thereby reinforces a visceral effect. Similar "things to do" are extended to the ball and chain, thumbscrews, the chastity belt, and the chopping block ("put your head on the block and have your photo taken"). Fittingly, the tour concludes with the "Torture Chair," described as a device to gain confessions from prisoners. Once the body was fully strapped, the back of the chair would be raised and tilted forward, forcing the victim to "sit on the edge of their seat." From that position, the torturer could easily apply a number of tools, including the tongue pullers. The poster suggests "things to do":

1) Think what they might do to you once you're strapped in the chair.
2) Guess what tools they might use on you.

While seated in the torture chair, penal spectators complete their visit with a mildly amusing moment: that is, having a personal picture taken with the museum's camera. The instructions read: "After your photo has been taken a receipt will print from the box on the wall to your left . . . Simply log on to your photo via the website where you will be able to download a copy to your computer to keep. You will also have the opportunity to order a variety of special gifts." Therefore, a trip to the Clink does not remain in the past; through state-of-the-art technology—not to mention merchandising—tourists can keep a living memory that forever connects them with the *sited-ness* of the former prison: "I was there."

Though themes of cruelty are prevalent in penal tourism, not all prison museums risk becoming a "morbid theme park" (see Williams, 2007: 102). Certainly, there is always much more to the visit. In their critique, Lennon and Foley (2010) propose that dark tourism posits questions and doubts about modernity and its consequences. Likewise, the case studies contained in this book decipher the complex narratives told through prison museums, including claims to progress, rationality, technology, and science. Moreover, critical analysis reflects on the manner by which prison museums—as story-telling institutions in Buenos Aires, Cape Town, Hong Kong, Johannesburg, London, Melbourne, Philadelphia, San Francisco, Seoul, and Sydney—issue a historical tale about their host city with respect to punishment and social control. Of course, the persuasiveness of those stories depends largely on techniques of positioning and distancing as well as on the overall force of the museum effect. Setting the tone for our exploration, we turn to a brief overview of museum studies, particularly as that scholarly field informs penal tourism within a wider cultural sociology of punishment.

THE DYNAMICS OF PRISON MUSEUMS

A museum, according to Paul Williams, is "an institution devoted to the acquisition, conservation, study, exhibition, and educational interpretation of objects with scientific, historical, or artistic value" (2007: 8). Rather than remaining static repositories, museums are appreciated for being dynamic, a quality that has attracted an interdisciplinary field of scholars devoted to museum studies (Bennett, 1995; Crimp, 1993; Prior, 2002). Among the many areas of interest belonging to museum studies is the overarching impact that museums have on their visitors, culture, and society. That *museum effect* is produced by a complex interplay between objects, images, and space (Casey, 2003; Malraux, 1967). Such interaction entails a good deal of positioning whereby visitors are situated within the museum for the purpose of receiving a certain pedagogical lesson on the institution's collection. Unlike when students are seated in a lecture hall, museums relay their messages through loco-motion. Recognizing that visitors' experiences are realized through their physical movement, museums (as well as fairs and exhibitions) aspire to "regulate the performative aspects of their visitors' conduct. Overcoming mind/body dualities in treating their visitors as, essentially, 'minds on legs,' each, in its different way, is a place for 'organized walking' in which an intended message is communicated in the form of a (more or less) directed itinerary" (Bennett, 1995: 6).

A museum's use of "organized walking" circulates visitors around specific objects and images contained within a larger cultural space. Let us briefly touch on these features of the museum so as to understand better penal tourism and the museum effect. Museums facilitate their narratives by putting on display objects intended to catch the attention of visitors. Williams writes: "The force of 'the museum effect' . . . is the enlargement of consequence that comes from being reported, rescued, cleaned, numbered, researched, arranged, lit, and writ-ten about . . . [It] enables objects from the past to be valued in entirely new ways" (2007: 28). As objects become part of the collection,* they undergo a cultural transformation, passing from use-value (in their initial incarnation) to signify-ing-value (in their current incarnation). Curators tend to select objects based on one of three criteria. First, the object boasts signifying-value by being rare or revelatory. At the Argentine Penitentiary Museum in Buenos Aires, for instance, tourists have the opportunity to gaze at prisoner-made drug parapher-nalia (i.e., a bong) that represents not only a deviant social world but also a means of psycho-physiological escape from the pains of imprisonment. Second, an object may be selected for being typical and representative of a category. The lashing triangle exhibited at the Sydney Barracks is virtually indistinguishable from the ones in the museums in London, Melbourne, Hong Kong, and Johannesburg. Finally, a curator might choose an object due to its remnant-themed iconography: that is, for having belonged to a remarkable person or group. Penal spectators at the Melbourne Gaol can deepen their appreciation of Ned Kelly's legend by beholding his famous sash as well as his pistol, which was nicked by a constable's bullet during the notorious shoot-out.

Regardless of the criteria for selection, objects on display can be inter-preted as *semiophores*—items prized for their capacity to produce meaning

---

* Pomian (1990: 9) defines a collection as "a set of natural or artificial objects, kept tem-porarily or permanently out of economic circuit, afforded special protection in enclosed places adapted specifically for that purpose and put on display."

rather than for their usefulness (Pomian, 1990). With respect to dark tourism, some objects have a sinister appeal and are "insidiously arresting, particularly because we assume that they were actually used in terrible acts" (Williams, 2007: 31). Consider, for example, the Clink's display of the "Scavenger's Daughter"—an iron contraption that compressed the victim into a distorted posture so painful that it caused bleeding from the nose and ears. The device is accompanied by a storyboard with a disturbing illustration of person caught in its grip. Indeed, that picture speaks to another dimension of the museum effect, namely, the power of images.

Whereas images belong to the larger category of objects, at times they are regarded as interpretive illustrations that allow visitors to connect with the past (see Alpers, 1991; Carrabine, 2012; Lawrence, 2012). Photographs, as modern images, are especially significant in museums due to their power to captivate as well as their authority to verify history: "Hence, the museum is crucial not only in its ability to provide photographs with the expert technical verification that establishes their truth-value, but also with the cultural verification, wherein the institution's decision to collect and display the image establishes its cultural worth" (Williams, 2007: 53). At the prison museum in Buenos Aires, a photograph of Severino Di Giovanni entices curiosity. The infamous (debonair) anarchist is introduced to visitors in three photographs: a headshot, a group shot, and one with him standing next to the chair where moments later he was executed by a firing squad in 1931.

Museum studies have been faulted for neglecting the importance of space and spacial effect, in part because the field has descended from art history, which concentrates more on the meaning of artifacts than on the larger institutional significance (Bennett, 1995; Prior, 2002). Museums housed in former prisons, however, tend to avoid that drawback because of their unique architecture, enhancing a sense of both internal and external space. The Melbourne Gaol, modeled after Eastern State Penitentiary (Philadelphia) and Pentonville (London), stands conspicuously in the city's central district. Order is expressed through its sheer size, scale, and symmetrical design. Upon entering the institution, visitors find themselves positioned in a long corridor with rows of cells stacked on three levels. Without hesitation, visitors look directly up to the lantern ceiling that filters shafts of light into an otherwise gloomy interior.

One scholar keenly observes: "Architecture matters because it lasts, of course. It matters because it is big, and it shapes the landscape of our everyday lives. But beyond that, it also matters because, more than any other cultural form, it is a means of setting the historical record straight" (Sudjic, 2006: 23). Setting the record straight is an important dimension of penal tourism because visitors are positioned in ways that convince them of the overall authenticity of the institution. Usually, that is not a difficult task, since by being housed in a former penal institution, prison museums are rightfully judged to be authentic. Moreover, because some prison museums were sites of execution (of famous people), they are often regarded as hallowed ground. Accordingly, the historical accuracy is rarely disputed: "this building was used for this purpose; these people were killed here" (Williams, 2007: 80). Touring the Melbourne Gaol, visitors are presented with the tale of Ned Kelly: in that context, the story seems rather hagiographic. The Gaol's advertising logo appearing on the brochure and the sign at the footpath features a drawing of Kelly's iconic helmet worn to shield him from police bullets during the famous standoff. After his capture, Kelly was transported to the Melbourne Gaol, where he was hanged on November 11, 1880 (see Welch, 2011c, 2012b).*

In sum, the museum effect relies on the mutually reinforcing relationship between objects, images, and space—all of which are linked to a particular site. To be sure, a defining characteristic of prison museums is their *sited-ness*. Such venues become a major draw for tourists because the prison and its pedagogy are viewed as authentic.

GOVERNING THROUGH MUSEUMS

In his decidedly Foucaultian approach in *The Birth of the Museum,* Tony Bennett locates parallels between the genealogy of the museum and that of the prison. Early on, both institutions were typically located at the center of the city, where they stood as embodiments of power to "show and tell." By doing so, they aspired to incorporate people in the processes of the state (see Simon, 2007): "If the museum and the penitentiary thus represented the Janus face of power, there was none the less—at least symbolically—an economy of effort between them" (Bennett, 1995: 87). Bennett mentions the prominent English social reformer James Silk Buckingham, who in 1849 issued a report ambitiously titled *National Evils and Practical Remedies, with*

---

* As we shall discuss in chapter 9 on memorialization, fieldwork for a portion of this project took place at the Melbourne Gaol on November 12, 2010, a day after the 130th anniversary of Kelly's execution. A floral display commemorating Kelly was set at the gallows, the very site of his death.

the Plan for a Model Town. His project was aimed at extolling the virtues of civilized man to establish a "higher state of existence" for Victorian society (224). The model town would be clean and neatly organized around such architectural beauty as statues, colonnades, and fountains. Ideally, churches, libraries, and art galleries would eclipse rowdy pubs, brothels, and the vices they incite. As Bennett points out, that Victorian program demonstrates an interest in conceptualizing the tasks of government. With the head of a family as its paradigm, government would assume gentle responsibility over its citizenry so as to give it a proper upbringing through carefully designed cities that would not only enhance surveillance but deliver incentives to partake in quiet sophistication embodied in parks, public lectures, and museums (see Foucault, 1978): "If, in this way, culture is brought within the province of government, its conception is on par with other regions of government. The reform of the self—of the inner life—is just as much dependent on the provision of appropriate technologies for this purpose as is the achievement of desired ends in any other area of social administration" (Bennett, 1995: 18).

What museum scholars, like Bennett, are placing at the forefront of their analysis is the refinement of cultural power (see Casey, 2003; Crimp, 1993). By the late eighteenth and early nineteenth centuries, the public museum was taking on its modern form and becoming regarded as a useful means for governing the subordinate classes, which, in the view of the elites, were in need of cultural improvement with respect to their habits, morals, and manners. Still, the sweep of cultural power would facilitate the civilizing of the population as a whole (Buckingham, 1849). Using Foucaultian logic, Bennett contends that by regulating social behavior, cultural power endows individuals with new capacities for self-monitoring and moral restraint. In the 1880s, Sir Henry Cole promoted the use of the museums (as well as parks and chapels): "If you wish to vanquish Drunkenness and the Devil, make God's day of rest elevating and refining to the working man" (1884: 368; Goode, 1895).

Though festivals and theatrical performances subject their audiences to the display of power, the downside is that those events are merely temporal. Hence, whatever cultural meaning is achieved is intermittent and tends to fade with the passing of time. So as to produce a better economy of cultural power, the enlistment of institutions allows government to use such sites as museums to deliver an ongoing influence. That progressively modifying form of cultural power is believed to have a more sustained effect on visitors' thoughts, emotions, and conduct, hence making them "cultured." The birth of the museum was very much a technological project (Bennett, 1995). True, the symbolic display of power remains important; still, the museum relies on a set of exercises through which visitors are transformed into the active bearers of the self-improvement that culture was held to embody. Toward that aim, the cultural technology of museums had to be carefully arranged. In contrast to private collections of objects, art, and artifacts, the museum was designed to be a public space so that the emulation of civilized forms of behavior might be recognized and acquired, becoming diffused through the entire social body.

Museums were not simply intended to evoke surprise. As a space for representation, the collection was displayed in ways that promoted knowledge, understanding, and enlightenment. Rather than remaining stuck in the past, museums were organized in ways that became a "nursery of living thought" (Goode, 1895; Key, 1973: 86). Overall, the museum utilized the principles of observation and regulation so that the visitor's body was taken hold of and molded according to the new norms of social conduct (Bennett, 1995; see Crimp, 1993; Elias, 2005). As we shall discover in this book, cultural power plays a crucial role in prison museums. It is through the transmission of meaning that such sites educate, enlighten, and, in some instances, even civilize visitors.[*]

CULTURAL SOCIOLOGY OF PUNISHMENT

David Garland (2009) is correct in noting that over the past twenty-five years the cultural turn in criminology has become more mainline. While many scholars look to an emerging field of cultural studies for insights into crime and punishment (Ferrell, Hayward, Morrison, and Presdee, 2004; Hayward, 2012; Hayward and Young, 2004), others prefer to return to some of the "great masters" in sociology, most notably, Emile Durkheim. This recent resurgence of the cultural sociology of punishment, however, has sparked some debate on the theoretical merits of Durkheim, especially in opposition to Michel Foucault (Smith, 2008; see Garland, 2009). While not giving into the putative polarity between those luminaries of social thought, the purpose of this analysis is to synthesize the insights of power-based theories (Foucault)

---

[*] Between 2008 and 2012, fieldwork involved at least one site visit to each museum (and sometimes several). The entire building and its collection were photographed (compiling a data base of approximately four hundred photos per museum). Supplemental materials such as scholarly publications, brochures, and gift shop books were also consulted.

with semiotics (Durkheim). For example, at the Argentine Penitentiary Museum, we detect the construction of a narrative about the birth of a modern Argentine prison that reaches beyond a reliance on pure disciplinary technologies geared toward transforming convicts into productive workers. At a deeper cultural level, there are important socioreligious influences at play. That museum goes to great lengths to display religious architecture and artifacts in ways that reveal unique relations between the State and the local Catholic Church as they pursue their own vision of prisoner reform. To be discussed in greater detail, religion and governance—as tandem forces—spill over into matters of power, modernization, social control, and gender (see Welch and Macuare, 2011).

In his influential work *Punishment and Culture,* Philip Smith contributes enormously to the cultural sociology of punishment by bringing into the forefront Durkheim's (2008 [1915], 2012 [1933]) socioreligious concepts, namely, pollution, the sacred, the mythological, and the cult of the individual.* Each of those cultural themes resonates in many forms of penal phenomena. For instance, the view that crime (the criminal) is something "dirty" and needs to be cleaned and purified stems from notions of *pollution* (see Douglas, 1966). The *sacred* refers not only to higher powers embodied within institutional religion but also to a wider sense of the supernatural that inspires awe.

Legends and stories rely on the *mythological* to spin enduring narratives about key historical figures, events, and social movements. Finally, Durkheim's insights into what he called *the cult of the individual* allow us to recognize an evolving sense of personal dignity that promotes mutual respect in a civilized world, even in the face of criminal prosecution, adjudication, and punishment.

In an effort to advance a cultural sociology of punishment, this work borrows Geertz's (2000 [1973]) method of *thick description,* whereby researchers deposit their observations into an in-depth network of framing intentions and cultural meanings (see Smith, 2008). Developing a thick description is indeed central to case studies by which a detailed interpretation draws from an array of objects, symbols, and narration. Consider thick descriptions of

* Smith's (2008) *Punishment and Culture* stems from a renewed interest in Durkheim shared by other scholars intent on advancing a neo-Durkheimian perspective that breaks from the "functionalist" and "positivist" tradition (see Alexander, 2005; Bellah, 2005; Riley, 2005; Smith and Alexander, 2005). By reworking Durkheim, there is much to gain for sociological, cultural, and criminological theory as they inform a deeper understanding of penal tourism.

socioreligious concepts in prison museums around the world.* Again, at the Argentine Penitentiary Museum, a gallery delivers a curious message about pollution being eradicated by modern purification, hygiene, and cleansing. Visitors are shown a white porcelain basin that at first glance seems to represent secular hand washing. However, the attached placard describes its use for "la clausura" (closing ceremony) by the religious staff as they prepare incarcerated women for release into the community. Similarly, a photograph of a bedroom reserved for conjugal visits captures the influence of Catholicism: a crucifix is conspicuously placed above the bed, suggesting that an omniscient deity oversees all human activities, including carnal knowledge.

Durkheim's notion of the mythological has tremendous purchase in prison museums. In the story of Ned Kelly as told at the Melbourne Gaol, curators underscore his legacy in Australian cultural history. A storyboard titled "NED THE LEGEND" describes the execution in literary fashion and issues a closing passage titled "Australian Icon": "The Kelly gang's 'flashiness,' courage, daring style and distinctive armour captured popular imagination. Despite his crimes, Ned Kelly and his iconic helmet remain for many Australians a powerful image, representing an emerging national identity celebrating independence, mateship, and 'a fair go.'"

As evidence of Ned's enduring mark on traditional and popular culture, the museum displays posters of movies inspired by the Kelly gang, most prominently, "Mick Jagger as Ned Kelly (Not Suitable for Children)." One cannot help make the connection between the (rock star) status of Mick and that of Ned (see figure 2).

Another important socioreligious concept is what Durkheim called *the cult of the individual,* referring to an evolving sense of personal dignity. Whereas such concepts as pollution, the sacred, and the mythological are pretty much self-evident, Durkheim's notion of the cult of the individual warrants a bit more elaboration since it merges his theories on punishment and religion. In *The Division of Labor,* Durkheim maintains that punishing criminal offenders is first and foremost an emotional response aimed at avenging an outrage of morality. Smith (2008) delves deeper into that

* Garland detects in Smith a tendency toward Levi-Straussian thinking, whereby the social and cultural order is understood to be patterned by binary oppositions and timeless universal codes. A chief problem in that way of theorizing is that socioreligious concepts become "so all-embracing as to rob them of precision (e.g., everything that is valued becomes 'sacred')" (Garland, 2009: 261). As a remedy, Garland proposes a Geertzian perspective from which cultural meaning is shaped by local usage (see Melossi, 2001).

FIGURE 2. A display of a *Ned Kelly* movie poster, featuring Mick Jagger (not suitable for children) (Melbourne Gaol). © retrowelch 2014

Durkheimian perspective, pointing out that even in the modern world penal law could never be entirely rational because it is embedded within cultural systems. Those systems, according to Durkheim, are forms of social control that are religious in character. Smith's close reading of *The Division of Labor* shows that under the condition of modernity there emerged a new kind of moral awareness, producing not only greater sentiments of tolerance but also a new grounding for the sacred known as the cult of the individual (see Garland, 1990; Lukes and Scull, 1983). The cult of the individual joins a cultural system committed to treating others with dignity and respect because the human person is sacred. From the religious standpoint that man is at once believer and god, Smith taps into Goffman (1967), who observed that social life is a series of ritualized encounters in which "the sacred status of the self is continually affirmed" (Smith 2008: 19). In turn, breaches of respect are commonly met with resentment or even disgust (see Elias, 2005).

Theorizing the evolution of punishment, Durkheim examines how punishments became less harsh and more humane. As a foreshadow to Goffman, Durkheim insists that ideal images of man are comparable to those of the deity. Moreover, in taking the role of the other, Durkheim repeats the Golden Rule: "Do not do unto others that which you would not wish done to you" (1983: 124–25). Durkheim goes on to explain that what tempers the collective anger, which is at the heart of punishment, is the "sympathy which we feel for every man who suffers" (1983: 125–26). Such sympathy—as a reflective emotion—tends to moderate punishment.

At the Hyde Park Barracks museum in Sydney, for instance, we are reminded of the significance of "The End of Transportation." The narrative promotes an emerging Australian identity that ultimately pushed back against the British. The last ship transporting convicts to Sydney landed in 1840, and nine years later the *Hashemy* was kept from reaching shore as a protest of five thousand citizens at Circular Quay "made their objections known." The local resistance to transportation marked a new era for Australia. Embracing the cult of the individual, Australians along with British parliamentarians (that is, the 1837 Molesworth Commission) concluded that the practice was "immoral, uneconomical and counterproductive to deterring crime . . . demeaning and close to slavery."

In formulating a cultural approach to punishment, Durkheim's socioreligious concepts are treated as fluid rather than static. In doing so, the project intends to show how they commonly interact and facilitate the maintenance of dominant (official) narratives. Furthermore, by attending to local history and culture, socioreligious themes add to a more layered interpretation of the story being told. As a vehicle for cultural transmission, prison museums often rely on poetic messages via plaques and literary references. A poster in the Argentine Penitentiary Museum cites a passage from the famous novel *La Vuelta de Martín Fierro,* whereby the penitentiary is depicted as a form of justice as well as a venue offering prisoners a new baptism. Perhaps no other item in the museum's collection captures the overlap of Durkheim's socioreligious concepts as well. Obviously, there is reference to the sacred along with the purification of pollution. And together they reinforce the myth of the progressive State and its commitment to the cult of the individual, whereby the personal dignity of convicts is preserved through a ritual of justice, delivering a higher (transcendent) form of redemption. As we shall address in coming chapters, the official narrative on Argentine justice omits the atrocities of the Dirty War carried out by the State's military apparatus between 1976 and 1983.

In a Foucaultian framework, a cultural sociology of punishment benefits from recognizing the power-control thesis. Prisons, as Foucault (1977, 1980a) theorized in great detail, are among the key sites where state power is exercised. Sharpening that observation, Foucault demonstrated how the institutional histories of penal regimes are grounded in the complex formulation of expert knowledge. In Europe and the United States, penitentiaries during the early nineteenth century had become laboratories designed to pursue the new sciences of surveillance, control, and discipline. The emerging modern prison, according to several scholars, served as a "museum for the display and diffusion of this knowledge" (Scicluna and Knepper, 2008: 503; see Ignatieff, 1978; Johnston, 1958, 2000, 2010; Rothman, 1971). Revealingly, a brochure explains that the Argentine Penitentiary Museum is "meant to work as a technical-cultural institution: its purpose would be to keep all materials that could witness past experiences of the penitentiary life" (museum brochure, English version: 4). The term *technical-cultural institution* should intrigue scholars interested in penal tourism, since it proposes that visitors are tutored in how to view the emergence of prison technologies alongside significant cultural interpretations. In other words, tourists are taught a particular lesson in the cultural sociology of punishment that does not dissociate the technical from its meaning. Indeed, state officials use the museum to communicate a tight narrative about Argentine penology and its role in state making.

The Hyde Park Barracks in Sydney also speaks to a wider imagination on *order*. At the perimeter of the museum, visitors are presented with a plaque titled "Control." It reads: "Convict constables and clerks occupied these two guardhouses between 1819 and 1848. This was the only entrance to the compound and they controlled the large numbers of people and goods passing through it." Though not a prison or jail per se, the barracks was tightly governed through a regime of strict rules and regulations geared toward keeping convicts in line. That disciplinary (Foucaultian) theme prevails throughout

FIGURE 3. A peephole for guards to keep watch over the dormitory (Hyde Park Barracks, Sydney). © retrowelch 2014

much of the tour. "Life at the Barracks," as described by a storyboard, reminds us that inmates did not have much privacy, free time, or personal space. Convicts would complain of the corrupt and sadistic practices of the superintendents. Still, the heavy-handed treatment of convicts appears to be held somewhat in balance by a system of fairness and incentives, or what Foucault (1977) conceptualized as a *microeconomy of perpetual penal power*. The staff served convicts only two meals a day, but extra food was issued in exchange for longer hours on the job. Conversely, rule breaking was penalized by restricting the diet to a ration of bread and water along with a stint in solitary confinement. Within the barracks, moral order was constantly being checked. A poster titled "Surveillance" gives visitors a sense that anxiety over the "crime" of homosexuality pervaded the dormitory, especially at night when lamps were extinguished. Along that theme, the tour features a "peep hole" outside the dormitory room into which the night constables would attempt to police "immoral" sexual contact among convicts (see figure 3). Put another way, such surveillance was intended to maintain a purified space from the contamination of *polluting* vice, thereby bridging the perspectives of Foucault and Durkheim.

At the Old Melbourne Gaol, we again witness how a particular prison museum tells its own story. Unlike the barracks in Sydney that served as secure accommodations for convicts, the Old Melbourne Gaol was Victoria's first permanent purpose-built prison. The architecture is imposing, reinforcing its semiotic message about what exactly it is—a penitentiary. By the 1880s, the Gaol deserved its reputation as a modern penal institution, again borrowing significantly from Eastern State Penitentiary (Philadelphia) and Pentonville Prison (London). Echoing Foucault's thoughts on discipline, an elaborate brochure describes how internal order was maintained: "Life in the gaol was hard—prisoners were kept in solitary confinement, communication was severely restricted, food was barely adequate and punishments for breaches of discipline were harsh" (Poultney, 2003: 1). That instrumentalist narrative on discipline persists throughout much of the tour. In developing the state's system of imprisonment, Victorians looked to the English model. A storyboard titled "Pentonville, Punishment and Penitence" quotes George Duncan, inspector general of penal institutions in Victoria (1871): "There can be no better test of a reformatory system than its success in developing and fostering habits of industry and self-control." The architects of the Melbourne Gaol replicated the design of Pentonville based on single cells, which had become a "model for prisons throughout the British Empire in the mid-19th century." That regiment, the poster concedes, was first developed in the United States. Still, much as with the American and British experiences, the practice of isolating of prisoners ("intended to break their spirit in order to re-form their character") was later abandoned in Victoria since it became viewed as ineffective, brutal, and degrading—a nod to the cult of the individual. While this analysis of prison museums pursues a cultural sociology of punishment by integrating the insights of Foucault and Durkheim, there is an effort to explore dark tourism by reflecting on a critique of modernity.

DARK TOURISM AND MODERNITY

Themes of modernity, reform, and progress figure prominently in the prison museums studied herein. As a historital starting point, the comparison begins in London, where from 1144 until 1780, the Clink served as a dungeon, or what could be described as a premodern prison. Next in chronological order, the Hyde Park Barracks offers evidence of an emerging modern penal institution; built between 1817 and 1819, the barracks served as secured accommodations for convicts arriving after the First Fleet (1788). The penitentiary in its early modern form, however, is witnessed at Eastern State Penitentiary (in Philadelphia), admitting its first inmate in 1829. That version of modern penal architecture was replicated at the Melbourne Gaol, constructed between the 1840s and the 1860s. Attending further to narratives on the birth of modern prisons, the Argentine Penitentiary Museum delivers a story of continued progress. Though its history is steeped in religious tension—much like that of the Clink—the museum in Buenos Aires shows visitors how a more secular penal sphere eventually eclipsed a theological regime.

Expanding the cultural sociology of punishment into the terrain of history, the chapters ahead rely on thick descriptions of penal modernity and its various components, including economics, governance, architecture, and science. As prisons became increasingly modernized, their means of production followed suit. Dating back to the 1820s, prison reformers adhered to the economic principles of efficiency and profit while advancing notions of humane treatment. In tandem, programs to transform convicts into productive workers as well as law-abiding citizens were realized in prison architecture whose innovative designs enhanced surveillance (see Foucault, 1977; Garland, 1990; Melossi and Pavarini, 1981).

Although early prison reformers viewed the modern prison as an alternative to corporal punishment, penal institutions remained rife with cruelty (Johnston, 1958, 2000, 2010). Curiously, prison administrators were soon attracted to the allure of science for the purposes of inflicting—and managing—calibrated degrees of pain (Welch, 2009a, 2009b 2011a; see Becker and Wetzell, 2007). A prevalent feature in penal tourism is the display of devices for maltreatment, torture, and execution, many of which appear to be adapted to humane reform through science. For example, the museum at the Melbourne Gaol goes to great lengths to document the role of science—physics, anatomy, and medicine—in pursuit of the perfect drop from the gallows. In its exhibition, a poster quotes Charles Duff's book *A Handbook on Hanging* (1828): "To achieve such a hanging, the rope had to be the right length. Mr Berry, an English hangman in the 1880s, worked out a table calculating the length of the rope required according to the weight of the person to be hanged. If the rope was too long it could wrench the head off, too short and it caused prolonged strangulation." A hospital senior warder wrote in 1918 regarding the hanging of Arthur Oldring: "Death was absolutely instantaneous. The best execution ever witnessed." The book *The Particulars of Execution,* replete with sketches (and later photographs) of fractured vertebrae, demonstrates the role of science in modernizing hangings. Moreover, such expert knowledge had a legal component, since under the Act to Regulate the Execution of Criminals (1855) death was to be "instantaneous."

Without losing sight of the cultural sociology of punishment, a comparative study of prison museums lends itself to a wider critique of modernity and tourism, especially dark tourism. Scholars remind us that tourism as an educative (and recreational) enterprise is closely aligned with the principles of modernity (Burkhart and Medlik, 1981; Cooper, Fletcher, Gilbert, and Wanhill, 1993). Developing their social critique of dark tourism and the attraction of death and disaster, Lennon and Foley (2010) propose that dark tourism posits questions and doubts about modernity and its consequences. They write, "Our argument is that 'dark tourism' is an intimation of postmodernity. We do not seek to enter any philosophical debates over the use of this term but, rather, aim to recognize the significant aspects of 'post-modernity' which are broadly taken to represent its main features. If these features amount to late capitalism, or late modernity, then so be it" (11).

Lennon and Foley sketch out their perspective on modernity and dark tourism according to three elements. In the first, dark tourism thrives on global communication technologies that possess the capacity to initiate interest. Nearly all the prison museums studied here have websites that draw attention to their site as an important tourist destination, whether one is traveling to Buenos Aires, Hong Kong, or London. Moreover, global communication technology—the Internet—crosses over into the realm of movies that can be streamed online (e.g., on Netflix or YouTube), giving greater exposure to such favorites as *Escape from Alcatraz,* featuring Clint Eastwood. Those virtual experiences have a phenomenological effect, since they allow for the exploration of global territory in ways that collapse space and time (see Ross, 1983).

The second aspect of dark tourism, according to Lennon and Foley, involves the display of selected objects, images, and spaces. Altogether they prompt anxiety and doubt the project of modernity. Holocaust museums, for instance, generate serious reflection over the "rational planning" and technological innovation used to carry out a highly modernized "Final Solution," which produced death on an industrial scale (Dekel, 2013; Williams, 2007). For penal tourism, a similar critique is leveled at the use of prisons to maintain state-sponsored racism. A visit to Constitution Hill (Johannesburg) and Robben Island (Cape Town) promises to deepen a critical understanding of apartheid and its unjust—though seemingly "logical"—separation of black and colored people from their white European counterparts.

Similarly, at Eastern State Penitentiary, penal tourists are given an opportunity to contemplate the enormity of mass incarceration. A poster titled "Prisons Today" explains:

> Pennsylvania's population has grown by just 7% since Eastern State closed in 1970. The number of people in prison, however, has grown by 800%.
> The expense has also increased. In today's dollars, the prison system in 1970 cost $185 million. Today it costs Pennsylvanians $1 billion, 900 million each year.
> Most state prison systems grew more. Nationwide, the prison population has grown by 1,000% since 1970.

The poster relies on large bar graphs to illustrate the skyrocketing increase in prisoners and costs as well as the international ranking of the United States vis-à-vis other nations (see Bruggeman, 2012). A caption reads: "The United States imprisons more of its population than any other nation. The American system is also the most expensive ever built. It costs Americans $74 billion every year." Reaching beyond numerical data, the placard includes a photograph of a contemporary prison dormitory jammed with bunked beds and scores of prisoners dressed only in boxer shorts. The image leaves onlookers with a sense that prisons today are simply (expensive) warehouses for inmates, thereby defying any claim to penal progress and rationality (see Foucault, 1980b, 2009; Welch, 2010b, 2011b).

Finally, dark tourism is accompanied by elements of commodification and commerce. At its very essence, an on-site visit is understood to be a product. Such consumption is most evident at the end of the prison tour as visitors exit through the museum's gift shop. While many of those stores are geared toward promoting further education via scholarly books and memoirs of celebrity prisoners, some add a sense of local kitsch. At the Melbourne Gaol, tourists are given an opportunity to purchase an array of Ned Kelly books, comic books, posters, stuffed dolls, key rings, caps, beer glasses, replica armor, helmets (priced at $150), and baby bibs (that read "The Kelly Gang" alongside cartooned figures of Ned and others) (see Pretes, 2002; Wright, 2000).

MODES OF ESCAPE

Of course, as the title of this book suggests, penal tourism involves elements of escape—a phenomenon that sociologists have pondered with deep reflection. Leisure allows people the freedom to flee the daily grind of work and responsibility, so it seems ironic that some vacationers would choose to visit a former prison. Perhaps they have an interest in prison history, a cultural fascination with punishment, or maybe a craving for an entirely different experience. The range of motives reminds us that there are several reasons why visitors attend prison museums; consequently, they each bring to the exhibit varied expectations and points of view. Cohen and Taylor's *Escape Attempts* and Rojek's *Ways of Escape* offer insights into the sociology of leisure by differentiating between the traveler and the tourist as well as the posttourist. Channeling Levi-Strauss (1955), Rojek maintains that high culture is attributed to the traveler while low culture dogs the tourist: "The traveler is associated with refined values of discernment, respect, and taste. Travel is seen as pursuing the ageless aristocratic principle of broadening the mind" (1993: 175). By contrast, cultural critics are often unkind to tourists, deriding them as unimaginative, unadventurous, and insipid. As they graze, tourists are all too willing to consume whatever the tourist industry feeds them (Carroll, 1980). Not only are those distinctions elitist but they are also superficial, since there is considerable overlap between traveling and sightseeing. Moreover, tourists frequently bypass the tourism agenda and script, thereby becoming the posttourist. Cohen and Taylor remind us that in the course of tourism, vacationers have the capacity to be cynical about what tour operators throw at them. Especially when searching for authenticity, tourists are "capable of ironically commenting on their disappointment in not finding it: they see through the staged authenticity of the tourist setting and laugh about it" (1976: 118).

In *The Tourist Gaze,* Urry recognizes the unique consciousness of the posttourist who is well aware of how commodification shapes the tourist experience. Still, rather than rejecting the contrived nature of many forms of leisure, the posttourist goes for the ride and treats the experience playfully: "The post-tourist knows that they are a tourist and that tourism is a game, or rather a whole series of games with multiple texts and no single authentic experience" (Urry, 2002: 100). Moreover, Urry notes that the posttourist willingly interacts with the different facets and representations of the tourist site. The crass commercialism of gift shops and themed food courts does not bother the posttourist; rather, those venues are simply accepted as part of the tourist experience. By contrast, the traveler and tourist maintain different expectations. The traveler is motivated by the pursuit of truth, knowledge, and one's relationship with the world. Conversely, the tourist commonly visits destinations in an effort to have a record of one's journey, which is ritualistically captured in photographs and home movies. What travelers and tourists have in common is that they both want a highly focused experience; toward that end, they react negatively to the nuisance of others who threaten solitude or merely interfere with snapshots and other features of the consumption experience (Rojek, 1993).

Travelers, tourists, and posttourists all share a sense of curiosity and the desire to escape their daily routine—even if that means visiting a prison museum. Most—not all—prison museums described in this volume tend to offer something for everyone, including travelers, tourists, and posttourists. In fact, curators are quick to understand that those social categories are overly simplistic since, at any given moment, we are all three. While at the Clink, for example, visitors can read the scholarly narrative on political and religious imprisonment and then take a photograph of their kid posing on the chopping block—all the while being aware of their experience. In the chapters to follow, critical attention is turned to prison exhibits, their content, and their story lines so as to reflect on the cultural pull of punishment as a means of escape. Still, what makes the prison museum experience possible is the full realization that the visit is temporary. Not many vacationers would enter such a site with the risk of being kept, mistreated, or tortured. No matter how authentic those museums appear, they are not real prisons—and everyone knows that.

THE TASK AT HAND

Penal tourism offers scholars unique opportunities to refine cultural concepts and interpretations of punishment in modern society.* Commenting on the project of cultural analysis in penology, Garland (2006) cautions that the cultural turn could add conceptual confusion into the field since the notion of "culture" is notoriously multivalent. Set forth by Sewell (1999, 2005), the term *culture* has two existing usages: first, culture as an analytical aspect of social relations ("the cultural"), and second, culture as a collective entity ("a culture"). Garland suggests that we blend cultural work into an explanatory platform, insisting that "we should isolate and analyze the 'cul-

---

* The term *penal tourism* is preferred over *prison tourism* because it seems to capture a wider fascination with the cultural history of punishment.

tural' elements of punishment only as a preliminary to more integrated analyses that fold cultural elements into multi-dimensional accounts of causes and consequences of penal practices" (2006: 436; see Smith, 2003a). With those proposals in full view, studies of penal tourism can contribute to a cultural sociology of punishment not only with historically driven research but also through comparative work, thereby enhancing cross-cultural interpretations (see Melossi, 2001; Melossi, Sozzo, and Sparks, 2011; Welch, 2012a, 2012b, 2013).

This book marks the culmination of years of international travel. With a critical eye on the cultural pull of punishment, the project explores ten prison museums scattered across Africa, Asia, Australia, Europe, North America, and South America. In alphabetical order, they are Alcatraz, the Argentine Penitentiary Museum (Buenos Aires), the Clink (London), Constitution Hill (Johannesburg), Eastern State Penitentiary (Philadelphia), the Hong Kong Correctional Services Museum,* Hyde Park Barracks (Sydney), the Melbourne Gaol, Robben Island (Cape Town), and the Seodaemun Prison History Hall (Seoul).

As remarks thus far suggest, the investigation is informed by a cultural sociology of punishment (Garland, 2006; Smith, 2008). In particular, the theoretical focus synthesizes insights of power-based theories (Foucault) with semiotics (Durkheim), thereby allowing us to appreciate the common ground shared by instrumentalist and communicative interpretations of prison museums (Welch and Macuare, 2011). When we venture into a wider critique, attention is directed at key dimensions of penal modernity and its benchmarks of progress, including economics, governance, architecture, and science. Observations are situated within the scholarly literature on museum studies, penal spectatorship, and dark tourism. In brief, that is the task at hand. Let us summarize some of the main areas and topics covered in the book.

The next chapter, "The Museum Effect," takes an in-depth look at how prison museums exercise their cultural power. Foucaultian notions of normalizing, gazing, and performing help us decipher the mission and techniques of penal exhibitions. Along the way, we realize that much of the cul-

---

* Technically, the Hong Kong Correctional Services Museum is not a former prison, although it is located within eyesight of the Stanley Prison. The building is situated next to the correctional training center and visitors are likely to witness staff marching and engaging in other outdoor exercises. The museum features transplanted prison cells and wall-length photographs of the interior of the Stanley Prison to give the impression that one is actually inside the prison.

tural authority that prison museums possess derives from socioreligious symbols, messages, and aura. We give thought to other phenomenological aspects of the museum experience, and special consideration is directed at the significance of objects, images, and space. Together they constitute the museum effect: the overall impact that those institutions have on tourists, society, and culture.

Similarly, chapter 3, "Dream of Order," begins with Foucault's reflections on heterotopias, which are physical representations of utopias. Museums are one such heterotopia insofar as they are dedicated to the accumulation of time and the collection of items. Whereas the "dream of order" speaks to a utopian agenda in pursuit of perfection, it is the penitentiary that serves as its tangible model. Penal ambitions, to be sure, manifest at the grand level as well as at the more mundane or institutional level. Still, due to resistance on the part of prisoners and their advocates, there is an alternative order driven by defiance. Prisons in South Africa and South Korea, for example, were used for purposes of political and social control, only to be countered by antiapartheid and prodemocracy movements.

Expressions of complete order typically make their way into the planning of penitentiaries. Chapter 4, "Architecture Parlante" (or "speaking architecture"), explores the communicative capacity of prison design. As a prototype, Eastern State Penitentiary blends neo-Gothic facades and Quaker philosophies of redemption into a quasi-panoptic radial design. More than three hundred prisons around the world have replicated that "cathedral of punishment." Such form, of course, had function. Critical discussion considers the ways in which Durkheimian semiotics interacts with Foucaultian utility. As we shall see, such semio-technology surfaces in different penal sites, including the island, the dungeon, the monastery, and eventually the model penitentiary. Matters of religion and governance, of course, influence not only the construction of prisons but also their maintenance (chapter 5). Entering former prisons, visitors are quick to appreciate the actual *sited-ness* while learning about the strict protocol of spiritual transformation. The historical relations between the Church and State with respect to the governance of prisons have been marked by tension and accommodation. So as to sort out some of those developments, special attention is directed at Argentine penology as it straddled the fine line between religion and politics. The chapter also delves further into the *sacred* by probing its darker affinities—or *left sacred*. Prison museums have enormous cultural pull due to themes of evil, murder, and execution. Visitors are intrigued by those manifestations of the left sacred; moreover, they might also wonder about a mystical afterlife. Many tours hint that the prison is haunted by ghosts.

Work and economics are common threads weaving through each of the prison museums studied herein. Accordingly, chapter 6 contemplates how prisons have been used to punish the poor (e.g., the Clink). From there, a more benevolent use of economics begins to take shape, most recognizably under the Pennsylvania System. While that regime focused on the individual inmate, other penal paradigms aspired to use convict labor for purposes of building the state, as in the case of Argentina and Australia. Curators also use occupational themes to give tourists a sense of what it is like to work inside a penitentiary, particularly given its reputation as a forbidden space. Displays of prisoner-made weapons (i.e., shanks) often are accompanied by stark photographs of assaults and riots, delivering potent testimonies on action, danger, and death.

Foucault reminds us that the early penitentiary was not only an institution for confinement but also an exhibition space used to display and diffuse an emerging penal knowledge. Today, prison museums maintain that narrative by explaining histories of scientific expertise, such as criminal anthropology and positivism (e.g., phrenology). Visitors are also given uneasy lessons on science as it was employed to refine the physics of hanging as well as various torture devices that deliver calibrated degrees of pain and suffering (e.g., waterboarding). With those concerns in mind, the chapter explores the paradoxes of science and rationality, as well as their claims of enlightened penal progress. The critique then discusses the reliance on prisons to advance colonial projects (chapter 8). Conversely, it also chronicles in detail celebrated forms of political, ethnic, and racial resistance: the campaign to liberate Hong Kong from the British, Korea's fight against Japanese imperialism, the American Indian experience at Alcatraz, and the struggle for racial equality in South Africa.

Memorialization is a major trend in museums, and prison museums are no exception. Chapter 9 examines cultural power as it activates solemn remembrance. Toward that end, many former prisons have been reinvented as heritage sites that honor famous political prisoners committed to noble causes. Analysis is organized around key styles of dramatization: hybridity, authenticity, minimalism, and absence. Correspondingly, sacred and mythological semiotics (Durkheim) facilitates the (Foucaultian) view that prison museums have the capacity to improve those who visit their galleries, thereby promoting introspection and civility.

The final chapter issues more testimony to the power of culture as it manifests in penal tourism. For instance, stories about prisoners who were convicted of murdering defenseless victims—namely, children—are especially disturbing, since those crimes brazenly violate the sacred. In a shift of emotional tone, discussion turns to techniques used by prison museums that give visitors a sense of "hands-on" power. Eastern State Penitentiary, in particular, invites tourists to engage in panopticism by allowing them to maneuver a camera perched on the guard tower. As the book concludes, we exit through the gift shop, where cultural consumption allows us to bring home souvenirs that reinforce our memories of the escape to prison.

TWO

The Museum Effect

While in Seoul, South Korea, visitors are encouraged to discover the Seodaemun Prison History Hall. As its mission: "The museum preserves and displays Seodaemun Prison signifying the suffering and pain of Koreans during the modern period. Here, independence activists and pro-democracy activities were jailed and martyred" (Seodaemun Prison History Hall, n.d.). Descending into the basement of the first building of the tour, we are given a harsh look at colonial control. The "Underground Torture Chamber" is the actual space where Koreans were interrogated and tortured by Japanese Imperialists. Through the use of mannequins and careful lighting, scenes of various tortures are displayed. One such reenactment is the "Water Torture," in which the interrogator is seen pouring water into the mouth of a prisoner who is suspended upside down with hands bound. The exhibits are accompanied by photographs and voice testimonies of men and women who survived "to show the reality of oppressive colonial ruling" (Seodaemun Prison History Hall, n.d.). In the next gallery, an even stronger sense of penal spectatorship is established by strategically positioning visitors inside the Shadow Image Experiment. There, one's face is projected onto a video screen as a silhouette in order to make it appear as if they are the person being tortured. With a runtime of ninety seconds, the interactive video takes the museum effect to another level of consciousness. By being superimposed onto the center of attention, one's out-of-body experience reduces the social distance of torture, thereby producing a closer affinity with the Korean victims.

As noted in chapter 1, technology—in the form of global communication—has the capacity to initiate curiosity in dark tourism (Lennon and Foley, 2010). Once the visitor steps into the actual site, technology is also used to enhance the interplay between objects, images, and space. Altogether, they contribute to the museum effect: the overall impact the museum has on its visitors, society, and culture (Casey, 2003; Williams, 2007). A significant feature of the museum effect is its ability to collapse space and time. That phenomenological shift is, of course, sharpened through technology. The Shadow Image Experiment at Seodaemun Prison History Hall not only compresses space (i.e., the Underground Torture Chamber) and time (i.e., the period of Japanese colonial rule), but also relies on positioning (Brown, 2009), whereby visitors are placed inside the virtual torture session. Ultimately, Seodaemun Prison History Hall, much like other prison museums, delivers a particular lesson on (political) imprisonment. At a higher degree of abstraction, the prison museum serves as cultural technology by transmitting to tourists a didactic experience involving the historical (time) and local (space) use of punishment.

In this chapter, the focus on penal tourism swings toward the museum effect. By tapping into the ten prison museums, special awareness is directed at objects, images, and space. While much of the analysis is inspired by the interdisciplinary field of museum studies (Lennon and Foley, 2010; Prior, 2002; Williams, 2007), it also stays on course with a cultural sociology of punishment (Garland, 2006; Smith, 2008). Once again, there is an effort to synthesize the Foucaultian power-control thesis with Durkheimian semiotics (Welch, 2012a; Welch and Macuare, 2011). So that we might properly comprehend penal tourism as a form of cultural transmission, discussion begins with a decidedly Foucaultian approach to the museum effect, thereby throwing critical light on normalizing, gazing, and performing (Bennett, 1995; Casey, 2003).

NORMALIZING, GAZING, AND PERFORMING

Foucaultian notions of normalizing, gazing, and performing figure prominently in penology, museum studies, and a domain where the two intersect (Bennett, 1995; Garland, 1990; Pearson, 1982; Welch, 2012). Mentioned previously, the early penitentiary and the museum were strategically located in the center of the city for purposes of showing their power; nonetheless, those institutions differed in their tactics for normalization. While the carceral system relied on "hard" measures of power, the museum opted for a "soft" application, thereby advancing the state's ambition to promote art and culture. In *The State and the Visual Arts,* Nicholas Pearson comments that the "soft" approach operated "by example rather than by pedagogy; by entertainment rather than by disciplined schooling; and by subtlety and encouragement" (1982: 35). The museum as a vehicle for the transmission of culture depends on voluntary participation. By instilling a sense of self-monitoring, the museum—much like its penal counterpart—strives toward making citizens "cultured" and thus more governable. Bennett (1995) elaborates on that phenomenon, proposing that both the prison and the museum sought to incorporate people within the processes of the state: "For those who failed to adopt the tutelary relation to the self, promoted by popular schooling or whose hearts and minds failed to be won in the new pedagogic relations between the state and people symbolized by the open doors of the museum, the closed walls of the penitentiary threatened a sterner instruction in the lessons of power. Where instruction and rhetoric failed, punishment began" (87–88).

In museum studies, the Foucaultian perspective reminds us that the birth of the museum in the nineteenth century had a rational and improving orientation, not unlike other cultural projects: international exhibitions, libraries, and public parks. Similarly, Bennett points to key features of the museum. First, the museum relies on the practice of "showing and telling": hence, exhibiting artifacts "in a manner calculated to embody and communicate specific cultural meanings and values" (1995: 6). Second, the museum is designed to be open to all people who are subjected to methods of regulating conduct. Toward that end, the museum aspires to move visitors in ways that constitute performance. Indeed, the museum is a space for "organized walking," where individuals ("minds on legs") are encouraged to explore the institution's carefully assembled collection of objects and images. Although visitors enjoy their own freedom of movement, they are still confined within a larger cultural itinerary that promotes self-improvement.

The museum's capacity to deliver cultural messages rests on its reputation as a strong—and legitimate—social authority.* To be sure, the power invested in being a trusted social authority is exercised quite strategically. In her analysis of the gaze and performance inherent in the contemporary museum, Valerie Casey directs critical attention to curators who regulate ways of seeing: "The museum is able to produce cultural knowledge by organizing how

* The American Association of Museums, in 2001, conducted a national survey, which found that 87 percent of Americans find museums to be one of the most trustworthy sources of information. Books were a distant second at 61 percent, and a majority of Americans find print and broadcast media and the Internet to be not trustworthy (Lake Snell Perry & Associates, 2001).

the materials it authorizes are seen—by controlling the Gaze" (2003: 2–3). Borrowing from Lacan (1978), Casey describes the Gaze as an act of involuntary participation governed by a cultural construction in which relationship between a Subject and the Object of its view is always mediated by a visual discourse. Visual exchanges are inescapably shaped by environmental, cultural, and physical conditions (Bryson, 1988). Moreover, the visual world (where Subjects participate) is mediated by the screen: an ensemble of signs and signifiers that determine how the Object is seen. Quite literally, the screen is curatorial information, whether in the form of labeled text, the design of the exhibition, or the narrative on an audio guide, all of which provides context that manages the visitor's understanding.

The tour of Alcatraz, not unlike other prison museums, is screened through the use of various storyboards, images, and photographs. Additionally, visitors rely heavily on the audio guide that instructs them not only where to walk and what to look at but also how to grasp key events. Perhaps due to its iconic location in San Francisco Bay, the theme of escape surrounds the narrative. Upon arriving at Alcatraz via boat, tourists enter a few galleries that serve to prime them for what they will witness later. An exhibition titled "Box Office" scans the manner by which Hollywood has portrayed Alcatraz (see figure 4). One can gaze at the familiar movie poster for *Escape from Alcatraz* from which Clint Eastwood stares back. Entering the Main Prison Cellblock, visitors are issued an audio guide that features detailed information on the famous escape. An authoritative voice matches the content of the labeled images, thereby enhancing the authenticity of the story. The principal players and their creative plot are described with flair.

> Using the unlikeliest of supplies, Frank Morris and the brothers John and Clarence Anglin made the most creative escape attempt in the history of Alcatraz. Placing dummy heads made of soap, cement, and paint under their blankets in the middle of the night, the escapees crawled out their cells through the small vents, scaled the utility corridor to the roof, slid down a stove pipe, and crept to the shoreline. The three men had reached the bay. As they slipped into the water—using a raft fashioned out of a raincoat—they met an icy current rapidly ebbing out to sea. They were never seen again.

The voice on the audio guide then directs visitors to step over to the actual cell, where the dummy head is tucked partially under the blanket so as to re-create the scene as it happened. At the back of the cell is the chiseled hole that enabled the breakout. The screen of curatorial information manages the way in which visitors comprehend the escape. Moreover, the tone of the narrative seems to even commend the prisoners for their ingenuity, suggesting that they somehow earned their newfound freedom.

Casey (2003) reminds us that even in the most informed or egalitarian environment, the prescribed curatorial meaning (the screen) facilitates perception and interpretation, delivering a particular museum effect.* As in the case at Alcatraz, visitors to Robben Island arrive by boat. The tour, however, is guided not by an audio device but by a former political prisoner who tells the collective story of confinement for belonging to a banned organization (e.g., the African National Congress).† Through that narrative, tourists are reminded of the brazen injustices delivered by the apartheid regime. Moreover, the role of the guide is vital to appreciating some of the most symbolic scenes of the tour. If it were not for the guide who physically points to the former cell of Nelson Mandela, visitors would not recognize it from the many other ordinary cells in the prison. It is remarkable for not being remarkable. But once attention is directed to the cell, the curatorial screen creates a sense of aura. The Spartan space contains only a red garbage can, a green night table with a metal dish, and a thin sleeping mat unfurled on the floor.

---

* Of course, even this text serves as another layer of screening, thereby telling readers how the author views and understands penal tourism in ten cities.

† Sipho Msomi served as my tour guide at Robben Island in July 2012. He is a member of the ANC and was a political prisoner on the island from 1984 to 1989. Again, I would like to thank him along with the others who made my trip possible: namely, Sibongiseni Mkhize, Boniswa Kondile, and Wendy Duma.

Despite their mundane nature, those objects seem to resonate greatness from the prisoner who, after enduring years of political imprisonment, would become President of a new South Africa.

From the standpoint of a cultural sociology of punishment that strives to incorporate Durkheimian concepts, one can recognize the socioreligious significance (Smith, 2008; Welch and Macuare, 2011). Although Mandela's cell is not decorated as a shrine, visitors gravitate to the site for its symbolic value that blends the sacred, the mythological, and the cult of the individual. In an almost ritualistic manner, tourists seem to fill the nearly empty space with their own admiration for Mandela, who stood as the eternal good against the evil of the racist state (see Katz, 1988). His mythic stature is enhanced further by his honorable style of leadership; by refusing to settle old scores, Mandela promoted mutual respect (Mandela, 1994). Altogether, those socioreligious phenomena contribute to an enduring sense of solidarity, even years after his presidency. Few visitors merely look into Mandela's cell and walk away; most of them revel in its semiotics. Unsurprisingly, tourists also photograph the space in order to preserve the moment of their pilgrimage. Unlike other tourist sites, which draw unruly crowds, Robben Island in general and Mandela's cell in particular tend to bring out the best in people, promoting a high degree of considerate behavior (see Shearing and Kempa, 2004; chapter 9).

In regard to the notion of the Gaze, it is important to realize that visual trajectory is reversible (Foucault, 1977; Lacan, 1978; see Welch, 2011d). By switching the panoptic direction, the watcher becomes the watched, or, as Casey (2003) explains, the spectator is then transformed into the spectacle. In doing so, reversibility induces a degree of self-consciousness so persuasive that it guides the Subject to maintain appropriate social conduct within a given environment: "In Foucaultian terms, the museum is an institute of discipline which indoctrinates appropriate behavior in the viewer. Foucault's critique reinforces the notion of the museum as a place in which cultural values are authorized and specific behaviors encouraged as a means to produce socially acquired knowledge" (Casey, 2003: 4; see Bennett, 1995).

An illustration of that reversible Gaze is detected at Eastern State Penitentiary, where deep down a narrow alley visitors can step into the Jewish Synagogue. The physical space stands out from the rest of the prison for the most part because it is a place of worship, prompting those who enter to assume a respectful demeanor. Perhaps more so than in any other space in the prison, visitors are self-conscious about their movement as they admire the restored woodwork, precious artifacts, and other socioreligious reminders. Even the presence of a staff member is more noticeable than in other areas of the prison, as if he (or she) is there to enforce a certain code of proper conduct. Likewise, the collection of Jewish emblems seems to impose an added layer of vigilance. The Star of David located on the ceiling oversees all activities in the synagogue—an intimation of Bentham's (1995) panoptic theory of an omniscient deity (i.e., a watchful God is everywhere). Religious poetics enhance the sacred space by issuing solemn words of wisdom (see Smith, 2008). Also printed on the glass ceiling are uplifting messages, for example, "Be your sins like crimson, They can turn snow-white; Be they red as dyed wool, They can become like fleece.—Isaiah 1: 18b."

Casey's (2003) analysis of the Gaze serves as a prelude to a genealogy of the museum effect. Accordingly, she distills museum practice into three evolving typologies: the legislating museum, the interpreting museum, and the performing museum. The legislating museum has its origin in the cabinet of curiosities that displays rare, exotic, and sanctified objects (Weil, 1995). Prior to the nineteenth century, such containers of items were the dominant form of exhibition. Over time, the legislating museum—with its wider sweep of knowledge—sought to put on view the paragons of the aesthetic and intellectual pursuit. Its narrative assumed a firm social authority by producing a venue for display, not debate: "Because the legislating museum deployed authority through objects, not information, it created a specific experience of the object which attempted to fulfill its institutional goals" (Casey, 2003: 5). Whereas each of the prison museums studied herein has remnants of the legislating museum, one site in particular seems to embrace it in greater holistic terms. Beginning in 1980, visitors have been invited to view the modern innovations in Argentine criminology by touring the Penitentiary Museum in Buenos Aires. Just as prisons have served as museums for the display of criminological knowledge, the Argentine Penitentiary Museum, not unlike other sites for penal tourism, is situated inside a former prison that dates back to 1860, thereby offering tourists a unique pedagogical experience in which local penology is displayed alongside a narrative on nation-building, modernization, and a dream of order (Welch, 2012a; see chapter 3).

Adopting a clear commitment to the legislating museum, the brochure explains that the Argentine Penitentiary Museum is "meant to work as a technical-cultural institution: its purpose would be to keep all materials that could witness past experiences of the penitentiary life" (museum brochure, English version: 4). The term *technical-cultural institution* should catch the eye of researchers since it suggests that visitors are instructed how to comprehend penal technologies alongside significant cultural interpretations. As mentioned, tourists are given a particular lesson in the cultural sociology of punishment that does not separate the technical from its meaning. Convincingly, those two themes are interwoven by state officials who use the museum to convey a particular story about Argentine penology and state making (Welch and Macuare, 2011; see chapter 7).

Sites for penal tourism operate as mechanisms for social production with respect to order. In the case of the Argentine Penitentiary Museum, visitors gaze at a carefully assembled collection intended to give them an official version of the nation's penal history. With an eye on Durkheimian concepts, the socioreligious narrative does not stray far from the story of state building (the mythological) alongside the influence of the local Catholic Church (the sacred). Themes of purification stem not only from religious rituals as part of the prison regiment but also from the secular sphere of science and medicine aimed at controlling social pathologies. From that perspective, the medico-legal apparatus applies positivist penology to create a healthy and productive state. All told, the narrative retains the cult of the individual, often blending socioreligious and secular poetics to communicate the State's commitment to human dignity and moral reform. Still, there is enormous tension between the museum's dream of order and the atrocities of the Dirty War (La Guerra Sucia). Unsurprisingly, because of its attempt to recite the state myth of a benevolent government, the Argentine Penitentiary Museum—as an example of the legislating museum—avoids sensitive topics that would dilute its local messages about justice. Philip Smith reminds us that there are "efforts to construct a narrative for an onlooking audience, to tell a story, to offer a commentary on events and statuses, to channel meanings in one direction or another, to open up worlds of significance, or to close off unwanted interpretive possibilities" (2008: 37).

In what could be described as cultural sanitation, the museum—which opened during the military dictatorship—offers no acknowledgment of the Dirty War and the military's brutal reliance on disappearances, detention, torture, and the killing of thousands of civilians between 1976 and 1983 (Feitlowitz, 1998). Even so, most foreign tourists visiting Buenos Aires—and the prison museum—are mindful of the Dirty War's ongoing aftermath, especially in light of frequent public protests organized by civil society. Most visible is the group Madres de Plaza de Mayo, made up of the relatives of those abducted by the military (www.madres.org). Indeed, it is precisely in response to a huge influx of tourists that the punitive state has mobilized campaigns to "show itself" as the product of progress, giving even greater resonance to cultural institutions such as the Argentine Penitentiary Museum, as sanitized as that exhibit may be (see Welch and Macuare, 2011).

In the next stage of curatorial evolution, as Casey (2003) observes, the contemporary museum shifted its course from legislating meaning through its objects toward interpreting that meaning. The museum became less an authoritative "temple" and more of a "forum" that invites multiple voices and perspectives (Cameron, 1972). Nevertheless, the role of curators and their use of the screen to filter information remain a key force in creating a museum effect: "Rather than having objects speak for themselves, museum professionals interpret cultural significance for visitors by structuring art and artifacts around easily identifiable chronologies, geographies, formal themes, and narratives" (Casey, 2003: 6; Ernst, 2000). At Eastern State Penitentiary, curators clearly move beyond the authoritarian "temple" in an attempt to incorporate other viewpoints on the historical use of prisons and their contemporary transformations. An entire wing of the penitentiary is devoted to contemporary artworks that throw critical light on imprisonment. In one exhibit, a prison cell is revamped as a (post)modern cage in which a sleeping mat, a bath towel, and shower shoes are surrounded by a chain-link fence. Without having to refer to the storyboard, visitors recognize it as a replica of the holding cells at Guantanamo Bay. The installation by artist William Cromar is titled "GTMO." Along with an entry on the audio guide, the written narrative explains to those peering into the cell:

> This cell is a recreation of a cell from Camp X-Ray, the now abandoned holding facility in the United States Federal Detention Center at Guantanamo Bay, Cuba. The Department of Defense replaced Camp X-Ray with a newer facility, called Camp Delta, in 2002.
>
> As of March 2006, the United States holds more than 235 "enemy combatants" at the newer Guantanamo Bay facility. Most are accused of associating with the Taliban or Al-Qaida.

By placing the Guantanamo Bay cell inside the Eastern State Penitentiary cell, Cromar illustrates "nearly polar opposite means used to find a nearly equivalent end." Where the Eastern State cell is massive, opaque, and stone, the small Guantanamo Bay cell is virtually transparent, reflecting a different attitude toward the prisoner and different expectations of the architecture. With this particular art exhibit, curators encourage visitors to reflect on the larger museum effect and its capacity to compare the past with the present. As the tour (and audio) guide explains, the architecture at Eastern State was originally intended to complement the Quaker philosophy of prisoner reform: "The interior of the prison was designed to resemble a cathedral to inspire penitence, or true regret, in the men and women housed there" (Dolan, 2007: 12; see chapter 4). Indeed, early prison reformers in Philadelphia believed that all persons were basically good; therefore, a stint in prison would serve to restore those virtues in convicts. That socioreligious commitment to the cult of the individual affirms the dignity of wrongdoers. By contrast, the war on terror—especially under President Bush—portrays terrorists as inherently evil. Correspondingly, institutions such as Guantanamo Bay were not designed to improve detainees. While some detainees have been considered for military commissions, others remain unjustly confined even years after being cleared of war crimes. Arguably, those detainees are being scapegoated (or sacrificed in the ancient sense) for the attacks of September 11. Along with being physically and psychologically abused, detainees at Guantanamo Bay are kept in a legal black hole—perhaps indefinitely (Welch, 1996, 2009). Cromar's "GTMO" offers a postmodern critique of the anxiety stoked by the war on terror. Especially by installing that artwork inside Eastern State, Cromar seems interested in raising serious doubts about modernity and its claims of rationality and humane penal reform (see Lennon and Foley, 2010).

In its final incarnation, the contemporary museum has become a space for performance where the task of conveying information relies less on objects and more on display. The move toward drama is a response, in part, to commercial incentives aimed at attracting tourists by promising them an entertaining experience: "In addition to conveying knowledge, the visibility of these modes of display highlights the museum as a medium for the production of culture, where the museum itself is on display" (Casey, 2003: 9; Kirshenblatt-Gimblett 1988). Keeping attention on Eastern State Penitentiary, we witness how it is influenced by each of the museal prototypes. Entering the prison, visitors are swiftly introduced to the mission of the legislative museum. In particular, John Haviland's architectural masterpiece (i.e., radial plan) is applauded for its impressive design: indeed, in the 1820s, it was far ahead of its time. Among the information dispensed by the tour (and audio) guide is the fact that Eastern State had indoor plumbing during an era when even the White House still resorted to chamber pots.

As noted, Eastern State also serves as an interpretive museum by sponsoring contemporary art installations. Interestingly, the exhibit by artist William Cromar (i.e., "GTMO") is supported by Eastern State's Halloween fund-raiser titled "Terror behind the Walls." Here we are able to connect the dots between the different types of museum practice. While Eastern State serves as both a legislative and an interpretive museum, it also operates as a performance space in the form of a haunted house during the Halloween season. By doing so, the prison museum emphasizes theatrics to deliver a jolt of excitement. The brochure reads: "Ranked the 'No.1 Haunted House in America' by AOL City Guide and 'One of America's Scariest Halloween Attractions' by The Travel Channel" (see Brown, 2009).

Of course, in terms of a museum effect, Eastern State's haunted house is geared at manufacturing fright. While some visitors might very well be startled, that emotional state is at best momentary. Therefore, the experience seems to ride on a condition of "pseudofear," since visitors know that they are ultimately safe. Still, what makes the performance worthwhile is allowing the museum to tap into one's wild imagination, conjuring thoughts of ghosts, goblins, and evil spirits (as the opposite and opponent of the sacred). Whereas Eastern State Penitentiary was founded on the Quaker belief in good health and the spiritual purification of convicts, the haunted house seeks to terrify tourists with threats of pollution (see Douglas, 1966). One segment of "Terror behind the Walls" is aptly titled "Detritus," referring to decay and decomposed bodies. Accordingly, visitors are supposed to be frightened by the (fictional) presence of ghoulish creatures coming back from the dead (see www.terrorbehindthewalls.com). In the realm of museum studies, the transformation of Eastern State into a performance space should not be overstated. By design, "Terror behind the Walls" is a temporary project from which proceeds are used to support the former prison as a traditional legislative museum (e.g., historic preservation), along with its interpretive offshoots (e.g., contemporary art).

In sum, Casey's typology classifying museums into different curatorial roles—legislator, interpreter, performer—serves as a useful analytical device. However, it has clear limitations in the study of prison museums. Few of the prison museums examined here fit neatly into Casey's scheme. Rather, most museums tend to incorporate one or more of those roles in the course of crafting a particular narrative. In the next sections, we delve deeper into the dynamics of the museum effect by exploring the significance of objects, images, and space.

Museum studies scholars write at length about the phenomenological and cultural significance of objects. As mentioned previously, the museum acquires social authority by managing ways of seeing; indeed, by utilizing a screen to filter curatorial details, the museum benefits from an established context. That environment facilitates the museal vision around which objects are arranged. Once placed on display, objects attain immediate meaning, thereby validating their status as something important and worthy of the Gaze (Casey, 2003; Malraux, 1967). Barbara Kirshenblatt-Gimblett (1988) adds further insight into that cultural transformation. Museums do not merely gather valuable objects; rather, they make objects valuable by gathering them. Such conversion involves a process of revaluation whereby objects pass from use-value to signifying-value. As a result, objects are rendered "emblems loaded with emotional and historical weight almost certainly greater than that enjoyed in their initial incarnation" (Williams, 2007: 28). Of course, in order to be appraised with a higher cultural value, objects must be chosen from an enormous pool of discovered artifacts. The selection procedure is usually guided by one of three criteria.

First, the object boasts signifying-value by being rare or revelatory. Consider the strange item on display at the Hyde Park Barracks in Sydney identified as a "parti-coloured suit" worn by recalcitrant convicts nicknamed "canary men" due to the ridiculously patterned yellow and black clothing that could be easily spotted at long distances. Those brightly colored uniforms not only improved the supervision of convicts working in the field but also served to impose a certain degree of public humiliation and penal spectacle (see chapter 6).

Second, an object may be selected for being typical and representative of a category. At the Clink museum in London, tourists can gaze at the cat-o'-nine-tails, "famous for the use onboard British Navy ships where the saying 'not having enough room to swing a cat' originates from due [sic] to the confinement below decks." Likewise, the cat-o'-nine-tails (known for leaving wounds resembling cat scratches on the back) is on display at the Melbourne Gaol as well as at the Hyde Park Barracks, where it was favored by superintendent Ernest Slade, who boasted that fifty lashes could look like one thousand. At the Hong Kong Correctional Services Museum, the "cat" is described as a "dreaded punishment" that "could rip and tear skin from the back of the victim, scaring for life." Although each of those prison museums marks the history of the cat-o'-nine-tails along with its cultural significance (for example, how it entered the vernacular), visitors are not given much detail on its demise. One exception is the Clink in London, where the museum provides an update on the controversy over corporal punishment. Visitors are informed by a poster that the cat-o'-nine-tails was used throughout the British Empire but that its use was abolished in 1948. Still, as that poster points out, comparable forms of corporal punishment were used in Trinidad and Tobago until 2005. In that brief remark, curators seem to embrace Durkheim's notion of the cult of the individual by suggesting that humane penal reforms eventually—albeit recently—landed on the outer rim of the (former) British Empire (see chapter 5).

Finally, a curator might choose an object due to its remnant-themed iconography: that is, for having belonged to a remarkable person or group. In Johannesburg, the prison museum at Constitution Hill offers tourists an in-depth look into the life and activism of Mahatma Gandhi, "Prisoner of Conscience." The sizeable gallery issues a retrospective on Gandhi, whose larger-than-life persona still resonates with mythic proportion. In addition to a series of elaborate storyboards, the room displays some otherwise ordinary objects that seem to "come to life" once associated with the world famous nonviolent leader. For example, a pair of sandals is culturally significant not only because they belonged to Gandhi but also because they symbolize his campaign against discrimination so as to preserve human dignity (i.e., the cult of the individual). In protesting the racist pass laws that restricted the movement of people of color, Gandhi abandoned European attire in 1912 (see chapter 8).

Once chosen, objects then enter the collection, thereby further validating their signifying-value. Altogether, those objects advance the museum's mission as a collecting—and normalizing—institution. Henry Flower, in 1898, wrote about the general requirements for public collecting institutions, which were aimed at maximizing their effect as vehicles for public instruction: "Correct classification, good labelling, isolation of each object from its neighbors, the provision of a suitable background, and above all a position in which it can be readily and distinctively seen" (1898: 3). Objects that appear to be from different historical periods allow the museum to convey a chronological narrative. The "walk through history" is a common technique in museums devoted to natural history, science, and art (see Bennett, 1995). Prison museums tend to follow that format. Inside many prison museums (e.g., Alcatraz, Argentina, and Hong Kong), staff uniforms from different historical periods are displayed, giving tourists a "walk through time" from which they are able to recognize themes of progress and professionalism.

At a higher level of awareness, those uniforms serve as semiophores that bring to the present (and visible) that which is absent (and invisible) such as the past (see Pomian, 1990) At the Correctional Services Museum in Hong Kong, the past is depicted in its colonial form. There, British officer uniforms are signifiers of the Queen's reach into China. Without much textual information, visitors understand the curator's message; that is, the British used the Victoria and the Stanley prisons to maintain colonial order over the Chinese. Moreover, the narrative on colonial rule benefits from an even thicker description as we gaze at the vastly different officer uniforms worn by Indians who themselves were brought to Hong Kong from the British colony of India. With the aid of vintage photographs, the theme of colonialism is layered: the British commanders watch over the Indian guards who watch over the Chinese prisoners (see chapter 8).

Under ideal circumstances, the museum effect encourages visitors to develop relationships with an object contained in the collection. However, as visitors try to get close—physically, intellectually, emotionally—they are often kept at a distance. Paradoxically, distance tends to strengthen the allure of an object and what it represents. With respect to that phenomenon, Casey (2003) explains the significance of the screen, distance, and desire: "Because the screen is merely an image of the Object, not the Object itself, the object of the Gaze can never be known directly. In psychoanalytic terms, the Object of desire always lies just beyond the reach of the viewer and is always intermediated by the screen. The Subject is perpetually propelled toward it, seeking but never sated" (3).

For the museum effect, desire is a powerful force, since it often renders certain objects unattainable: "Why look over and over again if not propelled by a deep unsatisfied curiosity?" (Casey, 2003: 3). That craving for apprehension is epitomized by the fictional story where visitors at the Louvre rushed to view the empty space left after the theft of the *Mona Lisa* (Leader, 2003). The tourists not only were intrigued by the scene of the crime but also were interested in furthering their understanding of the *Mona Lisa,* whether the painting was present or not. According to Casey, even when the object itself disappears, the cultural screen remains vivid. A similar phenomenon might be found in Philadelphia's Eastern State Penitentiary, where the cell of iconic gangster Al Capone draws legions of tourists (see figure 5). His imprisonment is described by the tour guide (as well as by the audio guide, which is voiced by famed actor Steve Buscemi):

FIGURE 5. The luxurious cell of Al Capone (Eastern State Penitentiary, Philadelphia). © retrowelch 2014

Capone arrived at Eastern State in 1929: he served eight months for carrying a concealed weapon. It was rumored that Capone welcomed his imprisonment during which time he dodged repercussions of the St. Valentine's Day Massacre in Chicago where rival crime bosses were gunned down. A visit to Capone's cell does not disappoint, culturally or phenomenologically. There he lived in luxury: among his comfort items were "tasteful paintings," fine furniture, oriental rugs, and a deluxe radio that played his favorite music (see Dolan, 2007). Visitors are drawn to gaze through the cell bars into the beautifully furnished cell; however, they cannot enter. Therefore, being kept a distance, tourists are propelled toward the space once occupied by the infamous gangster but never really achieve a sense of satisfaction. Those with an enduring fascination with Capone can stop in the museum's gift shop, where they can purchase full-color posters and postcards of his cell. In their own small way, those souvenirs transport the aura of Capone's legend into the daily lives of tourists who might display those items in their home or office (see chapter 10).

The allure of certain objects—enhanced via the screen—might also have a sinister appeal, a common theme in dark tourism, in which visitors gravitate to sites associated with tragic events for purposes of remembrance, education, or even entertainment (Lennon and Foley, 2010; Rojek, 1993). The sinister appeal in penal tourism contours the overall museum effect by injecting anxiety into the experience of visiting a former prison. Whereas the objects are clearly remnants of the past, the fact that they were used in such terrible acts as torture makes them "insidiously arresting" (Williams, 2007: 31). Much like the theme of colonialism found in the prison museum in Hong Kong, in the Seodaemun Prison History Hall the Story of Korea while under Japanese occupation is examined. Indeed, prisons were instrumental in controlling the local people, especially those committed to the resistance and rebellion. The torture devices on display possess a sinister appeal since they serve as evidence of brutality. Consider the Box Torture: "A torture by putting an individual inside a box stubbed with sharp nails and shaking the box to torture him or her." An actual torture box is placed on the floor of the gallery. Looking inside the box, one might have difficulty imagining how a person could actually fit inside a space not much larger than a footlocker. Once trapped inside the box, the victim was subjected to multiple punctures similar to those of the medieval torture known as the Iron Maiden. Along with an array of other torture devices, the prison museum in Seoul affects visitors viscerally (see chapter 7). As noted previously, the sinister appeal of objects in penal tourism serves to invert the "Disney" experience, becoming the opposite of "the happiest place on earth" (Williams, 2007: 99). Still, objects are just one part of the museum effect; as we move on to images—and later space—critical attention is turned to cultural and historical verification of the prison narrative.

IMAGES

The museum's social authority, to reiterate, is established by dictating the manner by which items are seen. Whereas objects seem to be the real thing, images serve to authenticate their historical significance. Museum studies scholar Paul Williams explains: "Images are both representations of the past and vestigial artifacts from it" (2007: 51). Due to their capacity to preserve history as it actually was, images tend to make a significant impression on museum visitors, including those touring former prisons. Images contribute noticeably to the visual space of the prison museum. Among the most powerful visual forms are photographs. Such images provide the museum and its narrative with expert technical verification and, in doing so, establish their truth-value. The curatorial message is rarely disputed: this incident really did happen. At the Seodaemun Prison History Hall, visitors are presented with disturbing images of war crimes and crimes against humanity. An exhibit titled "Traces and Sufferings from Torture" informs visitors: "The results from such unthinkable torture inflicted by the Japanese to Korean patriots included the cutting off of bodily extremities, the peeling off of skin, and rupturing of internal organs. Most of the imprisoned patriots were not defeated by such inhuman torture, but endured their imprisonment, but there were many who died in or out of prison after being paroled due to torture." Photographs show Korean political prisoners with bandages covering their injured faces and badly mutilated hands. The images offer compelling documentation of torture, further enhancing the truth-value of the entire museum.

Along with expert technical verification, photographs add cultural verification to the museum (Williams, 2007). In penal tourism, cultural validation often takes the form of local embeddedness in which the prison museum displays punishments that at first glance seem almost universal (e.g., public humiliation) but upon closer inspection incorporate the immediate cultural landscape (see Melossi, 2001). In the first portion of the tour at the Hong Kong Correctional Services Museum, photographs serve to verify penal practices under colonial rule. In one picture, two criminals are shown seated on a city street with their bare feet poking through the holes of wooden stocks. A description of their offense is written (in Chinese) on a large board placed under their chin. The photograph captures the local embeddedness of late-nineteenth-century spectacle: offenders are recognized as traditional Chinese with their hair braided in a distinctive queue. Behind them stands an Indian officer (wearing a turban) who supervises the public spectacle. The image seems to support Foucault's contention that "the convict would repay society twice: once by the labour he provided, and a second time by the signs he produced, a focus of both profit and signification in serving as a lesson on crime and punishment" (1977: 111).

The production of meaning embodied in the display of photographs becomes all the more stark when visitors are presented with the harsh reality of punishment. Among the most recognizable forms of visual narrative is the atrocity photograph that contains graphic evidence of what happened. There are two dominant types of atrocity photography: the action shot and the identification picture (Williams, 2007: 56). As one would expect, action shots are dramatic, "in the moment," and "frozen in time," thereby preserving a memory of horror. Upon entering one of the galleries at the prison museum in Hong Kong, visitors are cautioned: "Attention: Please be reminded that some Exhibits may be disturbing." Indeed, the photographs become progressively more violent in nature. For example, one image seizes the immediate moment after ten pirates were beheaded. As their lifeless bodies and heads lay scattered across the ground, British and Chinese officials pose for the cameraman. In reference to the museum effect, Williams explains: "the 'pain of looking' involves not only victims' agonizing experiences, but our discomfort at having to see" (2007: 62). Moreover, there remains an ethical dilemma, since those photographed "did not ask to play any part in making history" (2007: 71).

As another type of atrocity photo, the identification picture leaves much more to the imagination. Often in the form of a headshot, the image serves to identify the person with such details as name, age, and height. The context of the museum, however, produces a sense of tragedy, since it is presumed that the individual photographed was detained, perhaps disappeared, or even tortured. Inside the Seodaemun prison museum, three entire walls of a large room are covered with "inmate cards" of Koreans imprisoned by the Japanese military. The arrangement of photographs adds an unsettling quality to the exhibit: positioned in the center of the space, the visitor is stared at by hundreds of political prisoners whose blank expressions suggest they met a terrible fate (see figure 6). At museums committed to memorialization, similar displays of identification pictures are commonly presented in a grid style; although egalitarian, that format strips the person of their importance, their social rank, and even their individuality (Williams, 2007). The seemingly endless checkerboard of photos inside the Seodaemun gallery is at once neatly bureaucratic and dehumanizing. Consequently, visitors are subjected to a solemn—albeit disquieting—experience comparable to other dark tourisms (e.g., holocaust museums; see Dekel, 2013; Lennon and Foley, 2010). Even so, the room exudes a sacred tone that benefits from the revaluation of inmate cards that pass from their use-value as processing documents to their signifying-value as symbols of noble resistance. Accordingly, that cultural transformation of images prompts visitors to show respect to those who were unjustly imprisoned (see chapter 9). With those ideas in mind, let us now turn our attention to the importance of space.

SPACE

As noted in the previous chapter, museology stems partially from art history; as a result, there has been disproportionate emphasis on the meaning of artifacts rather than on institutional space (McLeod, 2005; Williams, 2007).

Fortunately, in the realm of prison museums, the significance of space is paramount, since an excursion to a former prison is deeply connected to its history of penal practices. From its inception, the modern prison was an architectural invention that incorporated space into the transformation of the convict (Bender, 1987; Evans, 1982; Meranze, 1996). What usually attracts tourists to a prison museum are its imposing facade and intriguing interiors. Together, those spatial features reinforce the prison museum's actual sitedness from which it acquires its social authority. Many prison museums succeed in having a lasting effect on its visitors because the tour occurs inside a space that possesses an undisputed authenticity. With their monolithic design—and fortress guard towers—Alcatraz, Eastern State Penitentiary, Melbourne Gaol, and Seodaemun Prison do not fail in conveying their chief semiotic message. That is, visitors know it's a prison because it looks like a prison.

Museums in general, and prison museums in particular, operate in two spatial registers. First, those sites serve as concrete objects in space intended to serve practical purposes (e.g., a building inside where artifacts are displayed). Second, the physical layout contributes to the mental images that visitors create, especially with respect to the topic at hand (e.g., a history of incarceration) (Williams, 2007). Visualization becomes an important dynamic in prison museums, since those sites tend to produce a vivid—albeit artificial—memory (see Urry, 2002). Touring Alcatraz, Eastern State Penitentiary, Melbourne Gaol, Robben Island, and Constitution Hill, one can easily imagine the presence of legendary prisoners: the Birdman, Al Capone, Ned Kelly, Nelson Mandela, Mahatma Gandhi. Often such visualization endures as a lasting memory—or psychological memento—of visiting those former prisons.

While helping to form psychological states embodied in memory, spatiality also has profound phenomenological implications. Consider the distinctions between place and space. Michel de Certeau (1984) explains that a place comprises an arrangement of interconnected parts that is static and permanent. By contrast, a space is marked by vectors of direction that suggest cadence and time. Streets and buildings, for example, make up the place of a city while its space incorporates the actual movement of people: "Where place is defined in formal stable terms, obeying 'the law of property' that ascribes one function to any single location, space carries a variety of meanings awarded by multiple users" (Williams, 2007: 103). In many prison museums, such as Seodaemun Prison History Hall, Eastern State Penitentiary, and the Women's Jail (Constitution Hill), visitors can gaze inside an actual prison cell that remains in a fixed place. Then, with the freedom of movement afforded through space, tourists are able to mill about the prison, strolling its long hallways radiating from a central rotunda.

Furthering a phenomenological appreciation of place and space, de Certeau (1984) characterizes maps as scientific representations of place that erase the itinerary that produced it. So as to inject life into those indicators of place, tours serve to reactivate movement. Along with narrative and meticulously labeled objects and images, the tour, whether through a personal guide, audio guide, or a mere map of the museum, relies on locomotion to transcend the mind/body duality: hence, treating visitors as "mind on legs" (Bennett, 1995: 6). To be clear, such "organized walking" is made possible by utilizing space. Tourists at the Hyde Park Barracks museum, for instance, are invited to walk over and around a large map of the city drawn on the gallery's floor. There "organized walking" features a "walk back in time" by prompting visitors to situate themselves in Sydney during its days as a penal colony. From a phenomenological perspective, that particular museum effect compresses time and place through an imaginative use of space. Williams observes that (memorial) museums tend to straddle two functions:

> On the one hand, they are unusually visible, vibrant, and unregulated locations in which visitors can "practice space" in their own idiosyncratic manner in casual outings with no fixed, determined structure. On the other hand, there remains a strong ritual component to visitation. Grave and often official impositions of meaning also firmly situate memorial museums as perpetual, reliable, city spaces, perhaps as functional as any other. Hence, memorial museums are especially interesting in the way they seek to support a wide, open-ended variety of practices in visitors, yet also aim to make some authoritative statement about where and how to remember the past. (2007: 103–4)

Consider the tours at two comparable prison museums: Alcatraz and Robben Island. Since each of those islands remains in the constant line of vision for those who live or vacation in San Francisco or Cape Town, they exude a strong phenomenological and cultural presence. Correspondingly, Alcatraz and Robben Island seem to enter the local psyche with respect to incarceration, becoming a major attraction for tourism. Both visits begin with a long wait in line, and then a boat ride that takes sightseers to a historical place that seems at once geographically close and emotionally remote. Curiously, tourists are lured to those sites of banishment and willingly embark on a voyage that is not very different from that of prisoners who were sent to Alcatraz or Robben Island. Once there, visitors might share a convict's experience of isolation from the city situated before them. Skyscrapers in San Francisco and Table Mountain in Cape Town sit monumentally just beyond one's reach. While both islands offer vacationers momentary "escape" from the hustle and bustle of the city, after a few hours they eagerly await their return to the comforts and convenience of the urban center (see Cohen and Taylor, 1976; Rojek, 1993). For prisoners confined to Alcatraz and Robben Island, the wait was obviously more prolonged; for them, the city symbolized not only freedom but also home, family, and friends.

To create a well-rounded museum effect, tourists are encouraged to appreciate Robben Island and Alcatraz for their thriving ecological environment that exists apart from the prison. At Robben Island, getting a glimpse of whales, seals, and penguins serves to momentarily distract visitors from the primary narrative on political imprisonment. Likewise, at Alcatraz, Park Rangers (sporting their Smokey the Bear hats) instruct sightseers to hike around the island and enjoy its wide range of habitat, including wild flowers and exotic birds. As the tour segues to the prison, the shifting emotional tone can be a bit jarring as visitors are torn from the natural beauty of the island in order to face the man-made reality of incarceration. That move across the pleasure/pain spectrum reinforces the museum effect at Alcatraz and Robben Island, although with different spatial registers. At Alcatraz, visitors are sold a "touristy" experience through the use of engaging multimedia galleries and legendary stories of the Rock. Although the audio guide delivers a sequenced narrative on major historical developments, visitors can (de)activate the device if they feel like it, thereby allowing them to explore the prison compound without too many boundaries.

By sharp contrast, those visiting Robben Island are subjected to a fixed, lockstep journey. Tourists are put into large groups (of fifty), herded onto large coach buses, and driven around the island. The driver gives short bursts of narrative while directing attention to the main points of interest: residential housing for prison staff, a church, a post office, and so on. The highly regimented tour continues on foot inside the prison with a former political prisoner serving as a guide. Unlike in Alcatraz (and other prison museums), visitors do not "practice space" per se. Rather, space seems to practice them, in a way similar to the institutional structures and routines that regulate the movement of prisoners. The barren landscape inside the former prison yards is not visually appealing, which, again, gives visitors the point of view of the no-frills life of an inmate. Overall, the tour at Robben Island is not geared at providing a recreational experience; moreover, its educational value is delivered through a spoken narrative, not through a collection of labeled objects or storyboards. While the group is kept together, the mood is relaxed but somber. As noted previously, the visit seems more like a (sacred) pilgrimage to honor those who sacrificed their liberty for the birth of a new South Africa. Tourists are reminded of the unjust treatment of political prisoners in particular, and black and colored South Africans in general. Still, the message is upbeat, suggesting that political imprisonment failed to contain a people's resistance to apartheid. A proud feeling of victory over oppression is conveyed throughout the tour of Robben Island—even the buses are decorated with vibrant colors and a mildly amusing slogan: POWERED BY FREEDOM. Williams (2007) summarizes the significance of the performance of memorial museums (including Robben Island) by noting that those sites continue to remain interesting and controversial because they are associated with serious historical narratives (see chapter 9).

THE INVISIBLE HAND OF THE CURATOR

Of course, objects and images do not interact with space merely on their own. The museum effect is the final product of the curator. While prison museums might seem natural in their presentation due in large part to their sited-ness, there is a good deal of planning, designing, and decision-making that takes place behind the doors of meeting rooms. Though it goes beyond the scope of this discussion to address specifically each of the prison museums studied herein with respect to their curatorial ambition, some broader themes and techniques deserve attention. Corrine Kratz (2011) offers important insights into the construction of the museum exhibitions, particularly since they serve as critical sites for establishing identity and worth. As story-telling institutions, museums communicate by way of the "rhetorics of value" and "designed space." The process of organizing an exhibition entails judgments that reinforce hierarchies of merit; still, designers rely on rhetorics of value ranging from the serious to the playful while at the same time trying not to draw notice.

Since the 1980s, the catchphrase among curators has been "poetics and politics" (Karp and Lavine, 1991). That double vision certainly made its way into prison museums. At the Seodaemun history prison, the presentation of inmate artifacts (e.g., uniforms and tools) is stylized to project repression as well as honor, thereby upholding their cultural worth. Similarly, other prison museums, such as Robben Island, rely on the invisible hand of the curator to "structure feeling" among visitors while delivering messages about a higher morality (see Harvey, 1990). Curators understand that visitors (whether travelers, tourists, or posttourists) often experience an exhibition socially, with family, friends, classmates, and so on. Moreover, they bring with them their own backgrounds and interests as well as political orientations and expectations. Museums, consequently, strive toward identifying with their visitors rather than clashing with them so that the experience is rewarding. That does not mean, however, that such topics as incarceration and capital punishment are trivialized (see Sabatini, 2011).

The invisible hand of the curator maneuvers according to several techniques; chief among them are lighting and text, both of which engage poetics and politics. Boutique lighting, for instance, not only shapes perception but also conveys the importance of certain objects, granting them a jewellike quality. At the Melbourne Gaol, visitors cannot help but see the replica of Ned Kelly's death mask, since it is carefully illuminated by a spotlight against an otherwise shadowed background. As Roberts (1994) points out, lighting is never neutral, since someone always determines it. By placing Kelly's death mask on display in that manner, curators seem to be putting his legend in a favorable light. That maneuver is consistent with much of the narrative about Kelly at the Melbourne Gaol, which for the most part is hagiographic. Exhibition planners also use color to reinforce the positive sensations of the museum experience; moreover, such tonality can express politics. Inside the Argentine Penitentiary Museum, each of the galleries is adorned with the national flag. With its cool light blue stripes, a firm sense of Argentine pride is conveyed throughout the tour. At the other end of the lighting spectrum, prison museums maximize their manipulation of darkness so as to re-create the natural environment of imprisonment. Visitors at Alcatraz, Eastern State Penitentiary, and elsewhere are drawn into individual cells contoured by their dark interior, producing a mood of depression. Further down the emotional scale, isolation cells—such as those at Number Four in Johannesburg—inject fear and terror. From the standpoint of the curator, that "structured feeling" goes according to plan.

The rhetorics of value are also structured by words in the form of text, captions, and banners, all of which direct vision. For more than a century, curators have advocated the "rigorous use of labels in order to transform [art] museums from mere 'gazing museums' into 'institutes for visual instruction'" (Bennett, 1998: 368). Most museum visitors not only actually read texts but also give them voice by repeating them in their own conversations, producing what curators call the "text echo" (McManus, 1989). Again, since the museum experience is often a social one, that "text echo" has a potent effect. Visitors to prison museums can be seen (and heard) reading text aloud to their friends and family. Their "structured feeling" is noticeable as voices seem to crack when learning the gory details of such torture devices as the Spanish Boot, the Scavenger's Daughter, and so forth. In that sense, curators literally put their words into the mouths of visitors (Kratz, 2011). Curators also use audio and tour guides as vehicles for delivering carefully selected words in the form of stories. To be sure, political agendas are barely concealed in the tightly crafted anecdotes, especially when dealing with such matters as racial inequality and apartheid. At Robben Island, for example, serious narration is given levity with subtle humor. As the tour bus approaches the snack bar and restrooms, the driver announces to visitors that they will have just a "short walk to freedom." (Those familiar with Mandela's autobiography *Long Walk to Freedom* get the joke.) While the tour guides at Robben Island are themselves former political prisoners, their narration is produced by a committee: hence, another reminder of the hidden hand of the curator. Behind-the-scenes research reveals that although the former prisoners share their personal experiences about being incarcerated, the larger collective memory is scripted by a team to ensure that all visitors feel that they are on a pilgrimage (Garuba, 2007; see Mbeki, 1991; McAtackney, 2013). In sum, the rhetorics of value rest on a variety of techniques to create a coherent and gestalt-like experience (Kratz, 2011). Along the way, the articulated agenda often carries a subtle and almost unconscious "system of highly political values expressed not only in the style of presentation but in myriad facets of its operations" (Vogel, 1991: 200; see Dekel, 2013).

CONCLUSION

As this chapter describes in detail, penal tourism relies heavily on the museum effect, whereby visitors are subjected to a multilayered encounter with objects, images, and space. While some prison museums do offer a degree of entertainment, the thrust of the museal mission is still aimed at delivering knowledge. Consider the clever instructional device at Alcatraz titled "Alcatrivia." Visitors are positioned in front of a large wooden cabinet displaying a set of ten questions. For example, "True or False? Alcatraz inmates lived in dungeons on bread and water." After a moment of thought, one lifts a small metal knob attached to the plaque, thereby revealing the correct answer: "FALSE: Inmates ate standard fare and lived in the cells you see. However, against Bureau orders, the first warden used cells in the old fort beneath the Cellhouse as punishment for inmates, who dubbed them 'the Spanish dungeons.'" Visitors with a wider stock of information might recall "the Spanish dungeons," since the controversy was revisited in the Hollywood movie *Murder in the First* (1995), based on the true story from the 1930s of Henri Young (Kevin Bacon), who was brutalized by the sadistic warden (Gary Oldman).

That particular "Alcatrivia" item dispenses knowledge in a few complementary ways. First, it attracts the attention of visitors by asking them a straightforward (nonthreatening) true/false question, not unlike in a fun game show. Second, in order to determine the correct answer, the visitor must open the tab; hence, by putting the body in motion, the experience incorporates "hands-on" learning. Third, similar to the movie *Escape from Alcatraz,* the museum draws links between popular culture and the Rock's history: specifically, the case of Henri Young. Finally, the nature of the question addresses both Foucault's take on penal discipline and Durkheim's notion of the cult of the individual. The answer to the quiz makes clear that the warden who sent prisoners to the "Spanish dungeon" was violating Bureau of Prisons guidelines; therefore, the willful mistreatment of inmates was the exception, not the rule. Altogether, "Alcatrivia" illustrates the significance of gazing (i.e., reading the question), performing (i.e., lifting the tab), and normalizing (i.e., condemning prisoner abuse). And in doing so, the learning task—as well as the entire tour of Alcatraz—is intended to promote self-improvement by acquiring knowledge.

In the chapters to follow, the museum effect will continue to be examined, especially with respect to objects, images, and space. Indeed, each of those elements of exhibition figures prominently in an array of forthcoming penal topics: architecture, economics, colonialism, and resistance. Still, the interpretation pursues a cultural sociology of punishment by integrating Foucaultian and Durkheimian perspectives, thereby shedding light on the significance of power, control, and socioreligious semiotics. Setting an additional stage for that analysis, the next chapter explores the manner by which "dead" prisons are brought "back to life" so as to project a particular dream of order (see Brown, 2009; Welch, 2012a). As we shall see, prison museums in cities around the world share a common interest in the emergence of imprisonment, but in their own unique way, they incorporate local history and culture into the narrative on penality.

THREE

Dream of Order

In the realm of punishment, notions of order are ubiquitous. Penal signs, symbols, and slogans all contribute to normative messages proclaiming "the way society should be." Such visions of order have a wider appeal with respect to penal tourism, whereby the public visits former prisons refurbished as museums. While tapping into a popular curiosity about punishment, those sites deliver a didactic—and cultural—experience relating to incarceration. Among the archetypal meanings conveyed via penal tourism are lessons on order and how that ideal has been pursued over time. Michelle Brown observes: "Dead prisons reconfigure living prisons, not in a clear chain of direct institutional transformation but in a larger cultural imaginary and its ability to justify the pursuit of a proper 'dream of order' and the proper place of prisons, punishment, and their targets in that chain of signs" (2009: 120; Welch, 2010a, 2012a).

Along those lines of inquiry, this chapter elaborates on the way prison museums establish their social authority, allowing them to narrate the construction of order. As we continue to discover, the official interpretation of punishment rarely strays from visual rhetoric on order, replete with monolithic architecture reinforced by rules, regulations, and routine. Toward that end, many of the museums examined herein share a common theme highlighting the prison's role in the formation of the State. Upon closer inspection, however, similarities tend to disperse as they blend into the immediate penal landscape shaped by emerging politics and economics. Those historical forces are pivotal in how emerging societies each move toward modernity. Consider, for instance, the Penitentiary Museum in Buenos Aires, where a main attraction is the large model of the National Penitentiary located in Buenos Aires from 1873 to 1961 (see figure 7). The design of the institution proudly combines fortress architecture with modern function as five spokes

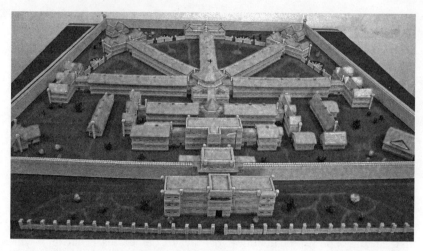

FIGURE 7. Model of the National Penitentiary in Buenos Aires from 1873 to 1961. The radial design borrows from Eastern State Penitentiary in Philadelphia (Argentine Penitentiary Museum, Buenos Aires). © retrowelch 2014

radiate from a central tower; indeed, it serves as a convincing symbol of symmetry and order not unlike Eastern State Penitentiary (Philadelphia) and Seodaemun prison (Seoul).

Projecting a thick narrative on local nationalism, the Argentine flag (with lettering from the First Unit of the Penitentiary Service) is situated above the replica. Adjacent walls contain numerous black-and-white photographs, including a wide shot and an impressive telescopic view down a main corridor of the institution. That dream of order is complemented with other pictures that reveal a decidedly industrial modern (instrumentalist) prison system as inmates are shown working in machine shops and an auto body repair shop, as well as driving rider lawnmowers (see Welch and Macuare, 2011).

With their strong sense of authority, prison museums operate as mechanisms for cultural production, delivering lessons on social order and the position of prisons within a particular imagination of punishment. So as to tease out the nuances contained in the dreams of order, we decipher how sites for penal tourism convey messages that seem at once to be universal and locally layered. While the interpretation maintains instrumental (power-based, Foucaultian) and expressive (semiotic, Durkheimian) perspectives, it ventures into three domains of order: grand order, institutional order, and alternative order. Before embarking on a multitiered analysis of the dream of order, let us conceptualize a bit more on phenomenology and culture.

In a lecture from 1967 titled "Of Other Spaces," Foucault delves into the notion of heterotopias vis-à-vis utopias. Utopias, he proclaims, are ideas or images of perfection. Still, they are sites without a real place, existing as unreal spaces. Heterotopias, on the other hand, are physical representations or approximations of a particular utopia. Somewhat schematically, Foucault identifies different types of "other spaces." To begin, there are heterotopias of indefinitely accumulating time:

> Museums and libraries have become heterotopias in which time never stops building up and topping its own summit, whereas in the seventeenth century, even at the end of the century, museums and libraries were the expression of an individual choice. By contrast, the idea of accumulating everything, of establishing a sort of general archive, the will to enclose in one place all times, all epochs, all forms, all tastes, the idea of constituting a place of all times that is itself outside of time and inaccessible to its ravages, the project of organizing in this way a sort of perpetual and indefinite accumulation of time in an immobile place, this whole idea belongs to our modernity. The museum and the library are heterotopias that are proper to western culture of the nineteenth century. (1986a: 26)

While some prison museums are relatively sparse in terms of their collection (e.g., Robben Island), others appear encyclopedic as they aspire to accumulate almost everything in their penal history. Consider the Argentine Penitentiary Museum. Even though its exhibit ignores the atrocities of the Dirty War (La Guerra Sucia), the objects and images on display offer a sweeping narrative on the emergence of the institution. The "walk through time" starts in the 1730s when the Jesuits expanded their missions into Argentina. It concludes with an installation of a contemporary prison cell. Along the way, tourists get glimpses of nearly every episode of the prison's evolution, including its lineage of weaponry, various work tools, and a hodgepodge of inmate artwork.

Foucault goes on to describe heterotopias as having a system of opening and closing that both isolates them and makes them penetrable. Unlike public places that are freely accessible (e.g., city parks), heterotopic sites have clear borders. In some cases, the entry is compulsory, most notably, with prisons. Along with psychiatric hospitals, prisons are referred to as heterotopias of deviation because they serve as "other spaces" where deviants and criminals are securely confined against their will. Other heterotopias, such as museums, are noncoercive institutions designed to attract visitors, then charging them an admission fee. The prison museum tends to combine both forms of boundary-maintenance: tourists gain entry by purchasing a ticket with the anticipation that they will experience what it is like to be incarcerated. The Melbourne Gaol takes that prospect to a higher sensate level. Its brochure boasts of "Australia's Most Wanted Experience." While exploring the imposing bluestone structure ("one of Victoria's oldest surviving buildings"), tourists have the option to extend their visit by entering the "Police Watch House," where they will "be arrested by a Charge Sergeant, get locked up in the cells and experience an environment unchanged since the police and inmates left" (Old Melbourne Gaol: Crime and Justice Experience, n.d.).

In some instances, the system of opening and closing is managed merely by having permission. In the prison museum in Buenos Aires, one such heterotopia is the office of the director, Horacio A. Benegas. The door remains wide open; however, visitors are not allowed to enter without an invitation from the director. One can still peer into the space that serves as both a current workspace and a repository with an array of items speaking to an encyclopedic history of the penitentiary system. The room contains a large desk, bookshelves, and a small church organ. The merging of socioreligious and secular themes is evident from the crucifix and portraits of San Martín that decorate the walls. The Argentine flag, along with a case containing a sword, projects a firm commitment to nationalism. Similarly, miscellaneous knick-knacks carry a military motif such as the desk lamp with an olive-green army helmet as its shade. A large metal sign displays the national coat of arms and lettering identifying the ministers of education and of justice and the national director of penal institutions. That theme of governance—education and justice—is maintained in various plaques on the walls of the room, such as one that has a quotation from Benegas himself: "The education . . . the home. The instruction . . . the school. The culture . . . the same." That local version of poetics clearly draws uninterrupted lines connecting family life, civics, and integrated culture in ways that defy a division of moral labor.

Other heterotopias are regulated according to deeper cultural imperatives, whereby one has to submit to rites and purifications. As Foucault explains, "There are even heterotopias that are entirely consecrated to these activities of purification—purification that is partly religious and partly hygienic" (1986a: 26; see Douglas, 1966). Inside the Argentine Penitentiary Museum, visitors can get a sense of how those socioreligious rituals involved prisoners. Recall the white porcelain basin used by the religious staff as they prepared female prisoners for re-entry into the community ("la clausura") (see chapter 1).

Likewise, a photograph of prisoners attending a religious ceremony reinforces the significance of sacred ritual and solidarity.

Expanding the notion of "other spaces," Foucault introduces what he calls crisis heterotopias: "forbidden places, reserved for individuals who are, in relation to society and to the human environment in which they live, in a state of crisis" (e.g., the elderly, the infirmed, and the disabled) (1986a: 24). At the Seodaemun prison in Seoul, visitors are likely to see a small cottage perched on an elevated tier of the prison compound near the guard tower. Walking up the concrete steps to get a closer look, one is met by a sign identifying it as the Leper's Building: "This building was constructed in 1923, and was used as a segregated leper colony to accommodate inmates suffering from leprosy." A companion book provides a little more detail with respect to the space: "Two small cells and one large cell are placed in parallel. Different from other jails, it has a heater" (Seodaemun Prison History Hall, 2010: 115).

Moving along the continuum of "forbidden places," Foucault discusses the "strange heterotopia of the cemetery . . . a place unlike ordinary cultural spaces" (1986a: 25). Until the end of the eighteenth century, the cemetery was conveniently situated at the heart of the city, next to the church. Then:

> Cemeteries began to be located at the outside border of cities. In correlation with the individualization of death and the bourgeois appropriation of the cemetery, there arises an obsession with death as an "illness." The dead, it is supposed, bring illnesses to the living, and it is the presence and proximity of the dead right beside the houses, next to the church, almost in the middle of the street, it is this proximity that propagates death itself. This major theme of illness spread by the contagion in the cemeteries persisted until the end of the eighteenth century, until, during the nineteenth century, the shift of cemeteries toward the suburbs was initiated. The cemeteries then came to constitute, no longer the sacred and immortal heart of the city, but "the other city," where each family possesses its dark resting place. (25)

While touring Robben Island, visitors get a quick glance at the leper graveyard. Although the bus does not even bother to slow down, those nimble enough to snap a photo will have an image capturing a blend of semiotics. The graveyard is dotted with crumbling tombstones and crosses, symbols of its decaying sacred status. Moreover, it is not just an ordinary cemetery; it is a forbidden space reserved for those infected by leprosy—a disease so dreaded that it stokes primal anxiety over pollution. Recall that for centuries leprosy was (falsely) believed to be highly contagious; hence, leper colonies were synonymous with isolation—even banishment. At Robben Island, the leper graveyard is located a noticeable distance from the prison and staff housing. In perhaps a cruel twist of fate, the lepers on the island constructed the church of the Good Shepherd (1895) as well as the graveyard where they eventually were put to rest (Claassen, 2010: n.p.; see chapter 5).

Foucault concludes his lecture by noting that some "other spaces" pursue perfection by adopting a general organization of terrestrial space. To illustrate the concept, he directs attention to the early waves of colonization in North and South America. As Puritans expanded their settlements in the north, they aspired to create "absolutely perfect other places" (Foucault, 1986a: 27). Those ambitions have been preserved in prison museums. Visitors at Eastern State Penitentiary are immersed in the remnants of the most determined experiment in prison history. There they can situate themselves with a dream of order delivered by energetic Quakers committed to good intentions. To further connect with the significance of ideal space, tourists can step inside the vaulted chapel-like cells designed to tap into the inner light of the prisoner's soul (Dolan, 2007; Johnson, 2010; Meranze, 1996; see chapter 4).

With even greater detail, Foucault marvels at the extraordinary Jesuit colonies founded in South America:

> [These were] absolutely regulated colonies in which human perfection was effectively achieved. The Jesuits of Paraguay established colonies in which existence was regulated at every turn. The village was laid out according to a rigorous plan around a rectangular place at the foot of which was the church; on one side, there was the school; on the other, the cemetery; and then, in front of the church, an avenue set out that another crossed at right angles; each family had its little cabin along these two axes and thus the sign of Christ was exactly reproduced. Christianity marked the space and geography of the American world with its fundamental sign. The daily life of individuals was regulated, not by the whistle, but by the bell. Everyone was awakened at the same time, everyone began work at the same time; meals were at noon and five o'clock; then came bedtime, and at midnight came what was called the marital wake-up, that is, at the chime of the churchbell, each person carried out her/his duty. (1986a: 27)

Similarly in Buenos Aires, one bears witness to the legacy of religious colonization expressed in city planning and architecture as well as penality. Set conveniently in the historical section known as San Telmo, the Argentine Penitentiary Museum receives a spillover from the crowd of tourists who mill nostalgically through the cobbled streets. Civic leaders promote the museum by including it on large maps posted on the sidewalks (along with a blurb from *Lonely Planet*). A plaque attached to the wall of the building declares that the site became a historical national monument in 1982. As noted previously, the edifice dates back to the 1730s, when the Jesuits were spreading their influence throughout the region. Approaching an imposing arched doorway that leads to the interior corridor and gallery, visitors have an opportunity to explore the early history of an emerging penal system as well as the site that currently hosts the museum. An archaeological display case preserves various objects discovered in the floor of the chapel dating back to 1840 (e.g., hand-painted pottery). Posters inform visitors that in 1860 the building was converted into a prison for both men and women, and thirty years later it became Asilo Correccional de Mujeres, a house of correction administered by a Catholic order known as Las Religiosas del Buen Pastor (the Good Shepherd). Near the reception desk are photographs demonstrating close ties between the modern State and the traditional Church as government leaders and clergy are pictured together. Likewise, the institution's disciplinary past is conveyed through photographs of women inmates working at sewing machines as well as pictures of them attending Catholic ceremonies with nuns.

The religious ambience of the site is enhanced as visitors are guided into the courtyard. There, they walk into the shadows of the neighboring parish church, San Pedro Gonzalez Telmo, whose tall bell towers loom graciously over the prison. White arches leading to the domed chapel of Nuestra del Carmen surround the serene open space. The wide doors to the chapel remain open, inviting tourists to enter a place of worship that seems more like a shrine. Behind the altar, an arrangement of three statues conveys a religious trinity and a cultural hierarchy: on the left is Jesus as a contemplative adult and on the right stands St. Joseph holding baby Jesus. In the center, a statue of St. Mary embracing baby Jesus is slightly elevated and illuminated, giving off a sacred aura. Situated behind the altar is an Argentine flag whose pole joins the symmetry of candlesticks pointing to the heavens above. Rows of polished wooden pews contribute to a sense of order: the central aisle paves a way for the faithful to put their body (and soul) into motion: to genuflect, kneel, and bow their heads in a coordinated act of physical and spiritual devotion.

The use of models in prison museums is a common device aimed at reinforcing the museum effect. As objects, models represent the actual space inside which tourists visit. Without too much thought, one can find the exact spot on which they are presently standing; hence, they too become part of the museum. In addition to creating that phenomenological moment, replicas of prisons also serve to enhance the notion of perfect order. In the back of the chapel of Nuestra Senora del Carmen is a sizeable model of Asilo Correccional de Mujeres. Even in miniature form, the prison speaks to an ambitious, carefully designed institution. Nearby, a poster of San Pedro (holding his hand to his heart) produces a higher sense of purpose. Gazing downward at the model, San Pedro seems to be blessing the penitentiary. In doing so, he sends a message of moral guardianship: that is, an omniscient deity oversees—and divinely ordains—the penal project. Overall, the site (both as a former prison and currently as a museum) exists as an interesting heterotopia, or physical representation of a particular utopia. In the next section, on grand order, we consider the significance of the prison as an ideal symbol of social and cultural perfection, or dream of order.

GRAND ORDER

So as to bolster its authority, many prison museums present visitors with a dream of order on the grand scale. There, ambitious testimonies by the State about the State offer fine details intended to deepen the national myth, especially with respect to ideal visions of justice (see Dussel, 1995; Gregory, 2004; Welch, 2009a). Since it stands as a prototype for such cultural production, we keep attention on the Argentine Penitentiary Museum.* Throughout the exhibit, one is reminded of the republic's myth, symbolized by an Argentine coat of arms along with multiple plaques commemorating its forefathers and key figures in world history. A plate cites the revered General José de San Martín, who led the movement for Argentina's independence: "Laws of a free people can be strict but never cruel." Other panels underscore a sense of Argentine justice in the formation of its governance: one plaque quotes St. Thomas Aquinas ("being good is easy, it is difficult to be just") while another borrows from William Shakespeare ("it is easier to obtain things with a smile than with a sword"). Similar tablets commemorate significant civil servants whose expertise served the nation's modern penitentiary system (e.g., Don

* As mentioned in chapter 1, discussion here relies on examples from Argentina and Australia. In later chapters, we return to how visions of order manifest in prison museums elsewhere, especially with respect to architecture (e.g., Philadelphia and Alcatraz), colonialism (e.g., Hong Kong and Seoul), and resistance (e.g., Johannesburg and Cape Town).

Raul Julio Pieroni and Dr. Juan O'Connor). Together, those quotations blend religious and secular lessons on ethical living, civic life, and the cult of the individual, thereby pointing to a key vehicle for the transmission of cultural meaning, namely, poetics (Smith, 2008). The power of poetics affords certain statements the capacity to dodge polarities and instead unite citizens with commonly shared values: what reasonable person could disagree with those words of wisdom? Interestingly, the popular appeal of Aquinas and Shakespeare is situated alongside major figures in Argentine penal history, producing a form of local cultural embeddedness (see Melossi, 2001).

As another expression of grand order, the Historical Records Room allows visitors to witness the emergence of the Argentine penal state as a modern bureaucracy, replete with extensive record keeping (Weber, 2002 [1904–5]; see Foucault, 1977; Szakolczai, 1998). The somber (if not cold) tone of the room is maintained by the presence of large bookcases displaying a vast collection of Argentine legislation and judicial judgments from the end of the 1800s to the early 1900s. Once again, there are poetic messages via plaques and literary references that contextualize the Argentine prison within a national (local) culture. As mentioned previously, a poster cites a passage from the famous novel *La Vuelta de Martin Fierro,* in which the prison delivers justice as well as a new baptism for criminal offenders.

The dream of order conveyed at the Hyde Park Barracks in Sydney resembles the Argentine narrative with respect to state building, modernization, and continued progress, without the conspicuous presence of the Church. Other significant distinctions should also be made. As a penal colony, Australia served as an outpost for the British Empire. Therefore, rather than striving toward an independent state, Sydney aspired to become a self-sufficient colonial city in New South Wales. As noted previously, the barracks in Hyde Park was not a prison, let alone a jail. It served as secure accommodations, providing meals and a hammock for some six hundred convicts resting from public work projects (e.g., clearing roads and quarrying) (see figure 8). The Hyde Park Barracks is nevertheless recognized as a starting point for the story that Australia tells itself (and others) about itself. National and personal identities can be traced to 1788 when the First Fleet landed with the initial shipment of convicts, which has been described as a "Noah's ark of small time criminality" (Hughes, 1986: front flap; see Hirst, 2008). Before transportation ended eighty years later, more than 160,000 convicts would be banished to Australia. Out of this "humane" experiment to ease the crowding of hulks (floating jails) in England, Sydney became a city in its own

FIGURE 8. The front façade of the Hyde Park Barracks (Sydney). © retrowelch 2014

right, built by convicts who with the benefit of the "fair-go" found redemption as emancipists (i.e., free citizens) (see Finnane, 1997).

The story of the Hyde Park Barracks is told in four historical parts. From 1819 to 1848, the barracks housed male convicts. Transportation was abolished in New South Wales in 1840, and eight years later, the remaining inmates of the barracks were transferred to Cockatoo Island. The next chapter of the barracks spanned from 1848 to 1886 when the institution became the Immigration Depot for single females. Then from 1862 until 1886, the barracks housed infirmed and destitute females. Finally, the barracks provided office space for the courts and government agencies from 1887 to 1979 when it became its present incarnation, the Hyde Park Barracks Museum (Historic Houses Trust, n.d. a; see Dewar and Fredericksen, 2003; Wilson 2004, 2008). According to the promotion for Convict Sydney:

> Explore Australia's convict history at the World Heritage listed Hyde Park Barracks. Learn about the forced transportation of convicts, their daily lives and how they built the colony.
>
> Wander the streets of 1820s Sydney on our giant map, try on a set of leg-irons, lie in a convict hammock, look for your relatives on the convict database and discover intriguing stories of some of the 50,000 convicts who passed through the barracks from 1819 and 1848.
>
> Bring your kids for dress-ups and our convicts Kids Trail. (Historic Houses Trust, n.d. b)

Built between 1817 and 1819, the Hyde Park Barracks inscribes itself into the Australian memory that retains (or revives) its convict past. Adding to its historical identity is the fact that architect Francis Greenway, himself an emancipated convict, designed the barracks: testimony that he could serve the public good. Although the museum celebrates that achievement, it consciously places the building itself at the center of its (mythological) narrative. Early in the tour, the museum posts an orientation message: "A significant architectural & social icon . . . the building should be properly regarded as a museum of itself, directly relating to its historic uses." Architectural, archaeological, and intellectual commentary maintains a sophisticated tone throughout much of the museum's layout. A prominently displayed poster quotes Karl Marx: "To discover the various uses of things is the work of history (*Capital*, 1867)."

The Hyde Park Barracks museum goes to great length to deliver a wider vision of the penal colony as it progressed toward modernity, though not without internal debate among its political appointees. "1817–1819 PENAL COLONY" titles a storyboard reading: "This land of convicts & kangaroos is beginning to rise into a fine & flourishing settlement." Below an illustration showing a young Sydney looking over the harbor is a series of questions regarding the destiny of the penal colony:

Was it to be:

Prison—dumping ground for unwanted Britons?
Plantation—exclusive gentry ruling an army of convict labour?
Colony—emancipated convicts prospering in town & country?

Dialogue over the direction of the colony pitted "exclusives" against "emancipists" over issues of power and privilege, the control of land, convict labor, and the authority of the governor: "Hyde Park Barracks, the site & symbol of convicts in government service became a focus for this debate." Visitors are introduced to the "players" who offered their own vision of grand order: Lachlan Macquarie (the governor) "aspired to a prosperous colony with public works built by convict labor"; Francis Greenway (the architect), who is described as an "uncompromising, outspoken critic of graft, bad workmanship & coercive labor"; John Bigge (the commissioner), an "elitist Tory lawyer sent to inquire into Macquarie's administration & to make transportation a greater deterrent to crime in Britain . . . [who] supported the 'exclusives' in opposition to Greenway's architectural pretensions and Macquarie's favours to emancipated convicts." So as to present a chronology of progress, companion storyboards attach time periods to their respective developments: "1819–1848 WORK, ROUTINE"; "1848–1886 INSTITUTIONS," which declares, "Useful public institutions . . . must be established . . . before you can hope for any lasting social improvement."

Enhancing a thick description, the museum employs a series of maps and panoramas not only to illustrate the growth and expansion of the colonial settlement, but also to highlight the vision of Macquarie (and his wife) and Greenway, who left an indelible mark on the future of the city. The plaque titled "Improving Sydney" testifies: "During their time in Sydney (1810–1921), Elizabeth and Lachlan Macquarie improved the town materially and socially. They wanted to impose more order, taste, and civility on the penal colony." The Macquaries set out to beautify the urban landscape with architecture and public gardens; still, a sense of order was maintained by strict segregation. The Botanic Gardens and the Government Domain were walled in, "creating a scenic promenade and carriageway for genteel citizens to enjoy . . . However, the enclosure of the Domain denied its use to convicts and working-class people—when they continued to use it, Macquarie had them flogged." The dream of order does not end there; visitors serve witness to continued progress in the decades after the Macquarie administration. The

"Founding a New Society" storyboard summarizes other key developments imbued with the cult of the individual, including the changing ideas on the treatment of prisoners, halting transportation, and embracing more enlightened regimes based on reform and social integration.

As noted in the opening chapter, an exhibition titled "The End of Transportation" blends an early sense of Australian identity with its own dream of order. By preventing the convict ship *Hashemy* from landing in Sydney, Australians sent a strong message to the British Government. Although some agriculturalists regretted the loss of convict labor, the movement to abolish transportation spread to other Australian colonies, and the final convict vessel landed in Western Australia in 1868 (see Godfrey and Cox, 2008). To commemorate this moment in Australian history, the museum presents a poster titled "UNCHAINED: 11 Australian Convict Sites on the World Heritage List." Giving the convict past international exposure, the World Heritage List "places Australia's penal origins within the global story of transported labor and colonial expansion in the 18th and 19th centuries." The text summarizes the changing national identity: "Talk of Australia's convict past was once taboo, a source of embarrassment. It is now treated with pride. Australians have come to value not only the social and cultural legacy, but also the objects and architectural remains that record and recall their convict past." The Hyde Park Barracks places itself within a wider consciousness of Australian identity alongside symbols of progress toward a modern state.

Turning to the Old Melbourne Gaol, we again witness how a particular prison museum tells its own story. With local history and culture in the background, a strong narrative about the gaol, the State of Victoria, and its legendary figures all contribute to a unique dialogue on the dream of order. Much like the prison museum in Buenos Aires, the Melbourne Gaol scatters poetics throughout the tour. However, rather than lofty and uplifting words of wisdom, poetics in the Melbourne Gaol attend to the misery of imprisonment. Upon entering the institution, a quotation by Oscar Wilde sets the tone: "I know not whether laws be right, / Or whether laws be wrong; / All that we know who lie in gaol / Is that the wall is strong; / And that each day is like a year, / A year whose days are long" (1898, "The Ballad of Reading Gaol").

Similarly, the birth of the penitentiary in Melbourne is situated in the context of political shifts as well as urban problems. As visitors walk farther into the museum, they read text telling the tale of early Melbourne as it "grew quickly in the 1830s from a collection small huts into a bustling settlement. It was a long way from Sydney and keeping the peace became increasingly difficult ... The majority of the population consisted of young male immigrants and former convicts released from penal settlements in other parts of New South Wales and in Tasmania." Of course, the gaol was not detached from events surrounding the Colony of Victoria as it earned independence from New South Wales in 1851, the same year gold was discovered. Consequently, the population leaped from 77,000 to 340,000. A plaque titled "The Gaol Boom" explains: "The crime rate shot up." An immediate response from the authorities was the expansion of the penal apparatus that soon added nine new prisons. At the time, rising crime was interpreted in even more ominous terms as "The Slum Threat."

> Melburnians in the late 19th century drew a sharp distinction between the grand boulevardes of Collins and Bourke Streets and the nearby narrow lanes and alleys. These they called the "back slums."
>
> Many thought that an under class of criminals inhabited the rough cottages and seedy hotels of this part of town, living off the profits of muggings and prostitution. To some extent this was true, but fears that the criminal class was out of control were greatly exaggerated. These fears were fueled by the belief that criminal tendencies were inherited.
>
> Authorities had a deep-seated fear about the many children of convict parents growing to adulthood in the 1870s and 1880s. Even though Victoria was never a major destination for transported convicts, it was feared that the dreaded "convict stain" might easily have infected the Colony. Hence the many calls for the Melbourne Gaol to play a greater role in punishing larrikins and reforming the criminal classes of the "back slums."

The summary informs museum patrons that early Melburnians discussed social problems in complex terms with a mix of references to the dangerous class and criminogenics as well as pollution and contagion (e.g., "the slum threat," "the convict stain," and "infection"). Such depictions of social pathologies not only had a strong positivist bent but also pointed to anxieties over urbanization. Correspondingly, the passage concludes that the prison was recognized as having the capacity to serve as a form of social defense against the tide of social ills. The same poster features a sketch of Melbourne from 1880: its panoramic view shows a concentration of churches, businesses, factories, and residences. To signal its importance in the rise of a major city, the Melbourne Gaol is identified as "a dominant feature." Precisely how Victorian authorities planned to deal with "The Slum Threat" reached beyond expanding the penal system. As we shall examine in the next section, an institutional regiment would figure prominently in establishing the dream of order.

INSTITUTIONAL ORDER

Whereas visions of grand order speak to the overarching purpose of prisons (what prisons are for), institutional order refers to prison conditions and the ways in which inmates are kept in line (what prisons are like) (see Carrabine, 2000, 2004). As is the case with the prison museums at the Hyde Park Barracks, in Buenos Aires, and elsewhere, the Melbourne Gaol reinforces its image as a prototype of institutional—and social—order by placing models of itself in full view. As one might expect, visitors probably view the replica not as a mere empty shell but as a representation of a penitentiary that in its heyday was filled with convicts held under tight control by heavy-handed guards. As noted, a brochure describes how internal order was maintained: "Life in the gaol was hard—prisoners were kept in solitary confinement, communication was severely restricted, food was barely adequate and punishments for breaches of discipline were harsh" (Poultney, 2003: 1). Inside a display case resembling a cabinet of curiosity is a set of carefully arranged objects that together send a message of institutional—even moral—control. The labels read:

> The Calico Hood (c. 1875): These were worn by all prisoners held in solitary confinement when outside their cells. The Pentonville system of reform aimed to isolate inmates from each other in all possible ways.
> Iron mask (c. 1860): An Iron mask was worn by male prisoners as an additional form of punishment.
> Leg irons (c. 1870): Used to punish prisoners.
> Truncheon: The outside casing of this truncheon is made of bamboo. The lead-weighted spring, displayed here, was inserted inside the casing for balance and to increase the effectiveness of the blow.
> Leather Gloves (c. 1870–80): This device was secure to the prisoner's hands in order to prevent "self-abuse" (masturbation).

While enforcing a strict regiment, the gaol was committed to degrees of modernization. A poster sketches out the physical improvement of the institution as it progressed between 1841 and 1864. The first cellblock, dating back to 1841, was a "stark building lacking the elegant architectural features of later additions." The harsh treatment of prisoners was compounded by overcrowding and primitive sanitation. By 1862, earlier cellblocks were overshadowed by a modern design with a grand entrance, a governor's residence and offices, visiting cells, an infirmary, and a chapel: "The debtor's cells were pulled out and replaced by a soaring central octagonal space with a lantern roof. This was flanked by four large cells on each floor and incorporated a new staircase and gallows."

In developing the state's system of imprisonment, Victorians looked to the austere English model. At numerous stops along the tour of the Melbourne Gaol museum, visitors are given an opportunity to see just how punitive the cells must have been. On display are the cramped solitary cells (measuring nine feet by five and a half feet) where prisoners were "warehoused" for twenty-three hours a day. Simulating church bells that synchronized social life in Christian cities, the Melbourne Gaol sounded "a series of bells [that] measured out the prisoner's day. They rang to tell the inmates when to eat, pray, exercise or sleep. Everything was regulated, silent, and anonymous." In accordance with the Pentonville model, prisoners at the Gaol (at least until the 1870s) were first placed in solitary confinement and were gradually allowed to mingle with other convicts and then to work in teams. However, overcrowding and the constant movement of inmates strained institutional order as work routines deteriorated: "Workshops were used ineffectively, the stone-breaking yard did not provide enough work and the prison was often treated as a home away from home by short-term inmates. By the 1880s police were describing the Melbourne Gaol as little better than a 'playground.'" With that simple admission, visitors are taught a brief lesson on the limits of instrumentalist, power-based practices of discipline as well as on the persistence of failed prisons (see Garland, 1990). Indeed, despite efforts to institute humane reform, the Gaol relied on corporal punishment—for offenses that ranged from abusing a warder to swearing—to maintain institutional order (see chapter 7).

Although the Hyde Park Barracks was not a prison per se, it emphasized security and institutional order. The "Life at the Barracks" exhibit reminds us that inmates did not have much privacy, free time, or personal space. Offering greater insight into the life of "government men," the curators tell us that convicts were permitted to do private work in Sydney; their earned wages provided discretionary cash to buy tobacco and other small indulgences. For momentary escapes from the control of the barracks, well-behaved convicts were allowed free time outside the institution: many of them would bolt to an area of town called the Rocks, a notorious section known for drinking, gambling, and bare-knuckle fist fights.

Order was also maintained by cracking down on reoffending. Recidivists were assigned to punishment gangs and harsh labor while shackled in leg irons. Working in remote areas, they spent their nights in portable jails. It is important to note that many of their "crimes" were job-related, such as refusing to work and stealing materials and tools. Some convicts who escaped became outlaws (i.e., bushrangers) and those who were apprehended by the authorities faced death. The dream of order was upheld by other work-related punishments, most notably, the treadmill: a mechanical device driven by convicts who stepped in motion, turning large wheels to grind grain. Although treadmills were supposed to replace corporal punishment, floggings continued as a means of instilling discipline. Moreover, greater innovations were aimed at maximizing the stroke of the cat-o'-nine-tails. Public humiliation was also a visible part of the penal spectacle. Recall the "particoloured suit" worn by stubborn convicts known as "canary men" due to the yellow-and-black uniform that could be monitored from a distance (see Hughes, 1986).

Themes of institutional order at the Argentine prison museum inscribe themselves into North American penal history. A placard lists the institutional rules for discipline at the National Penitentiary, specifically citing the regulations adopted previously at the Auburn Penitentiary (New York) and Eastern State Penitentiary (Philadelphia). (It should be noted that the National Penitentiary allowed prisoners to talk while working.)

Nevertheless, institutional order was maintained by a firm sense of militarism, paramilitarism, and professionalism. Toward that end, an entire room is dedicated to the Federal Penitentiary Service. An organizational chart maps out a hierarchical bureaucracy along with pictures and captions describing the contributions of key figures in the prison bureau, namely, Roberto Pettinato and Dr. Juan O'Connor. Color photographs of each of the current prisons in the system deliver a contemporary view of the enterprise. That bureaucratic image of the penal apparatus is also given a distinctive poetic style in promoting the virtues of the prison service. Recall the system's slogan: "Justicia y Fe Para Cumplir la Mision" (Justice and Faith to Fulfill the Mission).

The elaborate mission statement goes on to describe the prison service as being devoted to an innovative prison technology based on science, cooperation, and hard work from all its members. Here the local Argentine penal bureaucracy (Weber) depends not only on professional expertise (Foucault) but also on a commitment to shared values and solidarity (Durkheim). Not to be overlooked, a large section of a wall highlights the correction of women offenders from 1890 to 1978 in the institution known as Asilo Correccional de Mujeres (under the administration of El Buen Pastor). Old black-and-white photographs capture themes of discipline through the use of labor, household skills, and moral training as women inmates are shown working, sewing, preparing food, and attending a religious service. Those images demonstrate once again the normalizing theme of Foucault interacting with the socioreligious motif of Durkheim, particularly as they apply to female convicts (see Ruggiero, 1992; Caimari, 1997).

The next room highlights the penal institution itself. Visitors are met by two mannequins dressed in antique prison cadet uniforms from the national training academy (La Escuela Penitenciaria de la Nación), thereby reinforcing organizational and cultural imperatives of paramilitarism, expertise, and professionalism. The walls feature various items related to the National Penitentiary Service, especially from the standpoint of the security staff: for example, a letter of graduation and promotion from the training academy, a unit flag (from Unit 14), and various photographs of penitentiary personnel. Communicating the notion of prison work as a dangerous profession, the room displays a sizeable collection of weapons and security devices used to maintain order against the threat of disorder: pistols; rifles; machine guns; bayonets; riot helmets; gasmasks; tear gas grenades; and handcuffs used by the custodial staff. The exhibit offers a rich narrative by showing a linear pattern of modern progress toward advanced weapons technology. In a slight shift in tone, the narrative departs from its male-dominated story line toward acknowledging the work of women officers. That nod to feminism appears sincere as their professional contributions to the prison service are validated through the display of uniforms, (action) photographs, and award plaques.

Further enhancing the cultural side of a modern paramilitary hierarchy, the room includes various personnel uniforms and caps of ranking officers and an array of promotion stars, stripes, chevrons, and unit insignias. The Servicio Penitenciario Federal shoulder patch emblem suggests depth to its military origins by featuring a prison fortress with two rifles crossed. Similarly, the prison service boasts a fraternity (and solidarity) with the Argentine military by commemorating the soldiers who served in the war of

Las Malvinas against England in 1982 (known to the British as the Falkland Islands War). That famous battle off the coast of the mainland continues to be remembered as a pivotal moment for Argentines. More than thirty years later, posters of its war veterans are publicly displayed in such culturally charged landmarks as Plaza de Mayo, located in front of the presidential building, Casa Rosada.

So as to validate the claim that prison work is a dangerous profession, the gallery on prisoners depicts them as menacing. As a holdover from the days of penal colonies, there are security manacles used to secure hands and feet while transporting prisoners from the institution to the work site (much like with the Hyde Park Barracks). Still, that premodern version of convict labor appears to be overshadowed by symbols of modern disorder. A contemporary display board contains more than a dozen prisoner-made knives and weapons called "facas," "puas," "puntas," and "chuzas" (large curved knives, spikes, and sharp picks), along with a prisoner-made gun and a storage device concealing contraband and equipment used for escape. Prison life and subculture, according to the exhibit, also involve disorder and deviant behavior as pollution. The collection includes drug paraphernalia for smoking marijuana and prisoner-made tattoo equipment. Other vices, such as gambling, are captured in the form of prisoner-made dice and playing cards.

Themes of institutional order continue to pair the premodern with the modern, most notably in replicas of the prison cells. The contrast is striking and promotes the idea of progress and modernization in the practice of penology. An architectural draft of the two-tiered floor plan is available on the wall, showing the symmetrical organization of space within a contemporary prison. Advancing the notion of the modern prison as a model and symbol of order is a nearby photograph of a tall contemporary prison in Buenos Aires. Curiously, that institution, operated by Unit 1 of the National Penitentiary Service, appears remarkable for not looking like a prison; indeed, one could easily mistake it for any other office building in an urban center. In this instance, there seems to be some tension in the semiotic communication over what a real prison is supposed to look like (see Smith, 2008). The exhibit also includes a glimpse into the interior of a solitary cell. The narrative about what a contemporary prison cell is supposed to look like gets back on message. The Spartan cell boasts sturdy green bars and a food slot, a single cot attached to the wall with a brown wool blanket, a metal food tray, and a porcelain toilet and sink. Hinting at isolation and the anticipation of release is graffiti of Bart Simpson saying, "Cuando me voy" (When am I going). Nearby is a large hand-written calendar scrawled on the wall with several days crossed out (a nod to the temporal component of modern punishment that measures suffering by way of time spent behind bars). Poetic words "Libertad" and "Justicia" are written above, and below is a dagger with a snake climbing up and blood dripping off the tip of the knife.

ALTERNATIVE ORDER

Later in this book, we delve into the significance of resistance and the ways prison museums portray acts of defiance. For instance, penal tourism at Seodaemun Prison History Hall (Seoul) honors Korean independence activists jailed by Japanese Imperialists. Similarly, Constitution Hill (Johannesburg) and Robben Island (Cape Town) chronicle the injustices of apartheid and celebrate the hard fought freedom for South Africans. For the most part, visitors support those narratives since they appear to represent the truth, thereby setting the record straight. In other prison museums, themes of resistance are ignored altogether, such as the Argentine Penitentiary Museum, where curators seem to consciously avoid issues concerning detentions and disappearances during the Dirty War. While the Hyde Park Barracks recognizes popular resistance to transportation, it is the Melbourne Gaol that immerses tourists in controversies over an alternative order. In this final portion of the chapter, let us take an in-depth look at that particular museum effect.

The museum entrance calls attention to itself with a conspicuous sign on the footpath aimed at street traffic. It boasts "Old Melbourne Gaol: Best Heritage and Cultural Attraction in Australia." A logo featuring a recognizable helmet behind bars broadcasts to visitors that Ned Kelly, his gang, and his family figure prominently in the story about the Gaol (National Trust, n.d.). Thematically, the story of Ned Kelly offers counterbalance to the state's dream of order by highlighting how the Kelly gang sought to turn the table on the Victorian authorities. Toward that end, the museum activates the Durkheimian conceptualization of mythology, whereby legends express notions of heroism and related virtues often through such communicative devices as sensationalism (e.g., books, movies, and souvenirs). Of all the attractions at the Melbourne Gaol museum, it is Ned Kelly who takes center stage. His powerful saga continues to permeate Australian history and political identity. A brief (but thick) chapter on Victoria's past, "Ned Kelly—Man and Myth," summarizes the Kelly phenomenon:

> The figure of Edward "Ned" Kelly needs no introduction in Australia, but we are more familiar with the myths surrounding him than with the man himself. He is seen as a hero, a criminal, a larrikin, and a champion of the underdog.
>
> Since he came to the attention of the police, the media, and the general public, Ned Kelly's actions have been studied, analyzed and interpreted to create a cast of characters for this one person.
>
> Ned Kelly continues to be reinterpreted and remains an enduring presence within Australian literature, visual arts, cinema, and performing arts, music and popular culture. (State Library of Victoria, 2009: n.p.)

Self-consciously, the museum contributes to Kelly's persona as larger than life. Born in 1855, Ned was the eldest son of John (an Irish convict transported to Australia) and Ellen Quinn (an Irish settler). The Kelly clan's ethnic identity as "fighting Irish" bolstered Ned's reputation as standing "against authority" (State Library of Victoria, 2009). In northeast Victoria, the "rich had all the best land, while people like the Kellys ended up with small pieces, or 'selections,' of poor quality land" (Poultney, 2003: 23). Ned was in trouble at an early age, and at fourteen, he took to the road with Harry Power, "the last great highwaymen . . . and one of the best bushmen in Australia." Power, himself an Irishman transported to Hobart Town in 1842, had a "gift for blarney" and taught young Ned "the tricks of his trade and the art of surviving as a fugitive in the bush" (according to a plaque titled "Harry Power"). After a falling-out with Power, Ned accelerated his rebellious streak, serving prison terms for assault and receiving a stolen horse (see O'Malley, 1979).

If it were not the famous shoot-out between the Kelly gang and the Victorian Police in 1880, legend might have escaped Ned. A storyboard simply titled "CONFRONTATION: The Plan" puts the incident in its proper historical, social, and political context: "Land and restrictions imposed on Kelly sympathizers appear to have led Ned to dream of a republic in the north-east of Victoria. An independent republic would provide Ned and others like him with a safe haven away from government and police. But he needed to neutralise the police first" (see chapter 8).

In an elaborate scheme, the Kelly gang "herded over 60 hostages into a pub at Glenrowan, and then went about dismantling the railway lines. They intended to derail the police train and kill the policemen" (Poultney, 2003:

25). The plan went awry as the police were tipped off, allowing them to ambush the gang. Still, the Kelly gang would catch the police by surprise when they entered the firefight wearing large body armor and helmets made of steel. Police bullets did not penetrate the body armor, but Ned was struck in the legs and captured: "More dead than alive, Ned was brought to the Melbourne Gaol by train" (Poultney, 2003: 25). After two months in the Gaol hospital and another month in the old cellblock, he was given a two-day trial, convicted, and sentenced to death.

The museum's holdings give visitors a thick—if not altogether sympathetic—narrative on Kelly through the use of storyboards, photographs, sketches, and an interesting collection of memorabilia. A life-size replica of the body armor worn by Ned stands next to a huge photograph of the Glenrowan Inn where the Kelly gang battled the Victorian police (see figure 9). Describing "How the Armour Was Made," a plaque states that the panels were actually blades of ploughshares (also on display). The story behind the making of the body armor is given an added sense of aura as visitors are told that it "was made in great secrecy . . . in a hidden place in the hills known as the Devil's Basin." The exhibition also includes Ned's revolver: it is pointed out that the butt of the weapon was nicked by a police bullet, shattering Ned's little finger.

Ned Kelly was hanged on November 11, 1880, a historic date at the Melbourne Gaol. The museum preserves that event by turning attention to Ned's legacy in Australian cultural history. A poster headlined "NED THE LEGEND" describes the execution in literary fashion: "A few minutes after 10:00 AM Ned Kelly dropped through the trapdoor to ironic immortality. After hanging for 30 minutes, his body was taken to the gaol's dead-house for an autopsy and the making of a death mask. The body was then unceremoniously buried in the gaol burial yard."

Of course, Australians rarely recite the legend of Ned Kelly without acknowledging—even revering—his mother, Ellen. Examples of her "courage" are on display at the museum (and in supplemental materials):

> In April 1878 Constable Alexander Fitzpatrick came to the Kelly house to arrest Ned's younger brother, Dan. Although Dan submitted peacefully, a fight began when Fitzpatrick apparently tried to kiss 14-year-old Kate Kelly. The policeman later accused Ned's mother of hitting him on the head and Ned of shooting him in the wrist. As a result, Mrs Kelly spent three years in the Melbourne Gaol for attempted murder. The Kelly brothers escaped into the bush where they prospected for gold and distilled whiskey to earn money for Mrs Kelly's defence. (Poultney, 2003: 23)

FIGURE 9. Replica of Ned Kelly's body armor (Melbourne Gaol). © retrowelch 2014

Inside a cell in the upper tier of the Gaol, a sizeable exhibit is devoted to Ellen. It is headlined "Ellen Kelly: A Mother's Anguish" and features a large photograph captioned "Ellen in 1911 at the age of 79, with two of her grand-daughters, Lil and Alice Knight. Ellen had been a fiery Irish beauty who, at the age of 42, married Californian Geory King, 21 years younger than herself. Her fierce temper led to several brushes with the law." The storyboard "Ellen & Family" includes the subsection "Entry on Ellen Kelly" from the Victorian Prison Register: "Ellen Kelly was born in Antrim, Ireland in 1836. She arrived in Victoria in 1841 on the Indian and became a servant but could not read or write ... She is described as a member of the notorious Kelly family ... She had eleven children, including Edward (Ned) and Dan Kelly." Another panel describes the moment when Father Aylward, a priest from St. Patrick's Cathedral, told Ellen about the clash between the Kelly gang and the police at Glenrowan. He informed her that Ned was seriously wounded and was being held at the Gaol hospital. "Greatly distressed, she claimed to have dreamed of a fight between the police and the Gang only two nights before." Ellen and Ned were reunited at the Gaol. The day before Ned was to be hanged, she urged him, "Mind you die brave, die like a Kelly." At the time of the execution, Ellen was a few meters away, working in the prison laundry.

The museum imposes a critical retrospection of Ned Kelly by displaying a poster titled "Was Ned Kelly a Terrorist?" It features an authentic photograph of him but in the photograph an orange prison uniform and chains were superimposed (think Guantanamo Bay). The curators ask visitors to consider:

> How would Ned be treated today? ... With his barely concealed political agenda and his push for a breakaway republic in the north-east. Ned could have been tried under Australia's anti-terrorism laws. His attacks upon the police, his threats towards people in high office and his possession of a bomb at Glenrowan would have given the prosecution much useful ammunition. How much imagination does it take to see Ned in the dock, shackled and dressed in an orange boiler-suit?

That final segment of the tour seems to return to the dream of (an alternative) order in ways that consider the historical and political significance in the construction and exhibition of local Victorian culture. Of course, that intellectual exercise then segues into the museum's gift shop, where visitors are given an opportunity to purchase Ned Kelly history books (along with an array of memorabilia).

As examined throughout, penal tourism operates as a mechanism for social production, delivering what we identify as a dream of order. Toward that end, prison museums are unique heterotopias, or physical representations of a particular utopia. Correspondingly, those sites serve as vehicles for cultural transmission, projecting a particular narrative about the role of punishment in emerging societies. At the Argentine Penitentiary Museum, the official version of its penal history is one in which the nation's noble ambition toward modernity (the mythological) accommodates the interests of the local Catholic Church (the sacred). Narratives on purification also resonate from religious rituals as part of the prison regiment and from the scientific innovations aimed at eliminating social pathologies; together, those forces lay the foundation for a healthy and productive state (see Savelsberg, 2004). That two-part story retains the cult of the individual by weaving religious and secular poetics to communicate the State's commitment to human dignity and moral reform. However, to reiterate, the official narrative on Argentine penology as told by the State about the State appears to sanitize its history. The prevailing story omits human rights atrocities carried out by the military in the name of "defending the State" against left-leaning activists during the Dirty War (see Feitlowitz, 1998).

The dream of order conveyed at the Hyde Park Barracks museum also relies on a local story about progress and colony building in New South Wales. Unlike in the Argentine Penitentiary Museum, the collection on display does not suggest a strong influence of the Church. Nevertheless, the otherwise instrumentalist narrative does echo a few socioreligious themes, including the cult of the individual (e.g., abolishing the "immoral" practice of transportation) and the mythological. The overarching message conveyed at the Hyde Park Barracks is about how a small colonial settlement located on the other end of the world survived against all odds. Indeed, the fact that Sydney was built by convicts has entered the Australian consciousness in ways that shape cultural, national, and personal identities. With greater nuance, the Old Melbourne Gaol museum seems to promote not so much an Australian identity as a Victorian one. There, the government's dream of order is deliberately challenged by the legend of Ned Kelly, his gang, and his mother. The tour is imbued with reflections on power and (in)justice alongside symbols of resistance and struggle from below, which culminate as local heroism. That thick description is not merely deposited in the past; instead, it thrives as a living memory, honoring such virtues as courage and the moral willingness to stand "against authority" (State Library of Victoria, 2009). So as to elaborate further on the notion of order, the next chapter explores prison architecture and how prison museums utilize space to enhance museum effects.

FOUR

Architecture Parlante

The façade of the early penitentiary was intentionally designed to say something bold about itself. That *architecture parlante,* or "speaking architecture," is significant because it assumes an audience capable of being startled at the sight of a prison (Blondel, 1771–77; Kaufman, 1955). At Eastern State Penitentiary (ESP) in Philadelphia, such visual statements resonate from the past into the present as tourists are drawn to the site of the "world's first 'true' penitentiary," according to a large plaque titled "A National Historic Monument." There, visitors remain attentive to the enormity and complexity of the institution's story. In 1829, the year ESP admitted its first prisoner, the state-of-the-art prison was known internationally for its grand architecture, featuring a radial plan. While that spoke-and-hub design was exceedingly rational—aimed at improving surveillance on the inside—the architecture boasted a neo-Gothic exterior so as to instill in residents a sense of terror, a stark reminder of their fate if they ran astray of the law (Kahan, 2011; Johnston, 2010, 2000; Meranze, 1996).

To enhance its imposing presence, ESP was built on top of a hill, making it visible—and feared—from miles around. Its narrative architecture took into account the local people, most of whom were immigrants, "and for them, the castle-like structure conjured up thoughts of dungeons and torture, remnants of a feudal system that dominated Europe for a time" (Dolan, 2007: 11). Even the detailed ornaments served to intimidate, such as the fortress towers encircled by battlements strategically placed above arrow slit windows. For prisoners, however, neo-Gothic messages went unnoticed, since the interior delivered a different *architecture parlante.* Corridors and cells were designed to capture the solitude of a cathedral and its chapels so as to bring out the "inner light" of those confined (see figure 10). John Haviland's

architectural masterpiece earned praise for its ensemble of inner rationality and outer semiotics. An antique-style sign posted on the sidewalk reminds passersby that ESP became a "model for over 300 prisons around the world."

As discussed in previous chapters, the significance of space figures prominently in the museum effect. Arguably, spatial registers are even more dramatic in prison museums, since their actual sited-ness further validates their social—and cultural—authority. Monolithic structures, like ESP, possess unquestionable authenticity because they rely on an *architecture parlante* that succeeds in its semiotic message. That is, people know it's a prison because it looks like a prison. More than 180 years later, ESP still expresses a neo-Gothic message on power and deterrence. So as to explore in greater detail the importance of space embodied in prison architecture, this chapter continues to blend Durkheimian (communicative) and Foucaultian (instrumental) observations on the museum effect. In particular, we consider form and function as mutually reinforcing elements of penal architecture. That semio-technology helps us understand the various sites of penal ambition. As we shall see, punishment has been deliberately located in an array of spaces, including the island (e.g., Alcatraz and Robben Island) and the city, where it has occupied a dungeon (e.g., the Clink), a fort (e.g., Constitution Hill), a church (e.g., Argentine Penitentiary Museum), and a model penitentiary (e.g., ESP). Along the way, critical attention is turned to the interplay between prison architecture and society. As Robin Evans so insightfully notes in *The Fabrication of Virtue: English Prison Architecture, 1750–1840*: "[Prison] architecture, once the emblem of social order, was now one of its fundamental instruments" (1982: back cover). Setting the stage for some deep interpretations of prison museums, we elaborate a bit more on the emergence of *architecture parlante*.

NARRATIVE ARCHITECTURE

Haviland, the architect of ESP, himself an immigrant from England, brought to America a keen eye for the new prison architecture that was gaining popularity in Europe in the 1760s. During that era, the Enlightenment inspired a movement for the humane treatment of prisoners. Cesare Beccaria's *On Crimes and Punishments* (1764) laid the groundwork for prison reform along with a tempered system of sentencing, reflecting a commitment to mechanistic psychology (e.g., pain and pleasure principles) as it shaped deterrence theory. Toward that end, innovative prison design was maximizing its communicative potential. In *Imagining the Penitentiary: Fiction and the Architecture of the Mind in Eighteenth-Century England,* John Bender informs us that prisons began incorporating façades that were outwardly fearful, awesome, and intimidating. Among the sources for such imagery were the graphic arts, particularly the work of Giovanni Battista Piranese known as *Le Carceri,* a series of sixteen thematic etchings on "Imaginary Prisons" (*carceri d'invenzione,* c. 1745). The sketches re-created prison fantasies showing subterranean vaults, futuristic skywalks, and labyrinthian stairwells. Much like later drawings by M. C. Escher, *Le Carceri* produced infinitely distorted perspectives, delivering a haunting sense of institutional confusion and angst (see Wilton-Ely, 1978). Accordingly, Bender explains, "Prison interiors would shortly be reshaped into a powerful expository system in architectural portfolios and frontispieces, entry lodges, or gatehouses to the new penitentiaries. Their *architecture parlante* reminded all who would enter, or even pass by, of the power of confinement to alter the spirit through material representation" (1987: 21; see Pevsner, 1976; Rosenau, 1970). Much like ESP, Seodaemun Prison in Seoul (South Korea) and its neo-Gothic façade communicate a fortress-like strength. Along with its three octagonal watchtowers, a massive brick wall protects the elaborate network of cell-blocks. Here, it is worth noting that the prevailing semiotics of prison design seems to cross cultures. In Seoul, the penitentiary—a Western invention—is recognizable not only to the local Korean people but also to their Japanese occupiers who used it to suppress dissent (see chapter 8).

So as to activate *architecture parlante* as a moralizing narrator, the medium drew further from another source of aesthetics, namely, eighteenth-century painting. Bender (1987) examines the pictures of English artist Joseph Wright of Derby (1734–97), who immersed his audience into scenes of prisoners in isolation. The manner by which Wright constructed paintings relied heavily on stark images of architecture. With Wright's situating of the prisoner inside a cavernous backdrop, the viewer is invited to behold the subject and engage in an exercise of absorptive spectatorship (Fried, 1980; see Brown, 2009). With a decidedly theatrical technique, Wright's engrossing images project punishment into the imagination. By doing so, the absorptive aesthetic seems "to deny the beholder's existence and thus, paradoxically, to intensify his fascination with the characters to such a point that he may wish to address them, comfort them, or, in some paintings, even to enter their pictorial world" (Bender, 1987: 232).

Perhaps it is no coincidence that Wright's interest in the aesthetics of isolation added credence to John Howard's prison reform movement, since they shared a circle of close friends and patrons (Ignatieff, 1978). Art historians situate Wright within a "quiet pictorial revolution that will ultimately lead to the more programmatic realism of the 1840s and 1850s" (Rosenblum, 1968: 12; see Bender, 1987: 233, 309). Wright's realism captures, "with photographic truth, a flash bulb record of the incontrovertible facts of modern life" (Rosenblum, 1968: 12). In works titled *The Captive, from Sterne* (c. 1775–77) and *The Prisoner* (c. 1787–90), Wright's absorptive figures at once attract moral sympathy and keep spectators at a distance, thereby carefully managing their emotions. Lorenz Eitner describes *The Captive* as a "new type of prison picture . . . The whole emphasis falls on the pathos of man-inflicted suffering, witnessed at close range. [The figure affects us] with something of the stillness and solemnity of an *Ecce Homo*" (1978: 13).

To reiterate, architectural space plays an important role in influencing perception. Elaborating on the claustrophobic imagery contained in Wright's repertoire, Bender draws attention to the use of sculptural arches that suggest a massive entombment. Still, Wright maneuvers space into a visual field subjectively smaller than a ground-plot of architecture would show. From a single barred window, slanting light etches the shackled prisoner into his shallow cell. With respect to *architecture parlante,* Bender comments: "The image terrifies, it impresses, it moves, it provokes thought and moral sympathy; but in some measure it also asks to be seen in a theatrical mode" (1987: 236). The strategic use of narrative architecture facilitates the viewers' absorption, thereby entering a deeper consciousness.

So as to maximize their expressive potential, prison museums rely on techniques from the visual arts. Consider a similar use of painting at the Argentine prison museum, where a picture titled "La Mujer Del Preso" (The Woman of the Imprisoned) hangs along with other objects in the exhibit. Much like in Wright's theatrical style, the image features a compassionate woman visiting a prisoner behind bars. The background employs vaulted archways and a staircase that draws the eye downward to the dungeon-like cell. The prisoner appears to be grateful for the visitation, thus casting virtue onto "La Mujer." Although the picture is reminiscent of biblical times, the caption notes that the scene takes place in the Republic of Argentina; hence, it preserves the museum's nationalistic theme. Likewise, the dramatic use of props at the Clink museum puts inmates into a sympathetic light. With staged illumination directed at a mannequin dressed in shabby clothes, focus is on an outreached hand begging for sympathy. The scene amplifies the inherent injustice of the debtor prison. A caption brings into play a literary device to reinforce a Christian obligation to the needy:

Within the gate
They cry at the Grate
Praye remember our fate
And have Pitty!

Much like other performing museums, the Clink succeeds in taking visitors out of their own world and transports them into another place and time. Next, we continue our exploration of the significance of space as a cultural setting for punishment.

SITES OF PENAL AMBITION

As we move toward architectural sites where punishment has been strategically located, it is essential to contemplate their form and function. Together, those symbols and instruments animate the institution's semio-technology, giving it "life" as it expresses and pursues its ambitions. Outwardly, the early penitentiary aimed to communicate to all a degree of terror that would, in turn, strive to deter crime. The internal messages, however, were more nuanced, blending the religious with the rational so as to promote individual reform. Deferring to Beccaria and other secular theorists, John Howard (a devoted spiritualist) conceded: "We have too much adopted the gothic mode of correction *viz.* by *rigorous severity,* which often *hardens* the heart; while many foreigners pursue the more rational plan of *softening* the mind in order to [encourage] its amendment" (see Bender, 1987: 22, 261; Ignatieff, 1978). Those well-chosen words by Howard capture the crucial interplay between form and function.

Penal ambitions reside in multiple venues where their semio-technologies are easily recognized. Indeed, that is precisely the point of *architecture parlante:* to be immediately noticed so as to convey what it is and what it intends to do. As we visit different penal destinations, it is important to note that interpretation is directed at the prison not only in its original incarnation but also in its current one as a prison museum. Teasing out the many symbolic and instrumental features of imprisonment—and the museum experience— the tour ventures to the island and then returns to the city, where penality has entered the dungeon, the fort, the church, and the model penitentiary. Of course, remnants of those sites shall be explored further in the chapters on religion, economics, and colonialism. Nonetheless, emphasis here remains on the many forms and functions of penal architecture as they harness space and follow a particular objective, such as banishment, suffering, or reform.

THE ISLAND

Whereas banishment is among the most primitive forms of punishment, that kind of social exclusion took on even greater symbolism when villains, convicts, and those considered political threats were sent to a nearby island. Often located within sight of the metropolis, the punitive island communicated the fear of isolation and loss of belonging—a civic death. For tourists traveling to Cape Town and San Francisco, a vacation would not be complete without a visit to Robben Island and Alcatraz. Staring at those islands from the mainland builds anticipation and arouses curiosity. Tours at both destinations begin with a historical lesson on the use of banishment. Standing on

Table Mountain, high above the city of Cape Town, visitors can get a bird's-eye view of Robben Island. There a plaque titled "The Island" explains its significance: "Nelson Mandela gazed at this mountain from Esiqithini for Robben (Seal) Island, which for some 450 years served as a prison for European convicts, slaves from West Africa, princes from the East, lepers, the insane and thousands of South Africans punished for resisting oppressive rule." In San Francisco, tourists gain a similar perspective on Alcatraz. From the observation deck at Coit Tower in the North Beach neighborhood, the presence of "the Rock" commands attention as it sits noticeably in the harbor. While on the wharf, visitors waiting in line for their chance to board a ferry to Alcatraz are invited to read the many informative storyboards. They learn that from almost the very beginning, Alcatraz was a prison: in 1859, eleven military men were confined in the sally port basement. During the Civil War, Union soldiers convicted of assault, rape, murder, or desertion were incarcerated on Alcatraz along with Confederate prisoners of war and citizens accused of treason. Much as in the case of Robben Island and its banishment of indigenous people, Alcatraz exiled members of the Hopi, Apache, and Modoc tribes during the Indian wars of the mid- to late nineteenth century (Golden Gate National Parks Conservancy, 1996).

Compared to other sites of penal ambition, Robben Island and Alcatraz possess a distinctive semio-technology. As noted, both islands communicate to those on the mainland that it is a hopeless place of seclusion, secured by a natural—albeit daunting—perimeter. Even though Robben Island and Alcatraz feature man-made maximum-security units, it is the treacherous tides that deter escapes. At Alcatraz, sharks inhabit rough waters. So as to send additional messages about the dangers of escape, prison officials repeated folklore insinuating that the sharks were man-eaters. However, in its current incarnation as a prison museum, curators engage tourists so as to set the record straight. In the pedagogical exercise called "Alcatrivia" (discussed in chapter 2) visitors are asked: "True or False? Alcatraz is surrounded by man-eating sharks." The answer reads: "FALSE. There are sharks in San Francisco Bay, but none are 'man-eating.' The cold water and strong currents were greater deterrents to escape." Evidence of security at Alcatraz is apparent. Officials report that thirty-six convicts tried to escape: all but five were recaptured or otherwise unaccounted for. Three who were unaccounted for participated in the infamous escape involving Frank Morris and the Anglin brothers in 1962. The self-guiding information brochure tells visitors that those convicts "used raincoats as floatation devices and were presumably bound for San Francisco. Although their bodies were never found, they are assumed to have drowned" (Golden Gate National Parks Conservancy, 1996: n.p.). Visitors craving more details can purchase the one-dollar pamphlet titled *Discover Alcatraz Escapes: A Tour of the Attempts*. The opening passage highlights the message on deterrence. In 1926, Commandant Colonel G. Maury Gralle responded to a rumor of a planned mass escape: "Go Ahead, Swim!" The narrative continues: "The Commandant's common-sense attitude discouraged the escape that day. The frigid waters (58 degrees) and strong currents (6 to 8 mph) of San Francisco Bay caused many a desperate man to reconsider escape from Alcatraz throughout its 104-year prison history" (Golden Gate National Parks Conservancy, 1997: no page).

Similarly, Robben Island is fortified by a wave-beaten boundary that serves as a natural deterrent to escape. As a reminder of just how angry the cold sea can become, the shoreline is a graveyard for vessels. Legendary ghost stories still haunt the waters, most notably, the *Flying Dutchman;* according to ocean lore, the sight of the phantom ship foreshadows doom. On a rainy night in 1975, prison officers discovered in the thick fog a group of "soaking, exhausted, Taiwanese seaman, their clothes torn, oil streaking their bodies, struggling through a wind that threatened to cast them back into a sea that had crushed their ship . . . the *Fong Chung No. 11*" (Smith, 1997: 26). Even in the 1990s, three other ships wrecked, despite the nautical skills of experienced captains and crew.

Against all odds, some prisoners slipped into the frigid harbor undeterred by the tempestuous currents and man-eating sharks. Boats and rafts made of animal skins were the usual vehicles of escape. In 1659, prominent Goringhaicona leader Autshumato (Herrie die Strandloper) escaped by boat. Tragedy awaited many of the rest. Xhosa prophet Nxele Makana and thirty fellow prisoners attempted escape in 1820. Their small craft capsized just meters from the mainland. Most of them drowned, including Makana, who is remembered for shouting encouragement to his comrades as he clung to a rock. Two of the survivors were captured, hanged, and decapitated: their heads were fixed to stakes on Robben Island as a warning to others. Political prisoners from the 1960s to the 1990s called Robben Island by another name: Makana Island. This was in honor of the famous Xhosa leader who resisted the oppressive rule of the European settlers. Legend has it that Makana's ghost still walks the island (Smith, 1997; see Schadeberg, 1994; chapter 10). The site was declared a National Monument in 1996 and a World Heritage Site in 1999.

In surveying the sites of penal ambition, there is much to learn by considering the city, especially its innermost space. As Foucault commented, "The mysterious work of punishment will become near at hand, sometimes even at the centre of the cities of the nineteenth century, the monotonous figure, at once material and symbolic, of the power to punish" (1977: 116). Much like their punitive counterparts, museums also benefit from being strategically located at the focal point of the metropolis, standing as embodiments—both in substance and in semiotics—of a power to "show and tell." Hence, penitentiaries, museums, and now prison museums are deployed in public space, seeking rhetorically to incorporate people within the aspirations of the state (Bennett, 1995: 87; see Williams, 2007). Among those ambitions are efforts to educate and promote a sophisticated sense of history and culture, particularly with respect to punishment.

Long before the advent of formal prisons, punishment took place in the center of the city. In London, for instance, a small rotunda known as the Tun of Cornhill converted retribution into a spectacle, using open cages, stocks, and pillories for the display and mortification of offenders (Evans, 1982: 50, 425: Pugh, 1970). Recall that visitors to the Hong Kong Correctional Services Museum can see for themselves how the practice of public punishment took place in the British colonies. In a series of black-and-white photographs, a couple of young Chinese adults sit awkwardly with their feet bound by a single wooden stock. Their grimacing faces convey both emotional and physical discomfort. The caption reads, "Two criminals being displayed on the street with slogan telling clearly about their crimes."

Eventually, punishment was taken behind closed doors in city jails; however, those forms of penal ambition were a far cry from the orderliness of the model penitentiaries of the mid-eighteenth century. Londoners seemed to be well aware of the disorder in English jails, given the rich traffic between the city streets and the local lockups. The old Newgate Prison, for instance, earned a notorious reputation for its vice because outsiders could easily "penetrate the interior and witness the exploitive machinations of the keep and his deputies, the licentiousness, the overcrowding, the pervasiveness of mortal disease and moral contamination" (Evans, 1982: 2). A widely published illustration titled *Newgate—Prison Discipline, City of London System* (c. 1818) by George Cruikshank encapsulated the mayhem.

Across the Atlantic, a copy of Cruikshank's picture is on display at Eastern State Penitentiary museum. Tour guides explain that the disorderly jails were also a major problem in Philadelphia. The first city jail in Philadelphia in the 1680s was also a cage, not unlike the Tun of Cornhill in London. That strong, boxlike room, measuring five feet by seven feet, stood at the corner of Second Street and what is currently known as Market Street. Philadelphia's population growth prompted city officials to build a slightly larger jail (fourteen feet by twenty feet) but that soon proved inadequate. In 1718, the Old Stone Prison opened on the corner of Third Street and Market Street. In due course, that institution fell victim to overcrowding and chaos, prompting Philadelphia's Quaker elite to construct the Walnut Street Jail in 1773. Designed by one of the most prominent architects in the colonies at the time, Robert Smith, the jail was located opposite the yard of the State House (Independence Hall). It opened when only partially finished in 1776:

> The plan was traditional, consisting of a front building of three stories, flanked by two wings attached at right angles. As in British prisons of the period, inmates were housed together in large rooms. Aside from the handsome Georgian façade, which might have graced a city hall or a university building, the only architectural feature worthy of note was the use of brick vaulting to support the upper floors, making the building one of the earliest examples of relatively fire-proof construction in colonial America. (Johnston, 2010: 26)

The rapid expansion of Philadelphia consumed the Walnut Street Jail and it became synonymous with overcrowding, bad associations, idleness, and poor supervision. So as to accommodate an emerging system of separate confinement, the city's leadership embarked on what became known as the most ambitious penal experiment in world history, namely, Eastern State Penitentiary. ESP boasted an impressive *architecture parlante*. For the façade of the prison, Haviland chose a restrained Gothic style similar to that of English jails. The "keeper's house" at the front of the institution was, in the words of the architect, "'Anglo-Norman' style, complete with castellated towers and a portcullis and flanked by walls with blank windows and guard towers at each corner" (Johnston, 2010: 26). Overall, Haviland delivered a design that shunned the picturesque in favor of an austere, symmetrical exterior (Johnston, 2010: 109; see Johnston, 1978, 2000).

In the city center, the prison joined other distinctive architectural emblems, most notably, religious and governmental buildings. There, the prison, according to Bender, lay "deep in the syntactic structure articulating the space of the city. Viewed on the large canvass of world time, written narrative rests with the prison at the generative axis of the city as the enclosed seat of authority and the site of surveillance" (1987: 57). Architects took notice and coupled their own ambitions with those of the State, especially with respect to punishment and reform. In England, Augustus Pugin proposed a plan for a nineteenth-century town. Pugin's *architecture parlante* was stark, calling for a return to faith and Gothic buildings. His design challenged classicism and utilitarianism, both identified as aspects of the same malaise: "Pugin filled the immediate foreground of this picture with four modern enterprises: a gothic church rebuilt in the classical style, a lunatic asylum, a gas works, and right in the very centre, a new gaol, with central inspection, classification and unproductive labor to epitomize the age … Pugin's strident nostalgia turned the enlightenment diagram of progress upside down and pointed backwards from the cruelties of the present to gothic gentleness" (Evans, 1982: 394–95). The overarching ambition of Pugin was to situate the prison in a quaint social landscape that would complement the art of good architecture. Upon a visit to the Melbourne Gaol museum, one can gaze at a sketch that seems to capture precisely what Pugin had in mind. The caption reads: "Panoramic view of Melbourne in 1880 showing the concentration of churches, business, factories and residences in the city centre. The Melbourne Gaol, on the right, remains a dominant feature."

In a noticeable shift, the idea of a prison within the city was inverted, becoming the idea of a city within the prison. The blueprint by Richard Baldwin from 1782 for an English penitentiary was remarkable for its sequence of miniature town squares (Evans, 1982: 125–26). Although that architectural design did not reach the mainstream, it did influence the interiors of prisons as they maximized the use of space to direct the flow of traffic. At Alcatraz, tourists—like convicts before them—are oriented by way of street signs posted on corridors. Among the most familiar signs are Michigan Avenue, Broadway, and Times Square, reminiscent of Chicago and New York, respectively. Bender correctly reminds us: "Prison and the authority it assumes lie deep within the origins and structure of the city, but the city changes and so too do forms of confinement" (1987: 83). Moving forward, we shall witness how penal ambitions along with their semio-technology find expression in an array of urban institutions: the dungeon, the fort, the church, and the model penitentiary.

THE DUNGEON

Although the dungeon by its very nature constitutes a form of subterranean punishment kept from public view, it still resonates widely in the popular imagination. Its origin is traced to religious institutions, specifically to the monastery, where incorrigible monks were forced into hidden cavities of the building. Eventually, the practice extended to heretics, political enemies, and others targeted by the church or the monarchy (Mabillon, 1724). Robin Evans (1982) points out that a period of complete isolation became part of the execution process. In 1725, Bernard de Mandeville recognized that the procession to the gallows at Tyburn had become a travesty, or in other words a semiotic disaster (see Smith, 2008). The condemned were no longer intimidated by the spectacle; on the contrary, they often mocked it: "Their drunken and impenitent exit was distorting the dramatic meaning of public execution" (Evans, 1982: 75). To restore a fearful narrative to public hangings, Mandeville placed emphasis on the grotesque image of a prisoner as he emerged from the darkness. Altogether, his paleness, tears, and trembling limbs made him a terrifying sight, thereby conveying to the rabble class a message of the unspeakable agony brought on by such medieval confinement (Mandeville 1725; see Anonymous, 1701). Today, the horrors of complete isolation are displayed for penal tourism. At Eastern State Penitentiary museum, a large poster with an "action shot" photograph of a prisoner emerging from "the hole" documents the reality of solitary confinement. The prisoner's face is fraught with trauma and grief as he stares directly into the camera, making eye contact with everyone who falls within his line of vision.

While the use of the dungeon served the practical purpose of imposing harsh solitary confinement, its semiotic qualities warrant further consideration, especially as they surface in painting, literature, and opera: "It was the dramatic character of incarceration that gave it value, and its dramatic character overflowed easily into art. So it was that the architecture of the dungeon, as the scene of incarceration, was translated into an expressive theatrical setting" (Evans, 1982: 76). The opera scene, *Prison d'Amadis* by Daniel Marot, epitomized the theatrical use of the dungeon, imposing a histrionic effect on the audience that gazes at convoluted backgrounds of decayed caverns, vaults, and piers decorated with instruments of torture and confinement (Evans, 1982; see Bender, 1987). Recall that a visit to the Clink prison museum in London is very much a theatrical experience as tourists quite literally step into a scene for performance. The space of the dungeon is carefully lighted, accentuating the presence of mannequins who serve as actors portraying hideous prisoners. Audio recordings of wails, moans, and desperate pleas for help flood the scenery. Visitors are even encouraged to participate in the re-creation of torture by handling various props: the ball and chain, the Spanish Boot, the Scavenger's Daughter. As a performing museum, the Clink taps into the emotional world of the dungeon where inmates no longer reside in "the region of the damned, but in the region of the dead . . . a living hell" (Evans, 1982: 78, 91).

As we shall discuss again, solitary confinement remains a prominent subject in penal tourism. Nonetheless, some of the prison museums studied herein go to great lengths to capture the enduring legacy of the dungeon. At the Melbourne Gaol, the dungeon took on a modern veneer. Geared toward maximizing sensory deprivation, such punishment was designed to inflict psychological suffering more than mere bodily pain. A poster explains: "Both male and female prisoners were locked in these 'punishment cells'—cells with no windows—for days at a time. The purpose of these cells was to break the prisoner's spirit by total sensory deprivation—no light, no sound, no human contact and limited food." To add significant weight to that description, visitors are encouraged to peer down into the subterranean, cavernous space. Despite such scientific terminology as "sensory deprivation," penal spectators can see for themselves that the punishment cells amounted to little more than dungeons.

Visitors at the Seodaemun Prison History Hall in Seoul are directed downstairs to the "underground torture chamber" where an array of atrocities (e.g., waterboarding) occurred during the Japanese Occupation of the Second World War. The cell labeled "solitary underground confinement" gives tourists a close look at the dungeon-like chamber furnished with only a crude toilet bucket. Even more horrific is the "narrow room torture," where a room resembling a small wooden closet kept the prisoner from sitting down or standing up properly. The door of the cramped space was fitted with a tiny window located just below the chin, forcing the inmate to crouch in order to breath. Tourists are encouraged to step inside the box and close the door so as to experience its claustrophobic force. In a further reflection on the importance of sited-ness, the isolation chambers deliver a blunt message that is authentic and historically accurate: these cells were used for this purpose; people were actually confined here (see Williams, 2007: 80).

The so-called Spanish Dungeons at Alcatraz were a shadowy hole where unruly convicts "could be dragged, screaming and cursing, into a damp, echoing 'dungeon' cell—once a coal bin in the moat of the Civil War–era Citadel—then shackled to doors or ringbolts" (McHugh, 2007: 1). As noted in chapter 2, those subterranean cells were used selectively by the first warden and in violation of the rules of the Federal Bureau of Prisons. When the modern version of Alcatraz was completed in the 1940s, the D Block was reserved for solitary confinement, known as "the hole." Six of those units had solid metal doors with pull-down glass panels, and they imposed total darkness on prisoners, who were held there as punishment for a day, a week, or a complete session of nineteen days. Inside the bare steel walls, the convict was provided with not much more than a blanket (Stuller, 1998: 9; see Wellman, 2008: 34). Tourists are enticed to enter the isolation cell and even close the heavy door: amid the pitch black, they might imagine how they would cope under such conditions. The audio guide gives some suggestions. The voice of a former prisoner tells us that while held in "the hole," he would try to keep his mind alert by engaging in a few physical—and sensory—activities. For instance, he would pull a button from his uniform and toss it randomly in the cell. Then, he would crawl on his hands and knees around the floor to locate it. Once he found the button, he would start the game all over again. Unsurprisingly, visitors who step inside the cell and close the door behind them do not remain in the isolation cell for very long; after a brief moment, they are seen briskly extracting themselves from "the hole." Their nervous laughter is met with a sense of relief. Indeed, the isolation cell—as a performance space—succeeds in delivering a jolt of momentary captivity.

THE FORT

With the prominence of fort-like ornaments contained in Gothic revival architecture (e.g., Eastern State Penitentiary), it is fitting to examine such semio-technology in prison museums. Still, in many instances, the fortress theme is not merely an addition to *architecture parlante;* rather, the institution itself once served defensive purposes. As we shall explore, Alcatraz, the Old Fort at Constitution Hill, and Robben Island share a common heritage. That is, they all operated as a military garrison before being converted into a prison. Let us begin at Alcatraz, where the "mind on legs" tour is initially structured around carefully labeled objects and images on display in the former guardhouse. At this point, tourists rely on a self-guiding pamphlet (the audio guide comes later at the cellhouse).

The first stage of the "walk through history" experience involves learning about "Alcatraz, The Fort" and its military—and colonial—biography. For thousands of years, Native American tribes, mostly the Costanoan and the Coastal Miwok, occupied the region. In the eighteenth century, the Spanish invaded, establishing control over California, the San Francisco Bay, and what it called La Isla de los Alcatraces ("island of pelicans" or "island of large birds"). The exhibit displays the Spanish flag (a symbol of sovereign power) with a caption that reads: "The Presidio of San Francisco was the northern bastion of the Spanish empire from 1776 until the 1821 Mexican Revolution." The next flag in the sequence is that of Mexico, followed by the "Bear Flag Republic" with the label: "In 1846, American settlers on the northern frontier of what was then Mexico declared themselves an independent republic. On 14 June, they raised the 'Bear Flag' upon which the state flag of California is based." Finally, visitors step toward the United States flag (c. 1850), which is accompanied by a statement explaining that in the aftermath of the Mexican-American War, the United States claimed California in 1848, the same year that gold was discovered. Two years later, California would become the thirty-first state. In 1853, Alcatraz was in the full swing of being developed into a military outpost to protect San Francisco Bay from invasion (Wellman, 2008: 8; see Goodwin, 1963; Martini, 1990).

When the Civil War broke out in 1861, more than four hundred soldiers were stationed at Alcatraz. The fort was equipped with a line of heavy weapons, including a 111 smoothbore cannon and rows of open gun emplacements. A fortified gateway (or sally port) protected the brick citadel that crowned the island's highest point. Today, visitors can get a firsthand look at its semio-technology. The guardhouse, built in 1857, was designed to strike intruders with great intimidation. It was the first defense against the enemy: "It could only be reached by an oak drawbridge that spanned a 15-foot-deep dry moat. Two gun ports for 24-pound howitzers flanked the entrance and a chest-high wall with firing positions for riflemen capped the roof... Rifle slits lined the thick brick walls between the doors. Any invader who made it through the first door had to run a gauntlet of gunfire to reach the inner door. Defenders could also gather inside the sally port in front of the sealed inner door, and then burst out to drive off invaders" (Golden Gate National Parks Conservancy, 1996: n.p.).

In 1864, a twenty-five-ton Rodman cannon was installed. It had the capacity to shoot fifteen-inch, 440-pound cannonballs as far as three miles. The exhibit features a map of expected firepower with concentric circles emanating from Alcatraz (see Wellman, 2008: 14). By doing so, visitors comprehend the fort's semio-technology embodied in its awesome military might. During that period, Alcatraz also served as a military brig, holding Union soldiers convicted of crimes and Confederate prisoners of war. After President Lincoln suspended the writ of *habeas corpus,* conspirators and sympathizers were also imprisoned at Alcatraz: some of them sweated out their treason breaking rocks and shoveling dirt—while attached to a twenty-four-pound ball and chain (Stuller, 1998). The next wave of prisoners included American Indians captured during the Indian Wars (see chapter 8). Later, during the Spanish-American War, military deserters were held at the fortress prison. As pictured in companion booklets, the disciplinary regime was exceedingly strict. A photograph from 1902 shows a lineup for "noon verification": the count formation was called "nuts to butts," with army prisoners stacked into tight pairs, heal to toe (Stuller, 1998: 6; Wellman, 2008: 22).

By 1915, Alcatraz was recognized as a major engineering feat, becoming the "largest concrete structure in the world" (Esslinger, 2003: 2). By then, it served only as a military prison, since the fort was no longer considered to be an effective defense post. The compound switched from being under military authority to being under the authority of the Department of Justice in 1933 when it opened as a maximum-security penitentiary under the Federal Bureau of Prisons. Still, the island's military history resumed during the Second World War when an antiaircraft post was installed. Fittingly, it was those soldiers who gave Alcatraz its nickname, "the Rock" (Wellman, 2008: 8).

This portion of the tour of Alcatraz meets the tenets of the legislating museum since the narrative assumes a social authority that informs rather than debates: although that narrative takes a sympathetic shift when the topic of American Indians is discussed later in the visit (see Casey, 2003). Along those lines of pedagogy, the exhibit relies on objects to tell a story about the fort, in particular "A Soldier's Life," as one display is titled. Recall from chapter 2 that objects enter a process of revaluation from use-value to signifying-value. The objects here are deliberately selected to signify things that are representative of the typical routine of a soldier at Alcatraz. Accompanying a reproduction of a footlocker (c. 1863) is a storyboard that reads: "It was like any other western military post. Days were tedious, filled with training, weapons maintenance and inspection . . . These men served an important role in the defense of San Francisco through the years of international tension and civil war. Although over 100 canons surrounded the island, there was never a shot fired in anger." Through the display of objects and text, curators inform us that the fort was not a merely empty and impersonal edifice. Rather, its impressive (semiotic) architecture was animated by legions of soldiers who worked hard to keep the fort a defensive outpost. Visitors are given more details about life at the fort as army officers—and their families—are shown in a series of vintage photographs, thereby authenticating the historical record (see Williams, 2007).

As we journey to Johannesburg, attention is turned to Constitution Hill: a heritage site that includes the Old Fort, the Women's Jail, the notorious prison compound known as Number Four, and the Constitutional Court. It is important to keep focus on the Old Fort and consider its military and penal history, which together shaped its unique form and function. A large sign titled "The Old Fort" repeats a local story steeped in political economy: "After gold was discovered in 1886, the Witsatersrand was flooded with fortune seekers. In 1882, Paul Kruger, President of the Boer Zuid Afrikaansche Republiek, decided to build a jail on Hospital Hill to deal with the increase in crime in the rapidly expanding mining town." The narrative attends to the Fort's semio-technology: "Its strategic position also allowed the Boers to watch over and intimidate the *uitlanders* [foreigners, mostly English-speaking immigrants] in the town, who were considered to be a threat to the government."

In 1896, Kruger surrounded the jail's cellblocks with the Fort; this followed the Jameson Raid, which involved the *uitlanders* conspiring with the British to overthrow the Boer government. Convict labor built the ramparts around the prison and the larger military garrison. The Fort was fitted with Howitzer cannons on its two bastions overlooking the expanding town to the north and the south. Those armaments, however, were no match for the British, who returned with a formidable military. In 1900, the Boers surrendered the Fort—and Johannesburg—to the British. Six years later, when the British troops left the city, the Fort reverted to a prison. For nearly a century (from 1893 to 1983), the prison was racially segregated: whites were kept in the Old Fort and blacks were held in Number Four. The exception was Nelson Mandela, who was given a bed in the hospital wing of the Old Fort in 1962. Tourists are invited to visit the "Mandela Cell" exhibition, which contains personal documents and belongings from his days at the Old Fort and Robben Island.

The pedagogy on form and function continues. For instance, visitors learn that Sytze Wierda, a Dutch-born architect, designed the Fort. It took three years to build at a cost of forty thousand pounds. The main entrance, as described by another storyboard featuring a photograph dated 1899, looks like a gash in a hill. Interestingly, that opening is actually a tunnel built beneath the ramparts between 1896 and 1899. During the period of apartheid, police vans would drop off loads of prisoners several times a day. The mysterious gateway had its own *architecture parlante,* as "residents of Johannesburg imagined the dark tunnel to be a passageway deep into the earth." Today, tourists can peer through a large iron gate and down the tunnel. The foreboding passage collapses both time and space in ways that leave a lasting memory, making for a convincing museum effect (see Casey, 2003; Williams, 2007).

Inside the Old Fort, visitors gaze at its imposing fortress structure that oddly faces the interior rather than the exterior. A large poster explains: "One of the peculiarities of the Old Fort was that its façade was inside its ramparts, while the outside was designed to look like a hill." Special attention is directed at the Coat of Arms of the old Transvaal Republic that decorates the tunnel's inside entry way. The poster explains that Anton van Wouw, renowned for portraying Boer life in South Africa, carved the emblem. His other works include the Voortrekker Monument in Pretoria. Curiously, the text is accompanied by a photograph of British soldiers proudly posing in front of the Coat of Arms in 1900, a reminder that the Fort and its cultural symbols (e.g., the "Vierkleur" flag) were among the trophies of the Anglo-Boer War (1899–1902).

In the museum's gift shop, tourists can purchase an array of books about the prison. Curiously, in one of those volumes, there is a picture postcard from the early 1900s with lettering that reads: "Johannesburg. Main Entrance of the Fort"; "WITH BEST WISHES." Somehow, the idea of the Fort as a tourist site even back then seems strange, especially since the jail always had a brooding presence in the city (Segal, 2006: 9–11). Nevertheless, like much of the tour at the Old Fort and the rest of the compound, the narrative strikes an optimistic tone: "No longer needed for surveillance, intimidation, or incarceration, the ramparts now serve as a vantage point over Constitution Hill, the city of Johannesburg, and South Africa in the process of transition. They serve as a bridge between the difficulties of the past—as represented by the derelict old prison buildings—and the possibilities of the future—as represented by the Constitutional Court" (Segal, 2006: 018).

Off the coast of Cape Town, Robben Island has guarded approaches toward Table Bay for centuries. In 1672, when a French-British alliance challenged Holland, there was good reason to believe that the Dutch possession at the southern tip of Africa would be invaded. At least during that era, Cape Town was spared any major military intrusion. However, during the Second World War, the Germans and the Japanese took a strong interest in the Cape due to its prime shipping routes. Allied Forces, mainly the British, transformed Robben Island into a significant defense outpost. So as to become "battleship proof," the island was equipped with a battery of artillery, including 15-inch and high-angle 9.2-inch guns along with two Mark 7s and one Mark 9 (Smith, 1997).

Today, remnants of the military post are noticeable, beginning with the dock at Murray's Bay Harbour. The landing and its buildings (with their modest barracks-style architecture) were constructed at the beginning of the Second World War. It is there that tourists disembark the ferry and board a coach bus that drives them through the main gate. Waiting on the other side is a huge antiaircraft gun: the long barrel stares down everyone in its path. The intimidating weapon speaks for itself, especially since the tour guide does not even bother to comment on its presence. Robben Island is dotted with other military fortifications but none is featured in the visit. A picture book, *Remembering Robben Island,* provides photographs of bunkers and informs readers that during World War II, the Island had a maze of underground tunnels (Classen, 2010). Overall, the museum effect at Robben Island is one geared toward commemorating the political prisoners held during years of apartheid (see chapter 9). Unlike in the exhibit at the Old Fort in Johannesburg, the military significance of Robben Island is left unstated, with the exception of the antiaircraft gun that commands attention from all angles of the Island.

Although they did not serve as military garrisons, a few prisons studied herein express the fortress theme in their design, namely, the Melbourne Gaol, Eastern State Penitentiary, and the Seodaemun Prison History Hall. With imposing façades and thick guard towers, those institutions deliver an *architecture parlante* that conveys strength, security, and intimidation in Gothic proportions. As the next section demonstrates, another motif in penal ambition embraces religion, both in its form and in its function.

THE CHURCH

Though the next chapter is devoted to a full-scale critique of religion as it became infused in prison reform, this section focuses on the church as a site of penal ambition. As is the case with other forms of architecture, the church, whether expressed in all its grandeur (the cathedral) or more modestly (the chapel), relies on unique semiotics. People know that it is a special place of worship due to its obvious outward appearance. When the church intersects with penality, punishment takes on a higher purpose, most notably, redemption. Keeping attention on religious architecture, we discover the church in three settings. In the first, the church retains its own identity but joins the penal landscape, for example, at Robben Island. Next, it becomes an actual site where spiritual transformation is exercised, as witnessed at the Argentine prison museum. Finally, the church serves as a model for penal ambition, giving rise to a new form of prison architecture. That "cathedral of punishment" is best exemplified at Eastern State Penitentiary.

While being zipped around Robben Island via coach, tourists get a glimpse at the small but rich variety of religious buildings. In a settlement of the Island known as Irishtown stands the impressive Cape Gothic Garrison church. For more than a century, that Anglican Church served the "free" inhabitants; today it provides multidenominational masses, including popular Valentine's Day weddings. The Church of the Good Shepherd, on a separate stretch of the land, was reserved for the lepers, who built it in 1895. Unlike the towering Garrison church, the Good Shepherd was a compact, one-story prayer room. Visitors riding on the bus will notice that the church fallen has into disrepair. Picture books tell a more informed story about its history. Designed by Sir Herbert Baker, the structure had noble beginnings; still, its interior was remarkably vacant. The church had no pews, so lepers had to lie on the floor or stand during services. The building had inadequate windows, and the loosely fit nets could not prevent birds and bats from nesting in its rafters (Smith, 1997: 85).

In close range of the maximum-security prison, visitors can see the Kramat, a sacred site for Muslim pilgrimage and celebration. The bright green dome and doorway stand apart from the otherwise gloomy penal landscape. Built in 1969, the Kramat was erected over the grave of Sayed Adurohman Moturu. Also known as the Prince of Madura, Moturu was a political refugee who was banished to Robben Island, where he died in 1754. Legend has it that as one of Cape Town's first *imams* (religious leaders), he could materialize through closed doors to minister the Malaysian slaves. From the 1960s to the 1990s, the shrine became a point of homage for political prisoners who would ceremoniously bow to it as they departed the Island. Today, the Kramat is visited by descendants of Malay slaves on Sunday, and in February it hosts the feast of the Khalifa (Classen, 2010; Smith, 1997). Visitors interested in religious architecture at Robben Island will probably leave disappointed, since the tour does not include an inside look into its places of worship. Nonetheless, all tourists will recognize the sacred quality of *architecture parlante,* conveying spiritual messages to persons of different faiths.

For a deeper perspective on the role of religion in penal ambition, we enter the Argentine prison museum (founded by the Jesuits in the 1730s), where visitors will appreciate its actual sited-ness. In 1860 the edifice was converted into a prison for both men and women, and in 1890 it became Asilo Correccional de Mujeres, a house of correction operated by a Catholic order of nuns, Las Religiosas del Buen Pastor (the Good Shepherd). Whereas tourists at Robben Island are kept at a distance from its religious sites, visitors here are invited inside, where the museum effect delivers a lesson on Catholic objects, images, and, more importantly for this brief discussion, space. The spatial register is initially experienced as one passes through an arched passageway into the courtyard. There, the totality of its purpose as an uplifting institution is expressed through architecture. There is nothing Gothic or remotely forbidding about this design, as visitors find warmth in its peaceful square. Similarly, they are likely to feel inspiration from the two bell towers of the church San Pedro Gonzalez Telmo, the parish next door (see figure 11).

As described in the previous chapter, the serene ambience is enhanced by a series of white arches that navigate foot traffic toward the chapel of Nuestra del Carmen. Mirroring the spires of San Pedro, its dome is topped with a larger-than-life crucifix, symbolizing an omniscient deity that presides over those standing in the courtyard, whether they be the prisoners of Asilo Correccional de Mujeres or tourists in its current incarnation as the Argentine prison museum. At this phase of the tour, the museum effect succeeds in not positioning spectators within a closed interior that would create a sense of confinement. Rather, the openness of the patio in full view of the bell towers and domed chapel serves to connect visitors, at least metaphorically, with the "heavens above." Upon reflection, the space suggests that spiritual transcendence and redemption prevail over physical pain and suffering (see Welch, 2012a, 2013).

As the prison reform movement in the late eighteenth century adopted the church as its model, moral transformation became the chief objective. A key source of knowledge on the subject was Jean Mabillon, a Benedictine

FIGURE 11. The church San Pedro Gonzalez Telmo. Its bell towers loom graciously over the court-yard of the Argentine prison museum (Buenos Aires). © retrowelch 2014

monk who advocated redemptive imprisonment in his treatise *Reflexions sur les Prisons des Ordres Religieux,* written in 1724. Mabillon noted that while secular justice should terrify, ecclesiastical justice should save souls (Evans, 1982: 57). Mabillon proposed that every French province should open an independent monastic prison replicating a Carthusian cloister in which strict solitude was to be enforced: "There would be a number of cells, similar those of Chartreux, with a work room to train them in some useful labour. One could also add to each a little garden which could be opened at certain hours for them to work in and take the air" (Mabillon, 1724: 57). As a form of seclusion in austerity, the cell was an abode for the soul in communion with God, not man (Evans, 1982: 57; Knowles, 1963).

At Eastern State Penitentiary, tourists experience for themselves the chapel-like cells lined along a corridor with vaulted ceilings inspired by cathedrals (see Johnston, 2010). The museum effect deals with architecture and space in two ways. First, visitors gaze at a three-dimensional cutaway model that reveals the interior of an original cell. It shows three sections, each partitioned by a thick wall. The inner compartment is the corridor illuminated by natural light from skylights. Next is the living unit furnished with a single bed, a small table, and a bench. Since inmates were to serve their entire sentence (usually less than three years) in solitary confinement, the cells were considered large by contemporary standards: the original thirty-eight cells were eight by twelve feet with brick vaults ten feet high at the crown, where a skylight was installed. An iron latticework door coupled with a solid wooden door connected to the third segment, an individual, open-air exercise yard (eight feet wide and eighteen feet long). Initially, the only access to the cell was through the outside iron door in the wall of each exercise yard. Meals and work materials were passed from the corridor through an aperture that also had a small peephole that allowed the guard to observe the prisoner. So as to give visitors a sense of spatial proportion, a miniature prisoner is shown inside the exercise yard. Complementing the cutaway model is a vintage photograph of a prisoner working inside his cell, thereby giving visitors another perspective on space within prison architecture. The photograph, dated 1872, provides another layer of authenticity and allows viewers to recognize the monastic origin of cellular confinement. Above the door, a message reads: "I believe in God thy Father. And in Jesus Christ my savior. And in the Holy Spirit who comforts me, and leads me into all truth."

As a second spatial technique, the museum at ESP persuades visitors to step inside one of its cells. There is no mistaking the space for anything but a prison cell. While the skylight provides a refreshing beam of sunshine, the interior still retains the original purpose for confinement: to induce remorse and penitence. However, unlike the monastery, which serves as a spiritual refuge for those seeking their vocation (a calling from God), prisons are by their very nature coercive institutions holding convicts against their will. In the words of a prison administrator, the penitentiary is like "a monastery inhabited by men who do not choose to be monks" (Teeters, 1970: 8; see Johnston 2010: 47, 110; Meranze, 1996). Despite the apparent contradiction, ESP with its cathedral-influenced corridors and chapel-like cells became the model for penitentiaries built around the world.

THE MODEL PENITENTIARY

At Eastern State Penitentiary, it is easy to understand why tourists gravitate to the central observation hub where they can peer down eight separate corridors reaching outward to the end of the cellblocks. Even in its early years, Haviland's radial plan attracted many international luminaries, including Gustave de Beaumont and Alexis de Tocqueville (1833) and Charles Dickens (1842). Today, ESP offers visitors not only a genuine sited-ness but also a lesson on the ingenious use of space (see Bruggeman, 2012). The model penitentiary exemplified in ESP (and Pentonville in London) emerged during the first half of the 1800s when prison building was being recognized as a distinctive style of architecture. At the time, incarceration was becoming regularized within a larger campaign of penal reform, and because prisons were viewed as having a moral purpose, their architecture would be an instigator of virtue (Meranze, 1996). Toward that end, Haviland was known "as a good prison architect rather than a good architect" (Evans, 1982: 410, see page 1).

Standing at the epicenter, visitors can get a sense of the power contained in the space that once functioned as a command center for the guards. There, they experience ESP's semio-technology, in particular its concentric geometry that dictates both form and function. As Evans insightfully explains, circular architecture is traced to the temple and then to the chapel, to the roundhouse theater, and to the model penitentiary: "In the temple, the circle was used for its symbolic panorama of architecture, sculpture and painting to be contemplated by the observer. In the prison, however, the properties of the circle were employed otherwise, establishing the authority of the gaoler by displaying not the architecture and its decoration, but the inmates and their activities" (1982: 414). As one of the more than three hundred prisons claiming ESP's paternity, Seodaemun prison in Seoul gives tourists an opportunity to recognize the economy and strength of the radial plan based on a circular diagram. Seodaemun prison opened in 1908 under Japanese occupation, and for decades several cellblocks were added as more Korean resisters were imprisoned. Visitors are invited to enter the Central Prison Building that serves as the hub of the spoked design. A sign explains its architecture and purpose: "This 2-story central building was built in 1923 as a way to connect the 10th-11th-12th jails for effective surveillance along with office works and ideological persuasion." Once inside, tourists are drawn to the "Monitoring Location of Warder": an elevated wooden platform furnished with a desk and a chair, similar to a judge's bench in a courtroom. Museum staff members encourage visitors to step into the monitor station where they can gain the perspective of the guard who peers down the long hallway of cells. Interestingly, each cell is equipped with a "PAE TONG" for prisoners to inform the guard in emergency." The simple device is a stick that prisoners can push from inside of their cell, which falls outward and within view of the guard seated in the monitor station.

The radial plan borrowed heavily from Jeremy Bentham (1748–1832) and his panopticon, an architectural design aimed at maximizing surveillance. Initially proposed as the "ultimate penitentiary," the panopticon derived its name from the Greek, meaning "everything" and "a place of sight." Its architecture combines geometry (i.e., circular design) with economics (i.e., few guards watching many prisoners) while also embracing a sense of morality by imitating Christian ideas of ominiscience so as to promote personal reform. Citing the 139th Psalm, Bentham believed that the invisible guard in the central tower practiced a form of executive power analogous to an omniscient deity who could see everything at all times (Bentham, 1995; Lyon, 1991). In more secular terms, the panopticon was founded in the Enlightenment's quest for instilling order and control through observation, symbolizing what Virilio (1994) called the utopian vision machine. The panopticon (or "inspection house") benefits from a unique floor plan that manipulates interior space. At its center is an imposing column that serves as an indoor guard tower. Several tiers of cells are arranged in a circular formation, each of them facing the inspector tower. The design—a circle inside a circle—provides the watchers with a complete and continuous view over the watched (see chapter 10).

Foucault issues a forceful critique of the panopticon, noting that its circular design renders the prison population more transparent and thus vulnerable to control. The basis for inmate control is constant inspection, which represents power in two ways: it becomes both visible and unverifiable: "Visible: the inmate will constantly have before his eyes the tall outline of the central tower from which he is spied upon. Unverifiable: the inmate must never know whether he is being looked at any one moment: but he must be sure that he may always be so" (1977: 201; Foucault 1996; see Alford, 2000). Due to the conspicuous and mysterious presence of the guard tower, prisoners cannot always be sure whether or not they are the objects of observation. Consequently, the target of control is the mind rather than the body. While deeply aware of constant surveillance, prisoners internalize the gaze, thereby becoming their own self-monitor: "Hence, the major effect of the Panopticon: to induce in the inmate a state of conscious and permanent visibility that assures the automatic functioning of power" (Foucault, 1977: 201). It has been said that the panopticon was more a contraption than a building because it aspired to generate and stabilize an entire social system: "Here technology was not merely an aid to morality—it was a necessary precondition of the very morality it created" (Evans, 1982: 199). Perhaps Aldous Huxley best captures the oppressive potential of the panopticon when he called it the "totalitarian housing project" (Johnston, 1973: 20; Welch, 2010c, 2011d).

In Johannesburg, tourists can spend time at the Women's Jail museum located within the compound of Constitution Hill. At the center of its radial plan is an impressive atrium comprising a circular gallery supported by a team of classical columns. So as to stay connected with the outside, tall vaulted windows bask the interior space with natural light (see figure 12). Much like ESP and Seodaemun, visitors can exercise surveillance by standing at the midpoint and looking down each corridor. Its appealing design, however, seems to hide its chief rationale. A brochure explains: "Built in 1909, the grace of this Victorian brick building obscures the pain and humiliation suffered by the many women detained within it. The jail held black and white women in separate sections. The infamous murderess, Daisy de Melker, was held here, as were prominent activists Winnie Madikizela-Mandela and Albertina Sisula. Ironically, the vast majority of inmates were neither murderers nor activists. They were women arrested for pass offences or illegal occupations such as beer brewing." With respect to its current purpose as a museum, the pamphlet adds: "The hoarding, which protects the building, has been transformed into a temporary exhibition that honors the contribution of women in the struggle for freedom in South Africa" (Constitution Hill, Visitor's Brochure, n.d.; see Segal, 2006).

FIGURE 12. The circular atrium of the Women's Jail in Johannesburg (South Africa). © retrowelch 2014

So as to give a brief tutorial on its architecture, a storyboard tells visitors that the central oval hall with individual cells fanning out from it is based on the panopticon or roundhouse design by Jeremy Bentham: "Rather than confine prisoners to medieval dungeons, he said they should be under constant surveillance by the all seeing eye of prison authorities." Injecting the narrative with scholarly reflection, the sign quotes Audrey Brown, director of research at the Women's Jail: "Unlike the men's section, which does not conceal its primary purpose, this space beguiles the eye and misleads the mind. The light-filled atrium and the cells radiating off it conceal the very essence of a jail—punishment and subjugation. The architecture of the Women's Jail might be more subtle than that of a male prison in terms of power and control, but it is just as violent." The English version of the model prison at Pentonville, designed by Joshua Jebb in 1840, replicated Haviland's radial plan. Still, it featured a unique Benthamite innovation with its exercised yards:

> As with the cells, the architecture was enlisted in support of the ever more profound isolation of the convicts. Between the outspread fingers of the four cell blocks, areas of ground were demarcated with 108 wedges of walled space

with open railings at the ends, but partitioned from one another in such a way as to make each a private enclosure. These were to be the exercise yards, where, once a day, every prisoner spent one hour walking to and fro. At the center of the neat circles of yards would be a covered inspection lodge, from which an inscrutable warder, screened from the view of the convicts, could survey what was going on around him at a glance. (Evans, 1982: 361, see 350, 351)

At the Melbourne Gaol, a prison inspired by both Pentonville and ESP, tourists examine the fine detail of its architecture, especially as it is displayed in the form of a large model. Conspicuously present is the circular exercise yard just as Jebb envisioned it. For an even greater spatial effect with respect to Benthanmite architecture, Seodaemun prison museum restored the institution in a way that allows visitors to enter the "Gyeokbyeokjang" (exercise facility). The semicircled brick structure boasts a pie-chart symmetry with ten separate slices. An observation platform is situated at the hub where the guard can stare down into each section (stretching fifteen meters long and two meters wide). There, visitors can position themselves as the inspector, and then walk the length of one of the individual yards to get the point of view of a prisoner. A poster informs us that the exercise facility was designed to maximize monitoring while the individual compartments prevented the inmates from communicating with one another. The genuine sited-ness of the Gyeokbyeokjang is complemented by a vintage photograph that verifies its past.

Despite all the ambition to transpose an engaging blueprint into an actual prison, Bentham's panopticon was never built in Britain. Circular prisons, however, were built in Holland, in Spain, and on the Isle of Pines off the coast of Cuba. In the United States, the panoptic design was employed at Virginia Penitentiary and Western Pennsylvania Penitentiary. In Illinois, Stateville Correctional Center, built in 1919, continues to operate as a maximum-security panopticon. Stark photographs of Stateville are mainstays in books and magazines as well as in prison museums. At Alcatraz, tourists are given a glimpse of Stateville's interior design: the guard tower resembles a large lantern surrounded by four levels of cells. The picture is accompanied by a copy of one of Bentham's early sketches of the panopticon. A caption reads: "Jeremy Bentham proposed improvements in prison architecture to facilitate better discipline and moral reflection." Adding a bit more historical detail on prison architecture, the exhibit at Alcatraz includes an artist's rendition of the façade of Eastern State Penitentiary (c. 1830). A definitive remark states: "It became a model for prisons around the world."

At the Argentine prison museum, a main attraction is the large replica of the National Penitentiary, which was located in the city from 1873 to 1961 (see chapter 3). Its *architecture parlante* proudly combines a fortress façade with five spokes that radiate from a central tower. Its neat symmetry seems to suggest a blueprint for a larger sense of nationalism as Argentine flags hang above the replica. Wide-angle and telescopic photographs add historical verification of its semio-technology (see Welch and Macuare, 2011).

To recap, the model penitentiary as a site of penal ambition is best exemplified at Eastern State Penitentiary. Tourists marvel at its massive—thirty-foot—castle-like walls with a perimeter of half a mile. Making their way through the ornate portico (or barbican), visitors practice space by being able to stroll throughout the intriguing compound, all while under the gaze of the central guard tower. As visitors explore its wagon-wheel design, they can duck into a labyrinth of alleyways and dimly lit cells. A brochure tells us that ESP is "America's Most Historic Prison," and that it "stands today in ruin, a haunting world of crumbling cellblocks and a surprising, eerie beauty." So as to engage tourists, guides invite them to participate in "Hands-On History," a series of short interactive experiences. Here the museum makes contact with those interested in deepening their knowledge of prison architecture. The following are among the eleven lessons offered by tour guides:

Front Gate: Try your hand opening the penitentiary's complex and heavy front gate.

Punishment Cells: Descend into "the Hole" to see the windowless underground punishment cells.

The Ruins of Death Row: View the collapsing exercise yards of Death Row, one of the most ruinous spaces at Eastern State.

As tourists conclude their visit, they pass through the gift shop, where they can stock up on an array of books, posters, and decorative magnets, as well as a fashionable tote bag emblazoned with Haviland's blueprint of the radial plan. Available postcards not only deliver lasting memories of the day at ESP but also include more historical information. For example, one postcard features a striking picture of the façade at night: its neo-Gothic design and *architecture parlante* are embellished with strategic lighting. The caption on the back quotes the *Book of Minutes of the Board of Commissioners,* from 1922: "The exterior of a solitary prison should exhibit, as much as possible, great strength, and convey to the mind ... the misery which awaits the unhappy being who enters with its walls."

CONCLUSION

So as to illuminate the significance of space and architecture, this chapter delved into the many sites of penal ambition. Beginning with the island as a symbolic and feasible spot for banishment, discussion then turned to the city. There, prisons—and museums—rely on their central location to communicate a specific purpose. Of course, punishment manifested in a few different venues. The dungeon, for instance, had the capacity to strike fear in city dwellers even though it remained out of the public eye. The shift toward grand visual statements via penal architecture is clearly recognized at the fort, the church, and finally the model penitentiary. By incorporating punishment into regimes of militarism, religion, and correction, those institutions relayed their own unique semio-technology. Through the use of prison museums, those themes inform a cultural sociology of punishment concerned with both expression (Durkheim) and utility (Foucault) (see Smith, 2008; Welch and Macuare, 2011).

As prison architecture gained prominence in the early nineteenth century, a tighter coupling between form and function became evident. Borrowing from academic planning, the visual properties of neoclassical, centralized designs were gradually transmuted into "instrumental geometries that would finally result in the prison becoming an indispensible vehicle for the authority and order that earlier plans had set out only to symbolize" (Evans, 1982: 412). Indeed, the semio-technology of the model prison went well beyond the *architectural parlante*—Gothic revival—expressed in its façade; inside, prisoners underwent a distinct method of reform predicated on morality. Still, as Robin Evans insists, it was through architecture that moral authority was asserted. Moreover, a small but significant class of prison architects, including Bentham and Haviland, not only wedded discipline to building but also channeled their ambition toward maintaining society as a whole. In the next chapter, the role of religion in governance, as well as governance in religion, is treated as a crucial strand of penal history. As we shall continue to see, prison museums serve as insightful vehicles for culture, revealing both the instrumental and the expressive forces of punishment.

FIVE

Religion and Governance

At the Melbourne Gaol museum, the most noticeable overlap between religion and governance is relayed through a commentary on the chaplain. The division of labor in the execution protocol is explained: "After the sentence of death was passed, the Sheriff took charge of the condemned prisoner's body while the Chaplain took care of the prisoner's soul." For the Gaol, the Church of England appointed an official chaplain (though every major Christian religion was represented) who "supported the prisoner in the two or three weeks before execution, accompanied him on the scaffold and recited prayers as he was buried." While the exhibit clearly outlines the duty of the chaplain in facilitating the State's deathwork, it also informs tourists that over time, those spiritual leaders would oppose certain aspects of execution. A storyboard titled "HANGING: ENTERTAINMENT, JUSTICE OR LEGAL MURDER" contemplates the local debate over public executions: "The question that concerned mid-nineteenth century Victorians was not so much the morality of capital punishment or the right of the State to take a life but whether this should be done in public." Chaplain Keith Forbes weighed in on the controversy in a written statement: "It would be impossible for those who have witnessed, like myself, the 'brutal exhibition' of a human being launched into eternity to refrain from asking, 'Can this thing be justifiable in the sight of God?'" By raising ethical doubts over the use of public executions, the museum at the Melbourne Gaol offers visitors a sense of moral progress.

As discussed in the opening chapter, a cultural sociology of punishment benefits from Durkheimian thought, especially along lines of socioreligious constructs: the sacred vis-à-vis the profane, the mythological, and the cult of the individual. Those concepts, indeed, help us unpack the complexity of religion as it surfaces in prisons—as well as in prison museums. So as to introduce greater precision, we turn to Geertz's definition of religion: "(1) a system of symbols which acts to (2) establish powerful, pervasive, and long-lasting moods and motivations in men by (3) formulating conceptions of a general order of existence and (4) clothing these conceptions with such an aura of factuality that (5) the moods and motivations seem uniquely realistic" (2000 [1973]: 90). Continuing our exploration of penal tourism, we remain mindful of Geertz's description of religion while also employing his method of *thick description*. In doing so, the chapter sets out to deposit observations on religion into an in-depth network of framing intentions and cultural meanings. The field of semiotics (the study of signs), of course, enables us to sort out the subtleties and nuances of Durkheim's socioreligious concepts. Still, for the purposes of this analysis, we refuse to neglect power-based perspectives (i.e., Foucault), particularly with respect to domination and social control. However, a close reading of Durkheim reveals that punishment— even when intertwined with religion—is a matter of governance. As Garland writes, governance is concerned with the broader maintenance of a social enterprise whose moral character is not only complex but also political (1990; see Selznick, 1988). Toward that end, the discussion is organized around key intersections of religion and governance: namely, religious persecution (e.g., the Clink), the monastic effect (e.g., Eastern State Penitentiary), Church and State (e.g., the Argentine prison museum), and the Jewish experience (e.g., Eastern State Penitentiary). So as to inject our interpretations with a deeper sense of religious resonance, notions of purity vis-à-vis impurity are examined alongside the ways prison museums narrate the left sacred. After setting the stage, attention is turned to a renewed scholarly appreciation of Durkheim.

DURKHEIM REDUX

Over the past decade, a host of like-minded sociologists have embraced a campaign to revive the significance of Durkheimian theory (Alexander, 2005; Bellah, 2005; Riley, 2005; Smith, 2008; Smith and Alexander, 2005). Among their chief aims is to advance Durkheim's contributions in ways that break from the "functionalist" and "positivist" tradition. Toward that end, focus swings to the expressive elements of social phenomenon, including religion, punishment, and governance. Let us take time to review some of the main points in Durkheim's work, especially as they throw light on prisons and penal tourism. Durkheim's semiotic turn is recognized in his writings that investigate the communicative bonds of society as they reach into the individual and the mind (1895, 1915; Durkheim and Mauss, 1903). Thus, he was interested in mapping out socially constructed symbol systems that operate as mental frameworks, orienting the individual within the world. In that context, collective representations (e.g., conscience and consciousness) emerge as vehicles of communication that prompt people to perceive the world as classified into categories. A major classification is the binary separating the sacred from the profane—or *things set apart* from material interests. The sacred, empowered by a sense of awe, stands as a metaphor for the necessity of society's normative solidarity, group identification, and collective action.

"Undeniably, a certain amount of circularity exists in this model, as in all of Durkheim's work. However, he has located the major elements of a central problem in social and semiotic theory. Everyday experience testifies to the general correctness of his views" (Harkin, 1998: 207; see Lukes, 1975). Symbols that have political functions in modern society, such as flags, are capable of arousing emotional energy and, in turn, inspire and motivate citizens to support the state (Bellah, 1967; Welch, 2000). Consider, for instance, the Argentine prison museum and the ubiquity of national flags displayed alongside an array of religious symbols (e.g., the crucifix, pictures of the Virgin Mary). Together, those secular and sacred emblems help build solidarity and cultural pride among Argentines. For Durkheim, religion is not a mere social creation; it is society divinized. As people collectively worship, they pay homage to projections of the power of society; thus, "the collective consciousness is the highest form of psychic life, since it is the consciousness of consciousnesses" (2008 [1915]: 444; see Coser, 1977: 139). Indeed, collective consciousness, or common faith, crystallizes into communicable ideas. The museum effect typically taps into the collective consciousness to relay—without hesitation—the transcendent quality of certain religious artifacts. Those objects, from a Durkheimian perspective, allow people to celebrate sacred symbols and thereby visualize the power of their society (see Coser, 1977: 139).

Durkheim's interest in the sociology of religion allowed him to theorize more about morality and ethics (1961, 2012 [1933]). Still, a moral framework for society had to reflect the prevailing conditions of social organization. Modern morality, made possible by an advanced division of labor, gave rise to the cult of the individual: a constellation of related values such as dignity, tolerance, and freedom. Similarly, Durkheim viewed punishment as extending beyond retribution, becoming a moral phenomenon that contributed to social cohesion. Paraphrasing Durkheim, David Garland writes: "The state is thus conceived as a kind of secular priesthood, charged with protecting sacred values and keeping the faith ... For him, the institutions of penality function less as a form of instrumental rationality and more as a kind of routinized expression of emotion, like the rituals and ceremonies of a religious faith" (1990: 30, 35). At the prison museum in Buenos Aires, visitors gaze at a series of black-and-white photographs that document the close ties between the Catholic Church and Argentine state. In a group shot, clergy, government leaders, and prisoners are shown posing together in a gesture of cooperation and solidarity. Other pictures speak to a collage of institutional discipline, a local division of labor, and religious commitment as women inmates are seen working and praying with Catholic nuns.

Delving even further into the core of Durkheimian theory, Philip Smith (2008) issues a forceful and polemical critique. By doing so, he deepens our appreciation of Durkheim while building a cultural sociology of punishment that goes beyond the political and administrative toward signifiers of order and disorder, purity and pollution, the sacred and evil. Social control, from that standpoint, is a semiotic process, facilitated by cultural imperatives and rituals intended to transform disorder into order. Such a task is easier said than done: "Disorder is a perpetually moving target. When one form of the unruly, evil, or disgusting is eliminated others are found ... Creating cultural order is rather like trying to solve the Rubik's Cube. As you get one facet uniformly blocked out, things start to go awry where you are not looking" (Smith, 2008: 14; see Durkheim, 1958 [1895]). Smith reminds us that Durkheim (2012 [1933]) situated the primitive impulse—and moral outrage—to punish in the religious character of culture, including taboos and an array of evils, anxieties, profanities, and pollution that threaten the sacred. For Smith, punishment is not so much about justice, reason, and law; rather, it is cultural ritual intended to rid the world of evil without creating more of it in the process (see Welch, 2006).

As we transit toward the content of prison museums, a few final thoughts on Durkheim's sociology of religion brought to us by Harry Alpert (1939). The four functions of religion, as catalogued by Alpert, adhere to the following effects: discipline, cohesion, vitalization, and euphoria. In the first instance, religious rituals impose self-discipline and a certain measure of asceticism. Next, such ceremonies build solidarity by bringing people together to reaffirm their common bonds. Religious observances also maintain and revitalize the social heritage of certain groups, thereby transmitting their enduring values for future generations. Finally, religion has the capacity to deliver optimism, hope, and, in some cases, euphoria: "On the most general plane, religion as a social institution serves to give meaning to man's existential predicaments by tying the individual to that supra-individual sphere of transcendent values which is ultimately rooted in his society" (Coser, 1977: 139). Prison museums with their intended itineraries give visitors access to those touchstones of religion as they manifest in punishment, redemption, governance, and social control. As we shall see in greater detail, prison museums utilize religious objects, images, and space to craft a particular narrative.

RELIGIOUS PERSECUTION

Since the term *penitentiary* derives from the Latin words meaning penitence and repentance (and shares the same root with the words *punishment, pain,* and *revenge*), it is unsurprising to find religious themes in penal tourism (see Norris, 1985). Nonetheless, what should interest observers—and scholars—is how religion makes contact with government (and vice versa), producing key forms of social control. At the Clink museum, visitors are presented with numerous placards telling the story of its religious origins, which played out in the governance of early London. From the Middle Ages until 1780, the Bishop of Winchester used the Clink to hold various types of "offenders," most notably, debtors. Tourists are instructed to transport themselves to "mediaeval times" and consider being subjected to the whims of absolute power: "Just imagine that you are unfortunate enough to have been put here, in the Bishop's very own private prison for misdeeds whilst in his Liberty of the Clink."

The museum effect seems to create a sense of "hell on earth" as penal spectators descend into the Clink by stepping down a series of stairs. Indeed, as Evans observes, "Hell was the paradigm of penalties to which prisons were always being compared" (1982: 65). The callous subterranean conditions are intensified as visitors are funneled through dark, narrow corridors with images of prisoners being burned, boiled, and dismembered. Visceral reactions to such grotesque illustrations are tempered somewhat by intellectual engagement. Throughout much of this portion of the tour, visitors are also given a scholarly lesson on the history of London and its socioreligious forms of law. A poster explains that the "Liberty of the Clink" refers to jurisdiction under the power of the monarchy and clergy. The bishop was a freeholder of a large part of the manor. The Manor of Southwark was more generally known as the "Liberty of the Bishop of Winchester, or as the Liberty of the Clink": "The prison was its lock-up or small local gaol. The word 'liberty' implies freedom from a superior jurisdiction, usually that of the sheriff of the county, but the manor was of course always under the law of the land, the law of monarchs. The bishop exercised his local powers through the manorial court. In later centuries, the Liberty of the Clink was run simply as an estate as far as the bishop was concerned." A lengthy tablet reminds visitors that the Clink was also an instrument of religious persecution: "At each stage of these 16th century struggles, the prisons were occupied by the side out of power. Religious prisoners were regarded with strong distaste, they were treated worse than the general run of criminals." Again, the museum does not spare visitors the cruel imagery surrounding persecution, torture, and the execution of religious enemies (e.g., waterboarding). Amid the shifting tide of religious turmoil that followed Henry VIII's dissolution of the monasteries, "all whose belief differed from those in power suffered persecution." During Queen Mary's reign, Protestants like John Hooper, Bishop of Gloucester, were targets of the monarchy. A caption reads: "Even wealth did not protect religious prisoners. 'I paid like a baron,' protested Bishop Hooper, here being beaten in the Clink's grounds by Edmund Bonner, Bishop of London. 'They hath used me more vilely than the veriest Slave.'" In Queen Elizabeth I's time, it "was the turn of Catholics, as well as Protestant 'Dissenters.'"

Tension between Protestants and Catholics persisted for centuries; correspondingly, the Clink remained part of the local narrative. The museum concludes its story about the Clink by quickly forwarding to 1780 when the notorious Gordon Riots consumed London. In June of that year, Protestants demonstrated against liberties being extended to Catholics via a recent Act of Parliament, the Catholic Relief Act of 1778. A placard notes:

> In truth, it was a very mild change, which allowed Roman Catholic priests to work openly, but the religious passions of the age were stirred. To some, it seemed as if all the oppression and tyranny of the Middle Ages were about to return and subvert the nation. Rioters attacked Catholic chapels and property owned by Catholics, especially the Irish . . . But very quickly it changed into a more general riot against authority, and a chance to plunder . . . The mob also turned their attention to London's prisons. Inmates were set free, and the buildings were set alight and otherwise destroyed.

When the riots finally ended, several hundred people had died, including at least 285 vandals shot by soldiers. The Clink prison "was never revived after the destruction of the Gordon Riots." Upon reflection, visitors are left with serious doubts over the justness of confinement at the hands of religious authorities and their monarchical counterparts. During that period of English history, the tale of London—as told by the Clink museum—presents no evidence of moral progress, humane reform, or the cult of the individual. Overall, the museum effect at the Clink develops a narrative on religion and governance steeped in social control. Conveyed mostly through storyboards with illustrations, the subject matter demands that visitors consider the historical significance of religion without much tangible evidence. Hence, the tour is decidedly didactic but lacks the aura of religious imagery and experience. In Eastern State Penitentiary, visitors are immersed in religion that is embodied in architecture and monastic routine, thereby delivering a museum effect marked by spiritual reflection.*

THE MONASTIC EFFECT

For those visiting Eastern State Penitentiary, the local history plays an important role in telling a story about religion, governance, and penal reform. During the 1680s, the Quaker founders conceived the colony as a "holy experiment" (Dunn and Dunn, 1982; Meranze, 1996). Their influential leader, William Penn, understood the realities of religious persecution, for in 1670 he was imprisoned in England for his Quaker beliefs. Due to his high social status, however, he was sentenced to an inn rather than a common jail. Soon thereafter, Penn enacted the colony's penal code, which substituted the death penalty and corporal punishment with confinement, a dignified nod to Durkheim's cult of the individual. A century later, the city's municipal buildings reflected Quaker idealism, most notably, the Walnut Street Jail,

* Compared to the Clink museum, the significance of religion—let alone its relation to governance—does not resonate in the Australian narrative. Despite its vast collection, the Sydney Barracks museum mentions religion only twice. First, in the context of weekly routine, a placard states that convicts attend "Church on Sundays" and, second, with respect to some prayer books discovered by archaeologists. The Melbourne Gaol museum tends to give tourists a bit more detail on the role of religion in penal practices. However, the commentary fails to explain adequately how religion was locally embedded within penal regimes in Melbourne; rather, a poster titled "Pentonville, Punishment, and Penitence" merely notes that the famous London prison was the model of choice.

where imprisonment was understood as a progressive project. In the words of English traveler Isaac Weld, the building was not simply a jail; rather, it "deserves the name of a penitentiary house" (1799: 7, 9).

Drawing attention to the city's reformers known as the Philadelphia Society for Alleviating the Miseries of Public Prisons (later known as the Prison Society), a French investigator wrote in his report: "The Quakers were the chief promoters of this softened system . . . Public humiliation, . . . mutilation, . . . and whipping" were outlawed (Rochefoucauld-Liancourt, 1796: 6–7; see Johnston, 2010). Today, tourists at ESP get a glimpse at the significance of the Prison Society by way of portraits of its governing members: Benjamin Franklin, Benjamin Rush, and Bishop William White. So as to inform visitors about the unique departure from corporal punishment, other posters feature illustrations of past penalties (e.g., "Whipping at the Cart's Tayle," "Branding," "The Stocks," "The Pillory"). Especially against the backdrop of the stately pictures of the Prison Society, one gets the distinct impression that incarceration was introduced as a humane alternative to physical cruelty. Those messages set the stage for a tour of religiously inspired architecture directed at taming the mind as well as the soul.

At ESP, visitors appreciate the inventive use of seemingly sacred space. The vaulted ceilings reveal the influence of the cathedral, a reminder that the penitentiary was designed with a transcendent aim. Inside the chapel-like cells, that higher purpose—reform—would be idealized. There, the monastic effect was intended to take hold. Early on, prisoners served their entire sentence in a solitary cell measuring eight feet by twelve feet. A skylight channeled a celestial glow into the austere interior. At later moments of the tour, visitors are permitted to enter the cells for a firsthand experience of the monastic space. However, here the museum keeps tourists at a distance, allowing them only to peer deep inside the cell preserved in its original appearance. To verify its authenticity, several objects furnish the room: a bed fitted with a grey wool blanket, a pillow, and a bench. Nearby, a photograph titled "Life in Isolation" (1872) shows an inmate working alone in his cell. For the benefit of the visitors, the image conveys the monastic effect in motion.

The practice of solitary confinement is traced to a Benedictine council at Aix-la-Chapelle (Aachen) where in 817 an edict directed monasteries to place offenders in separate quarters with an attached workroom. Recall from the previous chapter that Benedictine monk Jean Mabillon (1724) praised isolation for its redemptive powers (Evans, 1982; Sellin, 1927). In England, John Howard (1726–1790) and his fellow Quaker "Friends" sought prototypes of prison reform. Like William Penn, Howard also experienced incarceration while a prisoner of the French forces. Prophetically, he contracted jail fever (typhus) during a visit to a military hospital in the Crimea, where he died in 1790 (Howard, 1958). During his extensive travels, Howard toured what he regarded as an exemplary institution in Rome, a juvenile prison known as San Michele. Among many observations, Howard was impressed with private rooms for inmates, a space that afforded ample time to reflect. Along with religious instruction, as was the practice in Rome, Howard advocated solitude, silence, and work (1929 [1777]; see chapter 6).

In Philadelphia, the Prison Society was well versed in the writings by Howard—and even corresponded with him. Today, tourists are repeatedly reminded that ESP was built on a moral foundation intended to foster the transformative potential of incarceration. As opposed to early prisons (and current ones), time behind bars was not supposed to be a purely punitive experience. Through the ingenious use of space and routine, the regime at ESP adopted a monastic effect aimed at humane reform. For visitors, that lesson on penal history might require a bit of imagination, since the prevailing culture equates imprisonment with punishment, incapacitation, and exclusion (e.g., "lock 'em up and throw away the key"). Nonetheless, ESP's impressive architecture allows us to interpret space as an ideal agent for personal and spiritual redemption. Such rehabilitation also demanded an important routine: religious instruction coupled with work. Philadelphia prison reformers believed that labor had intrinsic curative and moral value; moreover, it served to offset some of the debilitating symptoms of isolation such as anxiety and depression. With respect to governance, the Pennsylvania legislature passed a penal law in 1829 stipulating that labor would be mandated for sentences of solitary confinement. Interestingly, when ESP was undergoing construction, it was unclear whether the inmate regime would involve work; as it turns out, the cells were of sufficient size to accommodate the law of 1829. That same year, ESP officially opened. "All the elements were in place, and the great experiment could begin" (Johnston, 2010: 29).

Given its grand architecture and lofty ambitions, ESP attracted worldwide interest. From across the globe, emissaries, philanthropists, and prison reformers toured the institution to see for themselves how form and function cooperated to activate an idealistic penology. Fascinated by this new penal apparatus, these visitors focused attention on the role of religion. What foreigners discovered in surprise, however, was the absence of a formal chapel, a mainstay in European prisons. That puzzling inconsistency spread to other religious—and governance—matters. The penal law of 1821 noted that the chaplain would be unpaid, and all clergymen were to be volunteers. But by 1838, the "moral instructor" would be a chaplain selected by the board of inspectors and paid from public funds. Still, the topic of religion was subject to controversy. Some Philadelphians objected to the appointment of an official chaplain over concerns that it would lead to sectarian proselytizing. To offset those worries, clergy was recruited from different religious persuasions, including Catholic priests, rabbis, and various Protestant denominations. Because of all the spiritual fanfare that initially inspired the building of ESP, religious practices were carefully managed. In fact, it was not until the early twentieth century that prisoners were allowed to leave their cells to attend mass (Johnston, 2010). That degree of isolation—even from communal religious ceremonies—seems to have taken the monastic effect to an extreme.

Tourists at ESP might find the narrative on religion lacking range and depth. With the exception of the Jewish experience (discussed later), curators seem to restrict their exhibition of contemporary religion to a handful of storyboards. In a section of the prison that housed the Catholic chaplain's Office, there is a large poster labeled "Religion in the 20th Century." It shows an example of one of the murals painted by Lester Smith, a prisoner who found redemption in the 1950s. The image hones in on an inmate giving confession "while his soul receives comfort from Christ." Similar frescos are devoted to St. John the Baptist and the Coronation of the Virgin. A placard titled "Worship behind Walls" offers a succinct overview of religion at ESP: "Religion played a central role in the building of Eastern State Penitentiary. Quaker principles of innate humane goodness were foundational in the early policy of strict solitary confinement. In these early decades, prisoners were provided with a Bible, which would be their only reading material during their stay. Inmates were encouraged to worship communally by the 20th Century. In 1905, a multi-denominational chapel was added to the prison complex. A synagogue was added in the 1920s." The sign includes several photographs: a group shot of three chaplains (religious authorities), prisoners attending mass (an action shot of religious practice), and convict-convert Lester Smith. Smith's inspirational story seems to speak to the enduring monastic effect—even at a time when the concept of the penitentiary had been written off as a failure. The text explains that in the mid-1950s, Smith was serving a sentence of one to five years for armed robbery. It was at ESP that he was baptized into the Roman Catholic Church: "I used to mock the ministers and priests. Then one day I found I could not go it alone." Upon release, Smith was never rearrested.

Adding intrigue to the narrative, the story informs us that his family was unaware of his incarceration until 1994, when a newspaper article covered his artwork. In sum, the testimony of Smith and the aura of his murals appear to match Geertz's (2000) perspective on religion. The paintings involve symbols that induce long-lasting moods and motivations. Smith's realization that he "could not go it alone" has all the markings of a perceived order of existence based on communal—and spiritual—life. The storyboard on Smith serves as a sort of eulogy, concluding: "He died in 2004."

CHURCH AND STATE

Themes of religion and governance are unmistakable at the prison museum in Buenos Aires, where the story of state building accommodates the local Catholic Church. Of particular interest, Argentina's penal history contains separate methods of discipline according to gender. Whereas male prisoners were subjected to modern discipline guided by positivism and industry, their female counterparts were placed in a premodern regiment of reform in which their Catholic stewards resisted the appeal of modernization and secular rehabilitation. Before elaborating on the unique relations between the Church and State with respect to reforming prisoners, let us attend to how religious architecture, scenery, and objects set the stage for penal tourism in Buenos Aires.

As mentioned previously, the sacred ambience is enhanced by spiritual design, most notably, a series of white archways that surround the courtyard. In the shadows of that open space are the domed chapel of Nuestra Senora del Carmen (see figure 13) and the impressive church towers of San Pedro Gonzalez Telmo. Both places of worship use architecture to draw the eye upward to a seemingly omniscient deity. So as to connect visitors with the building's physical past, curators explain to visitors that the edifice in which the museum is housed dates back to the Jesuit missions in the early eighteenth century. A display case preserves various archaeological relics discovered in the floor of the chapel (e.g., hand-painted pottery, c. 1840). The building's religious origins merged with penal ambitions in 1860, when it was converted into a prison for both men and women. Eventually it was transformed into Asilo Correccional de Mujeres, a house of correction for women administered by the Catholic order Las Religiosas del Buen Pastor (the Good Shepherd).

FIGURE 13. Domed chapel of Nuestra Senora del Carmen (Argentine prison museum). © retro-welch 2014

Throughout much of the museum, tourists are exposed to a seamless over-lay of religious and secular symbols. Recall the office of the director, Horacio A. Benegas, where an array of objects reinforces the notion of a tightly cou-pled Church and State: a crucifix and church organ alongside portraits of San Martín and the Argentine flag. As noted in chapter 3, inspirational messages are delivered through the gentle words of St. Thomas Aquinas ("being good is easy, it is difficult to be just") and General José de San Martín ("laws of a free people can be strict but never cruel"). Once again, the Argentine peni-tentiary system's slogan is conspicuously posted: "Justicia y Fe Para Cumplir la Mision" (Justice and Faith to Fulfill the Mission).

The tour segues into an exhibition on the National Penitentiary that once stood in Buenos Aires. A dense narrative continues to inject religion into a historical story on the emergence of the federal prison service, underscoring the cooperative relations between the Church and State. Penal spectators are greeted once again by the Argentine flag prominently draped next to a crucifix attached to the wall. As mentioned previously, visitors are invited to gaze at the white porcelain basin used in "la clausura" (closing ceremony) as well as at a photograph (c. 1952) of a conjugal visit bedroom with a crucifix strategically placed above the bed. That portion of the exhibit delivers an uplifting message (poetics) about prisoner redemption in which a plaque reads: "There is more worth in one who falls and picks himself up than the one that has never fallen."

Much like Lombroso (2006), who collected prisoner art and handicrafts, the prison museum in Buenos Aires also celebrates the creative and inspiring side of inmates. On display are numerous carvings and paintings that promote a rich Argentine nationalism as well as reverence for Catholic tradition (e.g., a wooden plaque of the national coat of arms, a bust of San Martín, artworks devoted to the Virgin Mary and Jesus Christ). Moving onward to a neighboring room, tourists can glimpse into the interior of a solitary cell. A mannequin dressed in a contemporary prison officer uniform with a baseball cap stands nearby. Still, sacred themes linger. Behind the modern-looking guard is an antique picture of a religiously inspired scene of a woman visiting a prisoner during biblical times (see chapter 4). Through the display of architecture, artifacts, images, and text, the overall museum effect reinforces the intended message on penality in Buenos Aires; that is, modern incarceration operated by the State is not disconnected from its sacred origins.

Whereas the narrative portrays governance as progressive and benevolent, the interplay between institutional religion and the management of prisoners is more complex. Criminological positivists contributed to the remapping of class relations in Argentina in the early twentieth century by means of penal discipline intended to deliver a docile and obedient workforce for a stable nation (see Foucault, 1977; see chapter 6). Interestingly, elitist visions of a modern Argentina contained clear gender biases that prevented positivists from incorporating women into industry, since the prevailing concern was focused largely on immigrant men (Salvatore, 1996). As the prison museum shows, the gender divide was reinforced by unique relations between the local Catholic Church and the State, leading to divergent forms of penal discipline. Male offenders were sentenced to state-of-the-art correctional institutions modeled after positivism; by contrast, their female counterparts were sent to different facilities under the firm control of a religious order that dissociated itself from the new criminological science. The enduring continuity of the religious approach in the penal reform of female lawbreakers is evident in the influence of the nuns of the Good Shepherd (El Buen Pastor), who formally gained control of prisons for women in 1890 and maintained it until as recently as the 1970s (see Caimari, 1997).

Because of the rise of the modern Argentine state committed to seculari-zation and positivism, it seems out of step for the State to abdicate a signifi-cant part of its correctional apparatus to a religious organization. Deciphering that apparent contradiction involves more than an analysis of positivism versus religion. Attending to the role of certain social groups in the shaping of public policy seems to offer a more coherent explanation. Historian Lila Caimari reminds us that practical considerations were important as the gov-ernment leaned toward permitting the Good Shepherd to assume authority over female rehabilitation:

> Everyone agreed on the moral danger involved in leaving it to male adminis-tration. This prison needed a female staff that was trained and willing to live with the inmates. Such a staff did not exist in the state bureaucracy or in other religious orders, and it would take a long time to train one. Because they lived in convents—where they were often secluded in cells and used to severe regulations and all kinds of privations—nuns were perceived as natu-rally adapted to a penitentiary regime. Furthermore, their investiture gave them an aura of authority, vis-à-vis both inmates and secular members of the staff. (1997: 189–90)

Financial matters also figured into the State's decision to transfer the female prison population to the Good Shepherd, since the nuns requested a minimal budget to care for a relatively small number of incarcerated women. Still, once the deal was set, the Good Shepherd succeeded in keeping the State out of the operations of reforming women inmates. Apart from those practical considerations, theoretical assumptions about female criminality weighed heavily. Lombrosian criminology distinguished women from men, postulat-ing that females succumb to crime due to moral weakness, irrationality, and low intelligence (Lombroso and Ferrero, 2004). Moreover, since many of them had engaged in prostitution (which was not even a criminal offense), a religious solution seemed more fitting than criminal science (Guy, 1990; Rodriguez, 2006). Lombroso (2006: 344) himself advocated the use of con-vents over prisons in reforming female criminals: "Nuns can train them to replace sexual love—the most frequent cause of female crime—with religios-ity. Honesty and religious fanaticism will become substitutes for criminal tendencies. I have witnessed this process myself, even in a cellular prison where nuns were not trained to reform inmates." In their recent translation of Lombroso's *Criminal Man,* Gibson and Rafter comment: "The Italian state, like many Catholic countries, handed over the administration of women's prisons to orders of nuns in the nineteenth and early twentieth centuries. As a nonreligious Jew and a socialist, Lombroso generally opposed the interference of the Catholic Church in public affairs. It is a measure of his low regard for women that Lombroso recommends religiosity, as opposed to rational science, as best suited to mold their weak and immoral minds" (Lombroso, 2006: 399). Borrowing from anthropologist Victor Turner's (1967) notion of the "forest of symbols," Smith recognizes that there are "efforts to construct a narrative for an onlooking audience, to tell a story, to offer a commentary on events and statuses, to channel meanings in one direction or another, to open up worlds of significance, or to close off unwanted interpretive possibilities" (2008: 37). Similarly, Garland (2009: 262) notes that civil society plays a key role in promoting critical dialogue by renarrating the State's official story: ascribing new meanings to institutions and events and challenging governmental claims. In steering clear of other—unwanted—commentaries that threaten to contradict the *official* narrative being told through the Argentine Penitentiary Museum, civil society is conspicuously absent. As a result, other stories are completely ignored, even those that are central to a history of Argentine justice.

Consider, for instance, a critique of the religious group the Good Shepherd and how it succeeded in monopolizing the care of women prisoners. That story involves much more than the appeal of religion over science, especially since Lombrosian criminologists also explained female crime along the lines of immorality. The influence of certain social groups in formulating state policies is paramount when understanding how the Good Shepherd maintained its authority over female incarceration until the 1970s. Early on, the poor conditions of confinement at the Correctional House for Women (Asilo Correcional de Mujeres) became a concern of civil society, namely, law professors and students at the University of Buenos Aires. Those activists formed a group called the Patronado de Recluidas y Liberadas (PRL) in 1933: it campaigned to extend legal protection and improved care for female prisoners (the cult of the individual). However, Mother Superior deliberately undermined the work of the PRL by not granting them access to the correctional institution. Consequently, instead of introducing to female offenders advances in modern criminology such as individualized treatment, those women were "subjected to endless, useless religious speeches that forced them to see their crimes in terms of sin and forgiveness, completely dissociated from the reality around them" (Caimari, 1997: 205; see Ruggiero, 1992). Lawyer and criminologist Eusebio Gomez, an influential figure in the PRL, could not contain his contempt for religion, calling the clergy "parasites of superstition" (Caimari, 1997: 204)

Despite publicized complaints of prisoner neglect at the Correctional House for Women, the State did not alter its arrangement with the Good Shepherd, giving the religious hierarchy full reign over the reform of female prisoners for decades to follow. Caimari writes: "Limited material resources, combined with dominant conceptions about gender, crime, and work, seem to have conspired against applying the new criminological approach to the question of female crime" (1997: 208). Furthermore, she concludes that the creation of a well-invested penal apparatus for women did not interest government leaders because that population did not pose a significant threat to the project of a modern Argentine state. However, by the 1970s, hundreds of young women accused of being subversive activists were rounded up and sent to the prisons of the Good Shepherd, and soon most female correctional facilities were reassigned to state control (Caimari, 1997).

THE JEWISH EXPERIENCE

Returning to Eastern State Penitentiary, we gain more insight into the role of religion in incarceration. Compared to its exhibit on Christian (i.e., Quaker, Catholic, and Protestant) influences on punishment, the display of Jewish life behind bars is particularly extensive. Here the different functions of religion become evident. The Christian side of ESP is aimed at the first purpose of religion, namely, to impose self-discipline and a certain measure of asceticism so as to create a monastic effect. By sharp contrast, its Jewish counterpart lends support to the other functions. Jewish ceremonies build solidarity by bringing people together to reaffirm their common bonds. Likewise, Jewish religious observances maintain and revitalize social heritage, thereby transmitting enduring values. Visitors at ESP are given a fine anthropological lesson on the Jewish experience. The first sign of Jewish significance is a poster titled "Synagogue," which features a photograph (from 1959) of the congregation of inmates and volunteers from the community. The group shot shows them in front of the Torah ark inside the synagogue; together, they convey a strong sense of spiritual fraternity. The poster declares that ESP may have had the first prison synagogue in America: "It was built in 1924 in a set of workshops down this alley, and has been restored to its 1960 appearance." An arrow points tourists in the direction of the synagogue where they begin a two-part tour of Jewish life at ESP. The first section deals with the early history of the synagogue and its elaborate restoration project, and then segues into its current incarnation.

Throughout the exhibition, visitors are reminded of the civic contributions of Alfred W. Fleisher, who served as president of Eastern State Trustees beginning in the 1920s. Though unpaid, Fleisher and the board of trustees had tremendous influence in the governance of the institution as they oversaw all of its policies and operations. Fleisher, himself Jewish, is credited with leading the effort to build the prison's synagogue (see Dolan, 2007). In a series of placards, the importance of community support for "The Alfred W. Fleisher Memorial Synagogue Restoration" is officially recognized by a list of generous donors and a heartfelt note of gratitude: "Todah (Thank you). For sins of one human being against another the Day of Atonement does not atone, until they have made peace with one another.—*Machzor* (the High Holiday prayer book)." Curators seem eager to engage visitors by asking questions. For instance, one poster reads, "What Was This Space?" The answer: the rooms of this exhibit space began as an open-air exercise yard for prisoners, and the doors that once led from the cells into the yard are clearly visible. After the demise of solitary confinement—and the end of the Quaker experiment—the yards were converted into group workshops in the 1920s. Another sign (see figure 14) inquires: "A Synagogue in a Prison? It was not a large space, it didn't have many worshipers, and it required tireless support from the outside to serve its members. So why was it built? Who worshiped here? And why restore the synagogue today?" In order to deliver an informed narrative on the synagogue and Jewish prisoners, the exhibit takes visitors on a chronological journey from the early days of ESP, through the nineteenth century and the early twentieth, to 1970 when the penitentiary was closed. Large storyboards include smaller panels with concise historical material.

The Spiritual Prison

Religious instruction was among Eastern State Penitentiary's founding principles. The prison was designed not simply to punish, but to move the criminal toward spiritual reflection and change. Inmates were not allowed visits

FIGURE 14. An exhibit on the synagogue at Eastern State Penitentiary (Philadelphia). © retrowelch 2014

from family or friends. Prison officials believed that the inmates would accept the sin of their crimes only if they were cut off from a corrupt society. The early system of solitary confinement prevented gatherings for worship. The inmates in these years met, instead, with volunteer ministers and priests in the isolation of their cells. They were given Bibles and pamphlets on Christian faith. Choirs sang Christian hymns in the corridors.

But what about the Jewish inmates?

1845: First Jewish Clergyman Visits Eastern State

Philadelphia's Jewish leaders expressed concern that members of their faith might be pressured to convert to Christianity. But the prison administration seems to have been sincere to support any spiritual reflection within these walls.

The story line continues by citing several significant events, including "The Rite of Circumcision" of a baby born to a female Jewish inmate in 1851 and the first Jewish prison service in 1913. By the 1920s, the Jewish inmate population was rising. Out of 1,398 total prisoners, there were thirty "Hebrews."

That number increased to forty-two in 1927. According to the placard, there were reasons for the growth. First, the Jewish population in Philadelphia was expanding due to immigration from Eastern Europe and Russia. Second, Jewish Americans were playing a greater role in organized crime; those involved became known as the "Kosher Mafia." A photograph shows gangster, Max "Boo Boo" Hoff, posing with the prison boxing club in the 1920s. The caption explains that Hoff never served prison time but did visit many organized crime figures at ESP, including Al Capone. Attention is also directed at the intriguing story of Morris "The Rabbi" Bolber, who was a leader of a murder ring in Philadelphia. The gang targeted women who were willing to murder their husbands so as to collect on insurance policies. At least thirty victims were killed. Bolber was sentenced to life imprisonment and joined the Jewish congregation. Adding visual verification to the narrative, the display features Bolber's intake card. Along with his mug shot, key descriptions include his complexion ("med dark"), eyes ("trouty"), and nativity ("Russia"), as well as place of first papers ("New Brunswick, N.J."), and remarks ("accomplices: Arsenic Ring").

The Jewish population at ESP continued to grow into the 1940s but declined in the 1960s. The chaplain, Rabbi Rubenstein, said in an interview: "We had very few. If we had a *minyan*—do you know what a *minyan* is?—a quorum of ten adult males—that was a lot." After spending a few minutes at the storyboard, visitors move toward a series of objects that have undergone a cultural transformation from use-value to signifying-value. On display is what appears to be an old, ordinary door. But because it sits on a platform behind a security wire, tourists know intuitively that the door has special meaning. A plaque explains that this was the original synagogue door through which the congregation entered. Visitors are enticed to gaze even closer upon reading: "The paint layers bear the 'ghosts' of two Stars of David that once identified the room as a Jewish place of worship." Nearby is an exhibit intended to encourage participation in a Jewish custom: "Share Your Mitzvah! The Hebrew term mitzvah (literally 'religious obligation') loosely means any good deed in Jewish life." The poster commends the supporters of the Jewish congregation at ESP, who were motivated by a sense of compassion and responsibility to those in need. The display provides index cards on which visitors can write a good deed "You Have Done" or a good deed that has been "Done For You." The cards remain on view for visitors to read and for reflection on the kindness of others—another reminder that the monastic commitment to exclusion and isolation does not resonate here.

After the prison was closed in 1970, the synagogue—like the rest of the institution—was abandoned. So, according to another storyboard, "Why Restore the Synagogue?," the answer is couched in the cultural power of religion: "The synagogue was once a sacred space. It was a place of community and tradition, a refuge from the grim surroundings of prison life." Not only had the entire room had fallen into deep decay, but its key symbols had suffered damage, including the Torah ark. In 2004, the decision was made: save what could be saved, learn what could be learned, and "carefully piece this sacred place back together." The conservation team worked as archaeologists, trying to reconstruct the synagogue both physically and culturally. The exhibit delves into the minute details of the project. In a display case is a "Plaster Point of the Star of David" recovered from the debris. The conservationists guessed that the star had once decorated the synagogue ceiling. Visitors are drawn into the mystery with a caption that reveals: "The photo behind you—on the '1928 Panel'—was donated to Eastern State Penitentiary in 2006 and confirmed the theory."

From there, the tour exits into a long alley and toward the "The Alfred W. Fleisher Memorial Synagogue." Once inside, visitors are likely to understand what all the fuss was about. The sacred space is beautifully restored. Careful illumination puts a spotlight on the ornate woodwork and decorative plaster. Adding to the religious ambience, wall lights are shaped in the form of menorahs. Looking up to the ceiling, one can gaze at the hand-carved Star of David. Overall, the museum effect rests on religious objects and images to re-create the synagogue, a sacred space located in an otherwise coercive institution. Here, visitors of many faiths can appreciate the Geertzian conception of religion as a system of symbols that acts to establish pervasive moods and motivations. As a spiritual refuge from the harsh realities of imprisonment, the synagogue carries an aura of factuality, causing the moods and motivations to seem uniquely realistic.

PURITY AND IMPURITY

Recall, from Eastern State Penitentiary, the artist installation titled "GTMO" (by William Cromar) that introduces us to some of the cultural underpinnings of life in detention at Guantanamo Bay (see Welch, 2009c). Accompanying a replica of the fenced "cage" from Camp X-Ray, a poster inquires: "What's in the Cell?"

The objects in the cell are nearly identical to the materials issued to all detainees at Camp X-Ray. Much of the material is included to accommodate Muslim practices of washing, prayer, and the devotional reading of the Holy Quran. They include:

1 plastic canteen for drinking

2 white plastic five-gallon buckets (one for water, one for human waste)

1 pair of "flip flop" shoes

1 orange jumpsuit

1 foam mattress

1 sheet

2 blankets

1 washcloth

1 bar of soap

1 tube of toothpaste

1 toothbrush (inmate length)

1 bottle of Lively Salon anti-dandruff shampoo

2 towels (one for hygiene, one for use as a prayer blanket)

1 prayer cap

1 copy of the Holy Quran, in translation, suspended from the floor by a surgical mask in accordance with Muslim practice of keeping it away from uncleanliness.

Items on the list shed light on the cultural significance of the venerate. While traditional beliefs and customs dictate the separation of the pure from the impure, such observances, of course, depend largely on particular religious practices, whether Buddhist, Christian, Jewish, Muslim, and so on. As we shall see, the cultural relativity of the sacred is still very much part of the debate over Durkheim.

Recently, a collective of sociologists has returned to Durkheim so as to tease out and rework some of his theoretical claims (Alexander, 2005; Bellah, 2005; Smith, 2008; Smith and Alexander, 2005). Whereas Durkheim's *The Elementary Forms of Religious Life* (2008 [1915]) remains a touchstone for scholarly inquiry into religion, acceptance of his thesis is far from monolithic, since there are serious divisions in the trajectory of Durkheimian influence among subsequent generations of intellectuals (Riley, 2000, 2005). Those distinctions tend to revolve around Durkheim's description of the sacred. With frustration, theorists are quick to point out that Durkheim stacks the cards in his favor by maintaining his definition of religion after dismissing all competing views (see Garland, 1990, 2009). In essence, he insists that religion is what can be characterized as ideas and rituals oriented toward the protection of the sacred. That characterization of religion leaves investigators with the bewildering task of separating the sacred from the nonsacred, since those differences are largely determined by wider cultural imperatives. Indeed, what is considered sacred in one society might be viewed as nonsacred, or profane, in another (see Douglas, 1966). Simply saying that something is sacred because it inspires respect does not untangle the knot. Moreover, conventional Durkheimian analysis is drawn along the lines of binaries, most notably, the sacred and the profane; however, efforts to separate those opposites are often untidy. As Pickering convincingly argues, the sacred is not exclusively holy but can also be the accursed, "something devoted to a divinity for destruction, and hence criminal, impious, wicked, infamous" (1984: 124; Riley, 2005; see Duncan, 1996; Katz, 1988).

So as to resolve that theoretical dilemma, Durkheim proposes that the sacred—while retaining a remote relationship to the profane—maintains its own internal dichotomy. On one end of the spectrum, there is a pure, orderly, moral, healthy quality that gives the right sacred its beneficent power, and on the other end of the pole there is the left sacred, characterized by impurity, evil, disorder, disease, and death. Riley (2005) explains that for generations many (English-language) scholars might have misread Durkheim, in part because his early writings were not fully translated from French and Latin. Tracing the Latin etymology of the word *sacer*, one recognizes its contradictory meanings. In French, *sacer* can mean both the holy (e.g., *la musique sacrée*, or "sacred music") and the accursed (e.g., *un sacré menteur*, or "damned liar"). Somewhere those important dualities got lost in the English translation, leaving us with the former but not the latter (Pickering, 1984). Understanding the notion of the sacred as having a right (pure) and a left (impure) is not entirely original, as evidenced by the work of Robertson Smith (see Beidelman, 1974). Nonetheless, Durkheim and his followers developed it further and, by doing so, might have made things a bit more complicated (Hertz, 1960; Hubert, 1904; Mauss, 1979).

A sacred object, observes Durkheim, has the potential to become impure while not losing its holy traits. Consider the religious transformation of a corpse. Once dead, the body is in a state of decay and ruin and is perhaps even spooky. Then, as it passes through a ritual process (sometimes with the aid of an instrument of the deity, such as a priest), the corpse becomes sacred and supernatural as it protects the clan from evil spirits (see Hertz, 1960). Still, Durkheim never made clear whether the right sacred and its left counterpart exist as distinct states or as manifestations of a single power (Riley, 2005). For empirical purposes, he seems to suggest that the two can be separated, allowing for categorization. However, at a higher level of analysis, they both have the potential to become the other. That blurring of the pure and impure sacred seems to tap into our consciousness, whereby intense personal experiences—religious or otherwise— often comprise positive emotions of awe and negative feelings of fear.

With the benefit of Nietzsche, the Durkheimian concept of the left sacred gained more prominence:

> Much scholarly work has demonstrated the ways in which, beginning in the early 1900s, Nietzschean thought became a tool for French thinkers of this period looking to move beyond both the secular rationalist and the traditional religious alternatives to morality and meaning. Nietzsche's proposed means for self-overcoming and the heroic embrace of tragedy were adopted initially almost exclusively by poets, artists, and generally cultural figures, but soon the ideas began to be engaged by intellectuals in more culturally central locations. (Riley, 2005: 283; see Riley, 1999)

In the 1930s, conceptual development of the left sacred in French intellectual circles reached into themes of death and sensuality. Chief among those thinkers were Marcel Mauss (1979) and George Bataille (1986), who wrote at a time when fascism threatened their nation, especially its dissidents. Thirty years later, another political tumult impelled poststructuralists and post-modernists to consider the cultural implications of politics (Riley, 2005). Drawing on the influence of Bataille (1973), Foucault (1977 [1963]) maintained a strong interest in the left sacred, which was manifested in the Nietzschean themes of madness and death (see Macey, 1993). Tracing the birth of the asylum, Foucault (1973) considers the problem of confusing madness with unreason *(deraison),* since it undermines attempts to decipher the sacred through the experience of the "mad." Such "unreason" constitutes a form of transgressive knowledge that contains insights not accessible by other knowledges, particularly the scientific. Along those lines of inquiry, Foucault explored the transgressive power of the dangerous person who "establishes the ambiguity of the lawful and unlawful" (1975: 206; Foucault, 1988). A case in point is Pierre Rivière, a real-life character who, in the 1830s, killed several members of his family and then wrote a memoir explaining his motives and compulsions (Foucault, 1975; see Foucault, 1973)

Of course, Foucault's (1977, 1978) excursions into discipline and normalization remind us of the role of scientific discourses in creating categories of deviance in which specialists investigate transgressive knowledges (e.g., madness) that have the potential to deliver certain "immoral pleasures." Interestingly, Foucault condemned both liberal capitalist and communist societies for their attempt to "close off experience of the transgressive sacred" (Riley, 2005: 292). It is precisely because of the phenomenon of dark tourism—and the subset of penal tourism—that we are able to defy those boundaries and have safe contact with the left sacred.

NARRATING THE LEFT SACRED

Touring the Argentine Penitentiary Museum, visitors are subject to continuous visual messages on the sacred. The sheer ubiquity of crosses and crucifixes contributes to explicit and implicit narratives on Catholicism. While the crosses attached to the top of the domed chapel and the bell towers suggest an omniscient deity ("God is everywhere, and he is watching over us"), other crucifixes speak to a deeper belief in the afterlife. In the chapel, a large crucifix looms conspicuously over the pews. The wilting body of Christ hangs in a way that reinforces the Catholic message: "He died on the cross for our sins." That sacrifice is not the end of the story. According to standard lessons in catechism, Christ rose from the dead. Moreover, the sacrament of Holy Communion allows members of the congregation to maintain a personal and spiritual connection to Christ as the priest states, "The body of Christ," and the faithful responds, "Amen." From a Durkheimian perspective, the cross symbolizes a close alignment between the right sacred and the left sacred, since the trinity comprises the Father, Son, and Holy Ghost. (Physically doing the sign of the cross reinforces that spiritual belief.) As mentioned previously, the Argentine Penitentiary Museum seems to rely on the cultural power of the cross to convey the notion that the government's correctional apparatus is pure, benevolent, and divinely ordained.

The role of the right sacred—and left sacred—in organizing the world is contemplated at Robben Island, although in a very different and complex way. Inside one of the cellblocks, a series of photographs of former political prisoners is accompanied by a personal story. Jacob Sikundla, who was incarcerated from 1964 until 1983, explains that eventually the authorities abolished quarry work in favor of promoting skilled trades. Civilians were brought in to teach the prisoners. Sikundla recalls an Afrikaner who was hired to teach carpentry. Upon arriving, he expected to find people from another realm: "My grandfather told us that black people are born from the devil. They are not Christians, they do not belong to this country . . . [They] want to take over the country, kill white people and bring in communism." To his surprise, he encountered prisoners who introduced themselves as "politicians who were against the dirty laws of this country that governed white, coloured, Indian, and black people separately." Sikundla told the Afrikaner about the Freedom Charter. Other Afrikaners at Robben Island, however, were not as sympathetic. Naphtali Manana (a political prisoner from 1982 until 1991) remembers an instance when he heard Afrikaans warders wagering over which prisoners were to be executed: "Of course we were going to die but the way they treated us . . . They treated us like horses. They just betted on us and they enjoyed doing that." The callous treatment of prisoners—rejecting the sanctity of death—extended to the medical unit, where doctors would comment: "His kidneys are okay. We can take them out the day he dies." In that sense, the notion of the dead is conveyed not as a beneficent power but as an exploitive—even inhumane—means of perpetuating life. A strange form of biopower indeed (see Foucault, 1978, 2008).

At Number Four, the prison in Johannesburg, a storyboard about a prisoner directs attention to the violent capacity of the left sacred. Nongoloza Mathebula (Jan Note) had a long criminal history, including robbery, attempted murder, and an attack on a warder. He formed a self-styled militia known as the Regiment of the Hills, or the Ninevites, which was committed to political resistance and social banditry in the early twentieth century. While in prison, Mathebula organized a prison gang that still operates today and that is the oldest of the gangs—the 28s. He boasted: "I read in the Bible about the great state of Nineveh which rebelled against the Lord and I selected that name for my gang as rebels against the Government's law."

Themes of ghosts and evil spirits abound in prison folklore, thus elevating the significance of the left sacred, often embodied in a fear of the dark. Consider, for instance, the dreaded punishment of solitary confinement. At the jail in Johannesburg, uncooperative prisoners were stripped, hosed, and thrown into the wet "EMAKHULUKHUTHU—'Deep Dark Hole'" (see figure 15). A sign informs us: "The third cell was believed to be inhabited by a ghost. Prisoners were terrified to be locked in there." Tourists are allowed to enter those forbidden spaces, including the one believed to be haunted. Giving into temptation, they might even close the cell door so as to have some

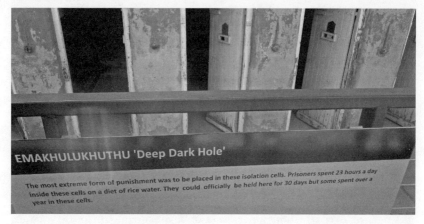

EMAKHULUKHUTHU 'Deep Dark Hole'

The most extreme form of punishment was to be placed in these isolation cells. Prisoners spent 23 hours a day inside these cells on a diet of rice water. They could officially be held here for 30 days but some spent over a year in these cells.

FIGURE 15. Solitary confinement cells at the Number 4 prison complex (Johannesburg, South Africa). © retrowelch 2014

safe contact with the left sacred. Also on display are huge photographs of the inside of the cell doors scrawled with graffiti. Looking closely at the graffiti, one can only imagine the emotional torment that prisoners endured, including an entry from "MAD-JOE."

The narrative on death is also used to attract tourists to the Old Melbourne Gaol. The promotional poster reads: "Walk the road to the Gallows in Victoria's oldest prison where 136 people, including infamous bushranger Ned Kelly, were hanged." While the legend of Kelly puts the place on the map, tourists will discover dozens of similar—even more ghastly—stories. A display located inside one of the cells explains that the gold rush brought prosperity as well as an increase in crime. George Melville preyed on travelers and isolated communities, and like Kelly, he and his gang were daring, becoming folk heroes to many who despised the authorities. Melville's undoing was the McIvor Gold Escort robbery. As the gang members attempted to flee the colony, they were captured, convicted of robbery with the intent to murder, and hanged on the morning of October 3, 1853: "After the execution, Melville's body was released to his widow. She decorated it with flowers and put it on public display in her oyster shop in Melbourne. Newspapers reported a brisk trade, with Mrs. Melville entertaining customers with a torrent of abuse against the conniving police force. There was such public outrage over this incident that from this time on, the bodies of all those executed in the Melbourne Gaol were buried within the wall of the prison." Transforming the corpse into an object for show demonstrates the aura of the left sacred. The Melbourne Gaol museum gives tourists an opportunity to come face to face with Melville's death mask, which is situated inside a secured glass case, thereby enhancing a sense of cultural power.

At Alcatraz, tourists get a glimpse into the predatory world of murder. A contemporary color mug shot is that of Harvy Carignan. His grandfatherly demeanor seems to defy the caption: "The Want-Ad Killer." Carignan is still serving a life sentence in Minnesota for homicide and assault with attempt to rape, having spent eight years at Alcatraz until it closed. The poster states: "He is responsible for an unknown number of murders, rapes and assaults across the U.S. He often placed want-ads in papers to lure his victims." Carignan's sentence does not expire until 2075. While he is unlikely to reenter society, there are others who have been convicted of homicide, have served their sentences, and are currently out of prison. Their stories are the subject of an exhibition at Alcatraz titled "Life after Murder" (photographs by Elisabeth Fall, video by Gabe Maxson, book by Nancy Mullane). The introduction asks: "Once a murderer, always a murder? Or can a murderer change and be redeemed?" Mullane, a journalist, examined the lives of men she met at San Quentin State Prison. However, Mullane concedes: "[Initially] I never thought I would meet a murderer face to face—at least I hoped I wouldn't. I suppose I lived my life with an unconscious fear that it could happen, but just as unconsciously reason if I was careful, I could avoid that most horrible of all encounters." As a finished project, she shares their stories of remorse, introspection, determination, and "unshakable hope for freedom and forgiveness." One of those ex-cons is Jesse Reed. His biographical data is listed:

Conviction: first-degree murder, 1985
Sentence: twenty-seven years to life without possibility of parole
Incarcerated: nearly twenty years
Parole reversed by Governor Arnold Schwarzenegger
Paroled: June 11, 2009 by order of Alameda County Superior Court

Along with his portrait, curators provide details about his "life after murder." Jesse lives in his own apartment in Oakland, not far from his family. He works for the state's Department of Corrections and Rehabilitation, counseling young men incarcerated in the Stockton facility. He spends his weekends singing second tenor with a Christian gospel group, the Redemption Band. The band members met at San Quentin, where they sang "God's praises" every Sunday morning. In 2010, Jesse became the first former prisoner to graduate from the Golden Gate Baptist Theological Seminary. His spiritual purification is matched by his vocation. Having worked as a janitor while in prison, he runs his own company: "Jess-Clean Maintenance: For a smart clean, call Jess-Clean."

Looking back on her interviews, Mullen says: "The men I met weren't anything like the monsters I envisioned. Instead, they were men who had worked hard to take responsibility for their crimes, and redeem their humanity." At the end of the exhibit, visitors are invited to write messages on yellow "post-it" notes and stick them on a display board. Responses were varied, ranging from unforgiving to forgiving to political:

> Once a murderer, always a murder. Jail forever, or kill them!
>
> The people they killed didn't get a second chance. Why do they?
>
> What about the families of those they killed—they serve life without their loved one.
>
> An eye for an eye leaves *EVERYONE* blind
>
> Where there is faith, there is *hope*
>
> Thank God they closed Alcatraz
>
> Are soldiers murderers too?
>
> If Bush and Blair can make millions after mass murder then I reckon these guys deserve a chance!

Capturing the essence of the banality of evil, one visitor commented: "I never would have thought normal looking people could be cold hard killers. They seem so nice!" Overall, the project illuminates a sobering version of the left sacred in which even some murderers are viewed as basically "good" people.

At Eastern State Penitentiary, curators are quick to promote the dark side of penal tourism by launching the Halloween special "Terror behind Walls: A Massive Haunted House in a Real Prison." With less fanfare, the regular tour also taps into the left sacred. Gazing deep into a decaying cell, visitors are asked to consider: "Is Eastern State Penitentiary haunted? Many people argue that if ghosts exist, they must be found here." For more commentary on that subject, tourists can listen to the audio guide, which features narration by actor Steve Buscemi *(Reservoir Dogs)* and author Charles J. Adams III *(Philadelphia Ghost Stories)*. More complex representations of the left sacred, however, can be found in posters discussing such taboo topics as sexuality. For instance one placard, "The Solitary Vice," explains that early prison administrators referred to masturbation as "'self abuse' ... They tried for decades to eliminate the practice among inmates." The audio guide (item 32) warns visitors about the commentary by criminologist Norman Johnston: "Parental Advisory: Adult Subject."

Similarly, an art installation titled "Beware of the Lily Law" carries the same caution. In this exhibit, the "forbidden" topics involve homosexuality and transgendered people in prison. As a starting point, artist Michelle Handelman refers to the Stonewall Riots in New York City in 1969, where police raids on gay and transvestite bars sparked intense public protests. The incidents at Stonewall marked the beginning of the modern gay rights movement; still, many of those issues have yet to be resolved inside prisons. Handelman explains: "Today, transgendered female prisoners (male to female) are incarcerated in male prisons, and transgendered male prisoners (female to male) are incarcerated in female prisons. They are often placed in 'protective' or 'administrative custody.' The resulting confinement, while safer for the inmates, is effectively a form of solitary confinement." The exhibit shows videotaped monologues based on the testimonies of real transgendered inmates. By doing so, sexual taboos in prison are brought to the forefront and strategically confronted.

CONCLUSION

The general thrust of this chapter moved along the lines of Durkheimian perspectives on religion as they interact with governance and punishment. Keeping focus on prison museums as cultural vehicles that transmit narratives on morality and social control, we elaborated on topics ranging from religious persecution to the monastic effect, Church and State, and the Jewish experience. While the Clink, Eastern State Penitentiary, and the Argentine Penitentiary Museum relied on objects, images, and space to give visitors a sense of how religion shaped incarceration, each of those exhibitions tapped into different emotional registers. At the Clink, the subject of religion dwells on the horror and the sensation of pain and misery. At a higher level of abstraction, religious power is depicted not as a positive social force but as a negative one, capable of delivering damnation to a *hell on earth*. By sharp contrast, Eastern State Penitentiary teaches a sophisticated lesson on the softer forms of religion; instead of targeting the body, the monastic regime took aim at the mind as well as the soul. Writing about the Quaker approach to incarceration, Foucault (1977) observes: "In absolute isolation—as at Philadelphia—the rehabilitation of the criminal is expected not of the application of criminal law, but the relation of the individual to his own conscience and to what may enlighten him from within. Alone in his cell, the convict is handed over to himself . . . He descends into his conscience . . . and the silent architecture that confronted it" (238–39). Inside Eastern State, visitors practice space inside this performing museum that encourages them to amble down the long cathedral-inspired hallways and step inside the chapel-like cells. While the cells were originally designed to impose a form of solitary confinement conducive to redemption, penal tourists are quick to realize the crushing experience of being trapped in a small tomb. As a result, they are likely to understand why the monastic model—though initially designed to be a benevolent method of imprisonment—ultimately failed.

In Buenos Aires, the narratives on religion and governance are so tightly coupled that together they seem to be a defining characteristic of Argentine culture,* or at least that is what its correctional service would like us to believe. Throughout the museum, visitors are given a steady visual tour of Catholic and nationalistic emblems along with placards boasting kind words of wisdom. The use of such poetics reaches into the religious potential for bringing people together to reaffirm their common bonds. Unlike the images of religious persecution at the Clink or of lonely prisoners abandoned in their cells at ESP, the photographs of Argentine inmates make them appear to be content and to even be sharing a sense of solidarity with the civilian and religious staff members. Similarly, prisoner artwork expresses a commitment to both the Church and the State. Tourists at the museum will also recognize the gender divide in discipline: positivism and industry for male prisoners versus religion and housework for their female counterparts (see Foucault, 1977). Still, the curators do not prompt their audience to think critically about those disparate forms of treatment; rather, in accord with a celebratory view of solidarity, that division of penal labor seems to maintain a larger Argentine society. Of course, the historical record as critiqued by Latin American scholars tells a different story about punishment and gender: in particular, they draw critical attention to the persistent governmental view that female offenders required invasive moral training supervised by religious authorities (Caimari, 1997; Guy, 1990; Rodriguez, 2006; Ruggiero, 1992).

* Until the reforms in 1994, the Argentine Constitution required that the president be a Roman Catholic.

At Eastern State Penitentiary, we get an informed look at the Jewish experience. Unlike with the themes of persecution, monastic isolation, and the alliance between Church and State, the exhibit depicts religion as a genuinely positive social force. Curators succeed in delivering a narrative that has the markings of Durkheim's perspective on religion. Inside the synagogue, Jewish symbols (e.g., the Star of David, the Menorah) clothe traditional rituals and ceremonies (e.g., Rosh Hashanah, Yom Kippur), offering a thick description of Jewish life in the penitentiary. Photographs of the cheerful congregation give a convincing look at a shared heritage and cultural solidarity. By comparison, images of prisoners at the Argentine Penitentiary Museum seem contrived. There, inmates do not appear to be sincerely engaged in the Church-State project; rather, they resemble props for a staged narrative on Argentine belongingness. At ESP, the synagogue—restored with the generous support of the Jewish community—speaks to the importance of enduring values of optimism and hope. Especially against the harsh backdrop of incarceration, the synagogue provided a sacred sanctuary for prisoners as they contemplated deeper existential predicaments and transcendent morals (see Alpert, 1939; Coser, 1977: 139). Of course, religion and governance are just two of the manifold forces explored in prison tourism. As we shall see in the next chapter, work and economics are also important elements of imprisonment.

SIX

Work and Economics

A vast exhibition on work in the Hyde Park Barracks museum in Sydney gives tourists a multidimensional view of a thriving penal colony. Through the strategic use of placards and illustrations, the story of Australian economics benefits from the presence of curious objects. Among them is a miniature treadmill. The model shows a contraption with five convicts stepping in unison on a flywheel that rotates a crank and, in turn, grinds grain. Teams of workers alternated shifts with rest periods of twenty minutes per hour. A caption tells us: "This monotonous task was supposed to be a reformative punishment, unlike flogging. It also put convict man power to good use, as they were helping to feed themselves. In 1825 Sydney's treadmills were praised for producing 40 bushels (1000 kilograms) of ground corn per day." Robin Evans, in his *Fabrication of Virtue,* traces the treadmill to an English civil engineer named William Cubitt. In the early nineteenth century, Cubitt's invention gained enormous support from philanthropists, magistrates, and prison wardens, since it had the capacity to convert natural energy into consumable produce. Aided by the dynamics of time and motion, the treadmill not only extracted labor from convicts but also instilled the habits of industry, thereby offering a moral component to the exercise. In Australia, a larger sense of ethics surrounded the treadmill as doctors and humanitarians intervened to ensure that the machine would not harm the health of those forced to toil for long hours. Museum curators inform visitors that an overseer recorded in the House of Correction Register each man's weight as they went on and came off the treadmill to make sure they were not wasting away.

Gazing deeply at the replica treadmill, penal tourists are cued to contemplate the complex interplay between convict labor, technology, and modes of production, none of which escapes the broader issues of morality. As we move forward, this chapter expands on religious forces as they shape work and economics within the orbit of punishment. Discussion begins with the controversy over debt as described by the Clink museum in London. Descending into that subterranean "hell hole," visitors are inundated with cruel messages on the consequences of financial ruin. The vivid museum effect covers the moral spectrum by putting on display prisoners who were "irresponsible" as well as those who were merely "unfortunate." Either way, tourists are likely to leave with a sympathetic view of the poor as they face the unforgiving penalty of confinement. Focus next turns to the Pennsylvania system of penal discipline and its unique combination of religion and work. Unlike the Clink where injustice knows no bounds, Eastern State Penitentiary—the prototype of the Pennsylvania regime—instructs visitors that the use of solitary confinement was originally planned as a benevolent form of intervention. Of course, tourists see for themselves that, in the end, total isolation can be as brutal as corporal punishment.

At the museum in Sydney and then in Buenos Aires, we witness the larger application of penal labor in crafting the state. Those governmental ambitions reach far into the realm of culture, especially national identity, civic pride, and a strong sense of solidarity manifesting itself in micro- and macro-economics. In both Australia and Argentina, prison work is depicted as serving the common good. Not only does forced labor transform convicts into productive citizens but it also contributes to the modernization of the nation. The theme of state building, however, takes a different turn in South Korea and South Africa, where issues of prisoner exploitation are investigated. At the prison museums in Seoul and on Robben Island, curators go to great lengths to provide evidence of harsh working conditions and mistreatment. Along the way, the narrative segues into positive tones on resistance and ultimately on freedom and independence. Finally, we look at the prison from the perspective of those who were employed as correctional officers and administrators. While the Argentine Penitentiary Museum maintains its script on state building, the tour at Alcatraz delves into the dangers of working inside a maximum-security institution. Relying on dramatic photographs, displays of weapons, and audio-guided storytelling, the museum effect at Alcatraz succeeds at startling visitors without crossing into the sensational. While the chapter keeps attention on prison museums, their contents, and their narratives, discussion incorporates scholarly insights on penal labor and economics.

The coupling of prisons and economics is a major theme in penal tourism at the Clink museum in London. There, the tale of the impoverished is conveyed through the use of positioning and movement; those internal spatial tactics provide visitors with a "walk through" history (Williams, 2007: 99). The Clink's museum effect is darkened as penal spectators step into a dimly lit, cramped space that previously functioned as a dungeon for debtors. A placard explains the Statute of Acton Burnell (1283 AD) that allowed "creditors to imprison their debtors till they were repaid." Henceforth, the Clink ("the prison that gave its name to all others") served as a debtors prison until the end of its days. A similar storyboard adds to that account, pointing out that until the nineteenth century, prisoners were expected to pay for their own imprisonment. Upon reflection, one can detect a certain neoliberal explanation as the text states that the prisoners "had, after all, brought it upon themselves." That commentary on blame is repeated on another plaque that injects religion with a punitive tone: "Said Chief Justice Montague (1550 AD): The prisoner should live on his own goods. And if he had no goods he should live on the charity of others, and if others will give him nothing then let him die in the name of God . . . for his own presumption and ill-behaviour brought him to that punishment." The harsh condemnation of debtors, however, is offset by other statements on the widely accepted practice of charity, hinting at the genuine ideals of the welfare state and the cult of the individual. A sign located near the entrance of the museum reminds visitors: "Many prisoners had to beg to survive, and in the cells of the Clink street-level gratings were thoughtfully provided for that purpose. Ordinary citizens did respond: in a cruel and chaotic age no-one could be sure they might not one day find themselves falsely imprisoned . . . Henry VII himself left 2,000 pounds for charity, including 300 pounds for 'miserable prisoners condemned for debt or other cause'" (see figure 16).

Since the Clink was intended to be financially self-sufficient, it did not pay the jailers; rather, their income was extorted from the prisoners and their families. Basically, all features of their "accommodation" were subject to a fee: food, drink, and clothing. Additionally, prisoners paid an entering charge and a departure charge to cover the cost of having their fetters fitted and removed. One of the early scenes of the tour shows a blacksmith attaching irons to a newly admitted prisoner: the sound of the hammer hitting the anvil is believed to be the origin of the Clink prison. The financial scheme of

FIGURE 16. A prisoner begging through street-level gratings at the Clink (London). © retrowelch 2014

the jailer's lot bred corruption as prisoners quickly accrued a debt to the keeper, further extending the length of their confinement and misery.

In sum, the Clink museum paints a detailed picture of London from 1144 to 1780, when the prison served as a mechanism of social—and economic—control by allowing creditors to jail the poor. That tale is relayed through a museum effect that relies on moving tourists through the prison in a chronological direction. Accordingly, the penal spectator is positioned in front of multiple storyboards and illustrations. Text and images are complemented by dramatization. Among those theatrical displays are scenes of women with their children. While drawing attention to the theme of "mothers in prison," curators seem to be reminding us of the enduring problem known as the "feminization of poverty," whereby economic hardship disproportionately affects single mothers (Marlow, 2009).

Like other "performing museums," the Clink uses theatrical displays to darken the emotional tone of its internal space—a subterranean, claustrophobic abyss (Casey, 2003). Visitors are transported into the past with scenes of prisoners in shackles. The exhibit is equipped with audio speakers that fill the room with recordings of prisoners pleading for help, thereby establishing a sympathetic view of those confined. Like other forms of dark tourism, the Clink edges very close to becoming a "morbid theme park" (Williams, 2007: 102); however, due to extensive erudite narrative, there is much to gain from a historical perspective. Upon reflecting on the emergence of the debtors prison, informed visitors might wonder whether prisons today also serve to manage and regulate the poor, especially given the huge presence of low-income (nonviolent) inmates (see Irwin, 1985; Welch, 2011b).

THE PENNSYLVANIA SYSTEM

While touring Eastern State Penitentiary, visitors are reminded of the early debate between the Pennsylvania system of confinement and its chief rival in New York. A large photograph (c. 1850) shows prisoners standing in strict formation at the prison in Auburn, New York. Tour guides (and the audio guide) explain the basic similarities and differences between the Pennsylvania and New York regimes of prison discipline, especially with respect to work and economics. Both penal systems relied on architecture, internal arrangement, and daily routine, all of which reflected an American vision of a well-ordered society (see Rothman, 1971; McLennan, 2008). Toward that end, the Pennsylvania and New York systems enforced prisoner silence for reasons of spiritual—monastic—reform as well as to prevent criminal contamination, which was believed to be spread through communication. From that point, those otherwise comparable penal systems diverged (see Foucault, 1977: 237–39; Ignatieff, 1978; Meranze, 1996).

The New York penal regime initially experimented with solitary confinement between 1821 and 1823, when prison officials declared it a complete failure, in part due to the adverse psychological effects of total isolation. In its place, New York prison reformers instituted the *congregate* system. Under the plan, prisoners worked, ate, and prayed together in silence during the course of the day but were confined to their solitary cells at night. Foucault observed the significance of social organization within the New York system, since its advocates viewed the prison as a "microcosm of a perfect society in which individuals are isolated in their moral existence, but in which they come together in a strict hierarchal framework, with no lateral relation" (1977: 238). Recognizing the integrative aims of that system of discipline, Foucault noted that, rather than keeping convicts under lock and key like wild beasts, they are assembled in useful exercises to form good habits (see Beaumont and Tocqueville, 1964 [1833]).

The Auburn penitentiary also offered a unique contribution to correctional architecture, namely, the tier system in which the cells (measuring three and a half feet by seven feet) were arranged on different levels. That design allowed the housing of inmates according to offense category (Lewis, 1967 [1922]; Lewis, 1965). So that visitors at ESP can further visualize the differences between Pennsylvania's radial plan and New York's tiered design, the museum displays a large photograph (c. 1920) that shows Auburn's south-wing cellblock, which resembles a large metal cake with three layers. Whereas prison life under the Pennsylvania system was intended to be a monastic experience, the Auburn regime introduced a quasi-military style of inmate control. Routine was maintained by a strict schedule of activities, including lockstep marching to regulate prisoner movement. Prisoners wore striped uniforms that were used as an early form of classification as different colors distinguished first-time from repeat offenders. Corporal punishment was used to enforce silence and instill discipline. Auburn's first keeper, Elam Lynds, was a staunch advocate of whipping, viewing all prisoners as cowards who needed their spirit broken before they could be reformed (Barnes and Teeters, 1946).

Due to congregate work, increased productivity became the hallmark of the New York system. Soon that regime emerged as the model for other penitentiaries. So as to make comparisons with Eastern State Penitentiary, Americans as well as Europeans toured the Auburn prison: among them were Alexis de Tocqueville and Gustave Auguste de Beaumont (see Beaumont and Tocqueville, 1964 [1833]; Klein, 1920). The Reverend Louis Dwight, secretary of the Boston Prison Discipline Society, praised the New York correctional experiment:

At Auburn, we have a more beautiful example, still, of what may be done by proper discipline, in a Prison well constructed . . . The whole establishment from the gate to the sewer, is a specimen of neatness. The unremitted industry, the entire subordination and subdued feeling of the convicts, has probably no parallel among an equal number of criminals. In their solitary cells they spend the night, with no other book than the Bible, and at sunrise they proceed in military order, under the eye of the turnkeys, in solid columns, with the lock march, to their workplaces; thence, in the same order, at the hour of breakfast, to the common hall, where they partake of their wholesome and frugal meal in silence. Not even a whisper is heard through the whole apartment. (Dwight, 1826: 36–37; also see Powers, 1826; Hall, 1829)

In contrast to the New York system, the Pennsylvania regiment adhered to a greater commitment to religion, through which separate confinement could activate individual reform. Consistent with the Quaker tradition, the Philadelphia Prison Society proposed that prisoner reform was not so much an "application of common law but of the relation of the individual to his own conscience and to what may enlighten him from within" (Foucault, 1977: 238). While the correctional operations of the Pennsylvania system concentrated on the conscience and the silent architecture that confronted it (239), there was considerable deliberation over whether inmates should be allowed to work. Advocates of solitary confinement argued that solitude would be more effective without the distraction of work: since "the guilty mind makes every effort to avoid reflection, and activity drowns out conscience, the prohibition of labor would mean that corrective results could be achieved in a shorter period of time" (Johnston, 2010: 29). Critics, however, insisted that labor possessed curative and moral powers insofar as the habits of industry improved the physical and mental health of the inmates. Furthermore, it was proposed that revenue from manufacturing could defray some of the costs of operating the institution. In 1829, the Pennsylvania legislature agreed, approving a penal law that required work for state prisoners. Nonetheless, ESP officials subjected prisoners to a stint in solitary confinement, reasoning that "when a convict first arrives, he is placed in a cell and left alone, without work and without any book. His mind can only operate on itself; generally, but few hours elapse before he petitions for something to do, and for a bible ... Thus work, and moral and religious books, are regarded and received as favours, and are withheld as a punishment" (Johnston 2010: 54). Those rewards were used to reinsert prisoners—morally and materially—into the strict world of the economy (Foucault, 1977: 124). Among the trades taught by the overseers was shoe making. After four days of instruction, prisoners produced handmade shoes that were sold to an outside agent despite opposition by labor unions, which condemned the practice as a form of unfair competition. Whereas other prisons contracted their inmates to outside firms that provided raw materials, ESP conducted its business independently. Eventually bowing to pressure from organized labor, prison officials scaled back their output (Johnston, 2010; McLennan, 2008). By the 1870s, many of the prison-made goods disappeared from the open market because, in large part, machine-made products dominated commerce. Decades later, most inmates at ESP were idle, engaging in repair work and making items used solely within the prison (e.g., blankets, clothing). With little evidence of revenue, proponents of the Pennsylvania system insisted that prisoner reform was more important than generating profit, hence giving penal discipline a higher sense of purpose (Johnston, 2010: 54; Kahan, 2011). Foucault, however, offers a deeper interpretation: "What, then, is the use of penal labour? Not profit; nor even the formation of a useful skill; but the constitution of a power relation, an empty economic form, a schema of individual submission and of adjustment to a production apparatus" (1977: 241).

Interestingly, even before ESP was completed, the Pennsylvania experiment with separate confinement was subject to much deliberation, especially in light of New York's rejection of complete solitary captivity. At international conferences, as well as in countless reports, penal reformers took aim at the Pennsylvania system, criticizing its overall costs, the adverse effects of solitary confinement, the degree of cruelty with respect to isolation, and, in the end, its claims of success. Philadelphians defended their penitentiary, arguing that its Quaker philosophy and institutional regime were quintessentially virtuous and humane, particularly as compared to the New York system's reliance on corporal punishment. Others disagreed, among them Charles Dickens, who toured ESP in 1842. Dickens wrote in *American Notes for General Circulation* that the separate confinement was "cruel and wrong ... I am persuaded that those who devised this system of Prison Discipline, and those benevolent gentlemen who carry it into execution, do not know what it is that they are doing... I hold this slow and daily tampering with the mysteries of the brain, to be immeasurably worse than any torture of the body" (1842: 238–39). Curators at ESP underscore the significance of Dickens criticism by displaying a large poster on *American Notes* along with commentary by the tour (and audio) guides.

Some disciplinary practices at ESP seemed to undermine its commitment to the spiritualization of punishment. In 1833, convict Mathias Maccumsey was punished for breaking the rule of silence. Prison administrators subjected him to the iron gag, a horrific contraption forced into the mouth and tied to the hands folded behind the prisoner's back. Producing a straight-jacket effect, the iron gag renders the body into a painful praying position. While bound, Maccumsey suffered convulsions and died. Penal reformers (and the legislature) defended the use of the gag, concluding that Maccumsey brought about his own death by struggling against its leather straps. In his insightful book *Laboratories of Virtue,* Michael Meranze reiterates Foucault by arguing that the iron gag epitomized the Pennsylvania penal system's reliance on corporal punishment, which, in turn, created resistance. Consequently, "prison officials had nowhere else to turn than to the body itself" (Meranze, 1996: 318). Unlike other prison museums that put on view various instruments designed to restrain inmates, ESP does not display the iron gag. Due to Meranze's research, however, an illustration of the device is prominently featured on the cover of his book.

Whereas the Pennsylvania system was often hailed in its ideal form, many work practices often violated its own rules. Even in the early days, some prisoners were released from their cells to perform such routine tasks as housekeeping, at times catering dinner parties sponsored by the warden. In 1834–35, a joint legislative committee found that female inmates were working in the kitchen, and on at least one occasion they were being returned to the cells intoxicated after a trip to the warden's liquor cabinet. The committee also observed a prisoner sitting next to a guard in the central rotunda, casually reading a newspaper (McElwee, 1835). That same legislative committee probed a well-publicized scandal involving Warden Samuel Wood and his staff members, who were accused of fiscal impropriety and cruelty toward prisoners. The inquiry also investigated charges that Wood committed adultery with the wife of his assistant (Mrs. Blundin). Pennsylvania's political establishment rushed to support Wood, exonerating him and his managerial practices. Mrs. Blundin was not so fortunate. She and her moral character were attacked and pilloried. Meranze (1996) suggests that the incident reflected reformers' anxiety over women exercising power outside the purview of strict patriarchal control (see Kann, 2005).

At ESP, the greenhouse was a unique worksite for inmates deemed physically or mentally "weak." With its array of flowers, the bucolic sanctuary was valued for being especially therapeutic (see Dolan, 2007). Today, visitors at ESP can gaze at the refurbished greenhouse: its windowed walls and rooftop offer a sharp architectural contrast to the fortified concrete surroundings. A poster informs us that the greenhouse was moved several times in the course of ESP's 142-year history: an etching from 1853 shows it situated along the north perimeter. Curators and conservationists celebrate the striking presence of the greenhouse behind the prison wall and had it restored in 2005 ("thanks to the generosity of our 2004 Supporting and Sustaining Members"). For more details, visitors can listen to an entry on the audio guide narrated by Donald Vaughn, an ESP guard from 1966–70.

Between 1877 and 1894, ESP underwent rapid population growth. Four new cellblocks were built by convicts to accommodate a census of more than twelve hundred (Johnston, 2010: 49, 50, 110). However, with only 765 cells, double bunking became standard practice. By the turn of the century, officials assigned as many as four convicts to a single cell. Thus, the Pennsylvania system and its claims of separate confinement were a mere public relations campaign used to draw attention away from the obvious overcrowding. Today, visitors can experience for themselves the cramped space by stepping inside one of the cells. As fellow tourists enter the same cell, human density creates a sense of tension, especially for those with strong personal boundaries. In 1913, the state legislature overturned its "antiquated" laws, paving the way for congregate "worship, labor, learning, and recreation," bringing an end to a long-held ideal of separate confinement (Johnston, 2010: 86, see 88, 113).

By the 1920s, power machinery was installed in the weaving shop, giving ESP a distinctly modern veneer, and during World War II, prison industries contributed to the American effort. The museum displays numerous photographs of prisoners working in what was transformed into a congregate system. Pictures put on display a proletarian prison where factory-based discipline, obedience, and docile behavior were to be instilled. Together those images hint at an economic market driven materially by prison labor (see Melossi and Pavarini, 1981; McLennan, 2008). A picture features inmates working in a machine shop (c. 1935) and another has them pressing clothes in the prison laundry (c. 1965). A group shot of cheerful inmates in a work crew (c. 1950) includes a caption: "Everybody, pretty much, was assigned to a job, and this place needed a lot of upkeep."

STATE BUILDING

Moving on to the Hyde Park Barracks museum in Sydney, we recognize themes of work and economics as intertwined in punishment and the building of a colony. Of course, central to the Australian penal—and national—story is the transportation of convicts from England and Ireland. Visitors at the museum are reminded of the significance of 1788, the year of the First Fleet, or what author Robert Hughes (1986) famously called a Noah's ark of small time criminality. Over the course of the next eighty years later, more than 160,000 convicts would arrive. The Barracks museum, however, does not dwell on the criminality of the banished population. Instead, curators draw attention to the *big picture* of Sydney as it evolved into a global city due to the hard labor of former convicts. Objects, text, and illustrations deliver a constructive and optimistic narrative. According to the museum's promotion for its exhibit titled "Convict Sydney," visitors are invited to "explore Australia's convict history at the World Heritage listed Hyde Park Barracks. Learn about the forced transportation of convicts, their daily lives and how they built the colony" (Historic Houses Trust, n.d. b).

The museum once again reminds us that the Barracks was not a prison but rather "secure accommodations" that furnished meals and a hammock for six hundred convicts who had been assigned to an ambitious public works project. A storyboard titled "CHAIN GANGS AND ROAD PARTIES" informs us that by 1829 nearly one thousand convict men were building roads at the edge of the settlement (see figure 17). A gallery displays a huge collection of tools that signify the presence of skilled tradesmen (e.g., arrow smiths, gunsmiths, and barrow makers). Thus, there is an effort to draw attention to the fine details of the penal labor force. A poster on new convicts, known as "new chums," explains that work was distributed according to their skills: "Convicts able to read and write became clerks, and military deserters would become constables. Most women were privately assigned as servants to work in shops, businesses or private homes or on farms. Badly behaved or unassigned women went to the Female Factory to weave woollen cloth, sew or do laundry." Visitors also learn that craftsmen, or "mechanics," were in demand and could earn extra money doing private work. But they were the lucky ones. Most convicts were subjected to harsh working conditions. Pit-sawing timber beams, for instance, was arduous work as Australian hardwoods were tough, and the sawyers remained in hot, airless pits with sawdust sticking to their sweat.

This segment of the tour delves into the many aspects of working in a penal colony, including meals. A video monitor inside a dining table gives visitors a point of view of convicts eating one of their two daily meals. Breakfast was hominy, a porridge of maize and sugar; dinner consisted of bread and soup. According to the caption: "The monotonous diet was high in salt and fat, with no fruit or dairy, but it provided enough energy for work-

FIGURE 17. A model of a portable jail designed to accommodate twenty convicts. At night, convicts were chained by the ankles. Each box was fitted with a urinal along with bibles and prayer books (Hyde Park Barracks, Sydney). © retrowelch 2014

ing men." The big picture of the colony's economic system includes statements about building materials and tools that were shipped from England. Several posters reiterate important facts about the Australian work structure, most notably, its advanced division of labor. At the lumberyard—the largest worksite in town—thirty-eight different trades were combined to maximize productivity: carpentry, coopering, leatherwork, and shoe making. Visitors are told that the convicts turned out a high volume of quality items, including fine furniture and coaches. The microeconomy of penal labor relied on strict time schedules (Foucault, 1977: 149) as specified in a storyboard titled "Task Work."

Task work was a way of setting the quota of work to be done in a specified time:

Tailors—two suits of convict "slops" per day

Pairs of sawyers—450 feet of timber per week

Brickfields gangs—30,000 tiles and bricks per month

In an effort to enforce quality control, all products were marked with a number identifying the gang that made them. In the event that items failed inspection, convicts replaced them while working on their own time. The convict economy also featured incentives. For instance, overseers could be rewarded when the gangs met quotas. Likewise, they were punished if they failed to meet the standards. With an eye on labor resistance, curators tell us that Australia's first strike was over task work: "Sawyers at Pennant Hills stopped work for three weeks in 1819 when the Chief Engineer tried to increase their quota." The labor apparatus was self-generating insofar as training provided young men and boys with opportunities to acquire valuable skills. Along those lines of interest, there lies an important—albeit implied—message on convict transformation. That is, penal labor not only was a means of discipline but also fostered redemption. Former convicts are described as being molded into law-abiding "emancipists" who are commended for taking advantage of their second chance, or what Australians still commonly refer to as the "fair-go." Perhaps the best example is the architect of the Hyde Park Barracks, Francis Greenway, an emancipated convict who proved that he could use his labor, skill, and ingenuity to advance the building of Sydney.

For penal tourists interested in the topic of economics, a trip to Argentina will not disappoint. There, the Penitentiary Museum in Buenos Aires offers tourists a pedagogical experience in which local penology is displayed alongside a narrative on nation building and modernization. As mentioned previously, the museum is introduced as a technical-cultural institution in which tourists are instructed about how to view the emergence of penal technologies as well as their social significance. Indeed, visitors are taught a particular lesson in the cultural sociology of punishment that does not separate the technical from its meaning. In that respect, state officials use the exhibit to communicate coherent themes involving Argentine penology and its role in micro- and macroeconomics (see Welch and Macuare, 2011).

As tourists enter the space, a large replica of the National Penitentiary in Buenos Aires greets them. Its sharp symmetry symbolizes an ideal convergence of science, technology, and economics. That state-of-the-art prison was deliberately modeled after the clinic, the laboratory, and the factory, becoming what Foucault (1977) would describe as omni-disciplinary. Inspired by English and American prisons of the day (i.e., Pentonville and Auburn), the National Penitentiary provided a unique venue where economic modernization intersected with institutionalized routine, thereby advancing Argentina's export economy alongside a commitment to a progressive and stable society. As Salvatore observes: "Rather than passively providing disciplinary solutions to a given labor regime associated with a certain cycle of the export economy, criminology provided a way of interpreting the complex social problems created by these social arrangements" (1996: 195; Salvatore, 2007).

Realizing that immigration into Argentina brought much needed labor along with such problems as vagrancy and disorder, influential reformers (e.g., José Ingenieros, Moyano Gacitua, and Francisco de Veyga) emphasized the centrality of work in the positivist constructions about delinquency. Ideally, work would serve to transform criminals into productive citizens by instilling a work ethic as well as teaching them a marketable skill. Such transformation, however, faced significant obstacles in the export economy (i.e., beef and cereals) that relied on a structure of labor demand that contained high fluctuation and required few skills. Moreover, due to the seasonal cycle in the distribution of goods, the export economy was vulnerable to a direct action by organized labor that could paralyze performance and shut down production, especially at peak times. "Criminologists' intellectual challenge was to present these tensions (unemployment, poverty, vagrancy, trade unions, marches, radical politics) as the result of individual 'anomalies,' to imagine social problems as part of a more general phenomenon—criminality—reducible to a systematic analysis, experimentation, and therapy" (Salvatore, 1996: 199). Positivists contributed to the remapping of class relations in Argentina in the early twentieth century by means of penal discipline intended to deliver a docile and obedient workforce for a stable nation (see Rodriguez, 2006).

As discussed in the previous chapter on religion and governance, traditional sex-role stereotypes influenced the divergent patterns of penal discipline. Compared to male prisoners, who were subjected to job training to meet the industrial demands of an emerging modern economy, women inmates were expected to find work as domestic servants, an occupation in high demand in early-twentieth-century Buenos Aires. Acquiring such skills as sewing, cooking, washing, and ironing could then be easily transferred to that sector of the labor market. Ideally, working as a domestic servant for a middle-income or wealthy employer meant that those women would be exposed to the virtues of family life on a daily basis (Caimari, 1997). Hence, it is fitting to note that compared to Italian positivists, the Argentines paid much closer attention to environmental forces in controlling criminality (Rodriguez, 2006; Welch and Macuare, 2011).

The significance of economics in Argentine penology is illustrated through numerous items and images displayed in the museum. Near an imposing arched doorway that leads to the interior corridor and gallery, visitors are positioned in front of a large antique wheel from a cart used in a penal colony (de General Roca in Rio Negro province), a reminder that prison labor was put to good use in building the nation's infrastructure while simultaneously imposing discipline. At many chronological stops along the exhibit, tourists can gaze at vintage black-and-white photographs of rugged prison life at Tierra del Fuego, a penal colony located from 1902 to 1947 in Ushuaia at the southern tip of Argentina. Strenuous prison labor is a dominant motif in the pictures, most notably, prisoners hacking down huge trees with axes. Amid the snow, the images confirm a cold, isolated, and dreary landscape. That Argentine version of a remote Siberian prison camp sharply contrasts to the thriving city of Buenos Aires.

The curators describe in detail various aspects of the social world of prisoners. A dominant theme of this part of the tour is the transformation of criminals into productive workers (see Melossi and Pavarini, 1981). Interestingly, that form of discipline merges with positivist rehabilitation described by a modern clinical term—"laborterapia" (labor therapy)—and gives that intervention a distinctly local meaning in Argentine culture. Laborterapia manifests itself in two principal settings, the farm and the factory. The Argentine Penitentiary Museum displays multiple photographs of prisoners working in agriculture. At a higher plane of thought, one might read into those images the idea that nature has the power of purification; however, this particular exhibit on the prison farm looks quite utilitarian. There is a mannequin in a prisoner uniform designed for fieldwork along with a sample of tools for agriculture, such as hay-hauling picks and machetes.

Visitors are likely to detect an effort to relay a perceived trait of convicts, namely, dangerousness. As a holdover from the days of penal colonies, there are manacles that were used to secure hands and feet while transporting prisoners from the institution to the worksite. Still, that premodern version of convict labor appears to be overshadowed by symbols of progress. Take, for instance, something as mundane as a metal seat from a farm tractor. Rather than having convicts strenuously hack the land manually, as in the penal colony Tierra del Feugo, the use of a riding tractor marks a modern innovation that not only contributes to efficiency and productivity but also inflicts less wear and tear on the convict who works more comfortably. Perhaps in a small way, that particular object also communicates the dignity of the convict worker as a productive member of Argentine society, producing an official narrative intended to shed a benevolent light on the penal state. That unique museum effect contrasts with those evident in other forms of dark tourism whereby the state and its claims of progress are called into question (Lennon and Folcy, 2010).

Although the display of prisoners working in agriculture could speak to the purifying quality of nature alongside the massive export economy of Argentina, penal spectators are kept focused on the factory, symbolizing an even more modern form of production and discipline. The visual narrative relies heavily on the exhibition of objects, including a red prison uniform for those assigned to work in the shops, a foot-pedal sewing machine, a steel moving cart, and photographs of inmates making pottery and baking bread. Contemporary pamphlets present office furniture currently being manufactured by prison industries, thereby helping visitors connect the past with the present. Overall, the Argentine Penitentiary Museum creates a narrative in which penal labor is depicted as playing a viable role in individual discipline as well as collective state building.

In a twist on that narrative, the subject of work is examined in more critical terms in prison museums in South Korea and South Africa, thereby exposing the injustices of penal labor. Especially compared to the favorable presentations of prison work at the Sydney Barracks and the Argentine Penitentiary Museum, the dramatic shift in tone at the Seodaemun Prison History Hall (Seoul) is decidedly unsettling. Its brochure keeps attention on the overarching themes of the tour by describing the museum as "The Place of Independence and Democracy." Even on the topic of prison labor, curators do not hide their contempt for the Japanese occupiers. At the Engineering Work Building, tourists are invited to attend three main exhibits:

Video of Laboring:

This place shows a video of the fact that the Japanese Imperialists exploited the labor force of inmates to produce various goods and military supplies.

Labor Exhibition:

This is the place that exhibits various types of labor, its record and relevant relics from the Prison during the Forcible Ruling Era by the Japanese Imperialists.

Special Exhibition of Independent Activists of the Month:

The Ministry of Patriots and Veterans Affairs selects an independent activist of the month and runs this exhibit all year long. (Seodaemun Prison History Hall, n.d.)

Visitors learn that the Engineering Work Building was built in 1932 for the purposes of stepping up prison labor, particularly during such peak times as World War II. Government supplies and uniforms were manufactured not only for prison use but also for the benefit of the Japanese military. Both inside and out, the two-story redbrick building with bars on the windows looks—and feels—very much like a factory within a prison. Along with a steady series of placards reiterating key statements on "Forced Labor for Exploiting Prisoners," the museum presents an array of artifacts. In a large glass case, two small items are displayed: a "Labor Statement" situated next to a "Clamshell for Making Mother-of-Pearl." By passing through a revaluation process, these relics are given greater signifying meaning; together, they speak to the fine detail contained in the bureaucracy of the enterprise as well as the skilled craftsmanship. Similarly, the museum makes us aware of the use of semiotics, which extends to objects as mundane as construction materials. A large storyboard titled "Forced Labor to Make Bricks" explains that inmate-made bricks were used to build the prison. The bricks were given an identifiable imprint that is still clearly visible in the prison walls. So as to enhance their signifying-value, two bricks are placed in a special display case.

Curators rely not only on objects (e.g., rice bowls of prisoners) and images (e.g., photographs of inmates laboring in workshops) to narrate the collection, but also on the personal testimonies of inmates "who were forced to work during the Japanese occupation," thereby emphasizing "their sufferings of endless labor without rest." A sizeable pie chart underscores the relentless work schedule: prisoners were required to work at least ten to fourteen hours per day. The circular graph shows the number of hours inmates spent laboring (i.e., from 6:30 AM until 6:00 PM) and sleeping (i.e., from 9:00 PM until 5:00 AM). Over the course of the day, workers were allowed two fifteen-minute breaks, a thirty-minute lunch, and a thirty-minute dinner. The demanding workday also included a daily degradation ceremony whereby inmates were forced to disrobe and jump naked over a wooden bar as a means to inspect whether they had concealed dangerous articles (see Seodaemun Prison History Hall, 2010: 121).

As we shall elaborate more in the chapter on colonialism and resistance, the story being told about work and economics at the Seodaemun prison museum centers on the cruel and unjust Japanese occupation of Korea and the exploitation of its labor. Still, the emotional register of the exhibition conveys a strong sense of cultural pride in the defiance of the forces of the Japanese Imperialists. The exhibition of Independent Activists sponsored by the Ministry of Patriots and Veterans honors some of Korea's political luminaries, including Lee Jung Eon (scholar), Kim Sang Deok (representative of 2/8 Tokyo Independence Declaration), and O Gwang Sim (leader of the Independence Army) (see Seodaemun Prison History Hall, 2010: 125; chapter 9).

Similarly, at Robben Island, tour guides—former political prisoners—explain how penal labor was used to demean inmates under the apartheid regime. Still, the narrative conveys a strong sense of hope, humanity, and determination to build a new South African nation. Though the idea of prisoners breaking rocks seems like an old movie cliché, inmates at Robben Island were subjected to that very chore. Walking around the prison compound, visitors can see for themselves the precise spot where political prisoners labored. In his famed book *Long Walk to Freedom*, Nelson Mandela recalls his experiences. Upon arriving at Robben Island, he found a white card stuck out of his cell. It read "N. Mandela 466/64," meaning that he was the 466th prisoner in 1964. Mandela was a forty-six-year-old political prisoner with a life sentence. His story echoes a harsh congregate work system dating back to the 1830s at Auburn prison in New York:

> We began to work in the first week, crushing stones with hammers in the courtyard. We sat in four rows, wearing hand-made wire masks to protect our eyes. We were not allowed to talk to each other. A huge container for the stones was placed in the courtyard and we were ordered to make it half-full by the end of the week. The next week, we were told that the container had to be three-quarters full. We worked hard and completed the job.
>
> The week after we were told to fill the container all the way to the top. Again, we worked hard and managed to fill the container. But we were angry and decided, there and then, that we were not prepared to work in such a way. The next week we started our first go-slow strike. The guards threatened us, but we ignored them and worked at our own speed.
>
> The struggle had now taken a new form for those of us on the island. We had a new fight on our hands—the struggle to keep our dignity and self-respect. (1994: 81; see Smith, 1997: 96–97)

Forcing political prisoners to break rocks was a practice that continued else-where on the island. Mandela later was assigned to a work crew that was driven to a remote lime quarry that he describes as a big hole cut into the hillside. Today, tourists take a similar journey to the lime quarry. It looks just the way Mandela remembered it, especially the blinding light that reflects off the white rock. Although Mandela and his fellow prisoners preferred to spend their days outside the compound, work at the lime quarry was more demanding than work in the courtyard. Lime is buried deep in the layers of rock and has to be extracted with a pick and then a shovel. Work in the lime quarry was intended to demoralize the political prisoner; however, as Mandela writes, it had the opposite effect, since it lifted their spirits. Nonetheless, the quarry produced physical ailments. By the end of the work-day, prisoners were covered in white dust, "which made us look like ghosts" (Mandela, 1994: 86). Even after a good scrub, the dust never seemed to wash away.

Even worse, the dust—compounded by intense sunrays—injured their eyes. In a press visit to Robben Island before his election as South Africa's first democratic president, Mandela posed for a photo opportunity at the quarry. Chiseling into a limestone, Mandela is shown wearing dark sun-glasses, because years earlier he underwent an operation to his tear ducts, which had been damaged by years of exposure to lime dust (see Smith, 1997: 91). Tour guides tell us that Mandela avoided flash photography, since it irri-tated his eyes. As visitors at Robben Island learn by witnessing the actual site, the lime quarry still resonates with the hope and resilience of the antiapart-heid movement. In 1995, more than one thousand ex-political prisoners gath-ered at the lime quarry for a symbolic reunion. With the press corp on hand, the former inmates reenacted their solidarity, singing in unison "Shosholoza"—work together (see Smith, 1997: 148, 150–51).

PRISON AS WORKPLACE

Now we swing focus from the kept to the keepers. Some of the prison muse-ums studied herein describe in detail what it is like to work in prison. By way of objects, images, and textual narrative, visitors gain a sympathetic view of the correctional profession. In many instances, attention is turned to the agencies that structure correctional work, thus enhancing their prestige and sense of purpose. At the Argentine Penitentiary Museum, an entire room is dedicated to the Federal Prison Service. An organizational chart maps out a hierarchical bureaucracy along with pictures and captions commemorating the contributions of local leaders, namely Roberto Pettinato and Dr. Juan O'Connor. Colored photographs of each of the current prisons in the system deliver a contemporary look at the enterprise. Thematically, the prison bureaucracy is promoted as being particularly virtuous. As mentioned, the system's slogan blends socioreligious messages: "Justicia y Fe Para Cumplir la Mision" (Justice and Faith to Fulfill the Mission). The elaborate mission statement goes on to characterize the prison service as being devoted to an innovative prison technology based on science, cooperation, and hard work from all its members. In that sense, the Argentine prison bureaucracy (Weber) depends not only on professional expertise (Foucault) but also on a commitment to shared morals and solidarity (Durkheim).

Entering the room dedicated to the penal institution, visitors are greeted by mannequins dressed in prison cadet uniforms from the national training academy (La Escuela Penitenciaria de la Nación), again enhancing the organizational and cultural tenets of paramilitarism, expertise, and professionalism. The walls are decorated with various items related to the National Penitentiary Service, especially items showing the importance of credentials: a certificate of graduation from the training academy, a unit flag, and several photographs of penitentiary staff. Portraying the notion of prison work as a dangerous profession, the exhibit displays an arsenal of weapons and security devices used to maintain order against the threat of disorder: pistols, rifles, machine guns, bayonets, riot helmets, gasmasks, teargas grenades, and handcuffs. The gallery offers a linear narrative by emphasizing modern progress toward a state-of-the-art weaponry.

Illuminating further the cultural side of a modern paramilitary structure, the exhibit displays personnel uniforms and caps for ranking officers and a range of promotion stars, stripes, chevrons, and unit insignias. As noted, a shoulder patch emblem reveals a certain depth to its military origins by including a prison fortress with two rifles crossed. Correspondingly, the prison service claims a fraternity (and solidarity) with the Argentine military by memorializing the soldiers who served in the war of Las Malvinas against England in 1982 (known to the British as the Falkland Islands War). That confrontation off the coast of the mainland is remembered as a monumental event for Argentines (thirty years later, images of its war veterans are proudly displayed in such politically significant venues as Plaza de Mayo and in front of the presidential building, Casa Rosada). As mentioned previously, the museum recognizes the women officers in the prison system. There seems to be a conscious effort on the part of the curators to emphasize feminist gains whereby secularism prevails over the long history of religious governance.

The next room exhibits furniture and photographs from the National Penitentiary and the former prison at Tierra del Fuego. By far, the items displayed here form the most eclectic part of the tour. Visitors are greeted once again by the Argentine national flag prominently draped along with a crucifix attached to the wall. In tandem, they reinforce the firm relations between the Catholic Church and the Argentine state with respect to the penitentiary service. With greater theoretical nuance, those symbols connect the sacred with the mythological in maintaining a dense narrative on the emergence of modern Argentine penology. That particular legend—as part of state making—is told in part by introducing tourists to key figures in Argentine penal history. Passing by a metal plate dedicated to the former inspector general Francisco Jose Sanz, we approach a display case commemorating the famous warden Antonio Ballve (1867–1909), to whom the museum is dedicated. Among the items on view are his desk, his typewriter, and multiple placards describing his career, work, and professional contributions to the development of a modern penitentiary. Objects from secular prison administration continue to be complemented by the sphere of the sacred; for example, the collection includes a photograph of the interior of the former Asilo Correcional de Mujeres (currently the museum). Interestingly, the picture of the Asilo is paired with a register book of admissions and releases from the institution, suggesting that it too operated along the lines of a bureaucratic procedure. Nearby is another photograph showing a contemporary regional prison, highlighting progress toward modern—secular—confinement.

In a subtle change of theme, visitors cannot help but notice the large manual printing press used by prisoners to copy notes and various administrative documents. Numerous items from the former penal colony at Tierra del Fuego underscore the bureaucratic theme of modern prison operations: a large desk, a switchboard, a bookcase, and a metal storage box. Still, that modern veneer contrasts with the harsh reality of the penal colony. Vintage photographs show a Siberian-like terrain with snow-capped mountains and a prisoner shackled at the ankles. The museum effect relies on the careful arrangement of objects to convey special importance. A mannequin dressed in an officer's uniform appears to watch over the collection, thereby suggesting that the items are valuable and in need of safekeeping. Nationalism, once again, provides a cultural backdrop by displaying several Argentine flags. Overall, the prison museum in Buenos Aires depicts correctional work and the prison service as benevolent, delivering noble contributions to a modern Argentine society.

Much like the Argentine Penitentiary Museum, Alcatraz delves into the subject of correctional work. Before tourists enter the maximum-security cellblock, they spend time in an exhibit dedicated to the officers and a larger bureaucracy committed to security. A huge montage features a life-size photograph of a prison guard standing next to the phrase "The Most Controlled Prison in the Country." Here curators establish a recurring theme, namely, danger. The display includes the front page of an issue of the *San Francisco Examiner* from 1946: "14 GUARDS SHOT, 1 DEAD IN RAGING ALCATRAZ BATTLE; CONVICTS HOLD HOSTAGES." The text tells us that maximum control did not prevent the breakout attempt that turned Alcatraz into a battleground, ending in death for three would-be escapees. Two officers, Harold Stites and William Miller, are remembered for being killed in the line of duty. In his memorial address, James Bennett, then director of the Bureau of Prisons, expressed socioreligious sentiments while recognizing the risks of prison work: "When men of courage and steadfastness lose their lives in the faithful performance of their duty, there is little that need be said by those of us who did not face this danger . . . [We are] saddened with a very real sense of loss when two such heroic men make the supreme sacrifice." A snapshot of the mourning families brings sympathetic viewers into close range of the tragedy. Despite that deadly event, the storyboard restores order by explaining: "With one officer for every three inmates, there was less opportunity for prisoners to attack one another. The prison with the toughest inmates was one of the safest. Loss of privileges and isolation also influenced behavior, as did the prospect of transferring to a less restrictive prison."

With a lighter tone, a panel within that same storyboard is titled "Life as a Correctional Officer." It informs visitors that prison work at Alcatraz was plagued by high turnover and low wages. Although some officers stayed for ten to twenty years, at times nearly one-third of the staff had less than a year's experience. Curators offer a bit more detail on the so-called guard culture by telling us that after four weeks of training, new recruits benefited from on-the-job advice from senior officers: "Those who were easily intimidated or lax about the rules never made it past the one year probation period." A group shot of four officers posing behind an interior prison gate allows us to visualize

FIGURE 18. The tower at Alcatraz. Widely regarded as the worst job at Alcatraz, tower duty meant eight long hours in a cold, windy metal perch. © retrowelch 2014

a job behind bars. Nearby, another caption hints at time and space in the local work regiment. Officers made twelve counts each day but never followed the same routine in making their rounds. The worst job at Alcatraz was the tower duty—"eight lonely hours on a cold, wind-blown metal perch" (see figure 18).

A significant portion of the exhibit on working at Alcatraz is sponsored by a cooperative effort of the National Park Service and the Federal Bureau of Prisons so as to commemorate the one hundredth anniversary of the creation of the Bureau of Prisons (1891–1991). A quotation from criminologists Norval Morris and James R. Jacobs ("Proposals for Prison Reform") places the Bureau of Prisons within a progressive framework that embraces *the cult of the individual:* "The administration of day-to-day life should be dictated by standards of humane concern for fellow human beings." With three photographs, the display puts faces on an otherwise impersonal bureaucracy, namely, directors J. Michael Quinlan (1987–1992), Kathleen Hawk Sawyer (1992–2003), and Harley G. Lappin (2003–present). Much like the prison museums in Buenos Aires and Hong Kong, visitors at Alcatraz can gaze at the paramilitary uniforms; adding a certain layer of prestige and respect for authority, those items are placed inside a large display case.

Similarly, themes of danger recur as attention is turned to weapons used by officers to secure the institution. Prominently featured are three intriguing objects from the 1930s. First is a Tommy Gun from the Alcatraz armory; with a round ammunition can, it resembles one from the Prohibition era when the G-men (e.g., the Untouchables) launched their fight against the mob. The next item is a Billy Club. However, it is not one issued by the prison bureau; rather, the weapon was handmade by an inmate for an officer at US Penitentiary Leavenworth. The stick was crafted from leather shoe heels glued together over a metal rod. The final gadget is a Gas Billy, a brass Billy Club fitted with a tear gas canister. Across the exhibition room is another display that speaks for itself. Titled "Security," the sign is embellished with the razor wire used to surround medium- and high-security prisons. A contemporary two-way radio and body alarm are put on view along with a statement informing visitors that correctional officers do not carry firearms inside the institution.

Once inside the cellblock, visitors experience the space where the guards once worked. The imposing cage-like interior conveys security as well as intimidation. So as to deepen the narrative on the social world of officers, the audio guide includes testimonies from those who patrolled the institution. Among those stories is the legendary "Battle of Alcatraz." Tourists are told that on May 2, 1946, convicts Bernard Coy and Marvin Hubbard overpowered Officer William Miller and seized his keys that opened the cells, allowing them access to the rest of the prison. These inmates then used an ingenious wrench-like instrument to pry apart the bars at the gun gallery and they took weapons. The missing part of the plan was Key 107, which would have enabled the would-be escapees to exit through the recreation yard. After searching everywhere, they located the key, which was hidden inside the toilet of the cell where the hostages were held. In their haste, Key 107 was inserted into the lock of the yard door but it would not open. Unknown to the convicts, the sensitive keys jammed if they were used incorrectly. The plot was foiled. Coy, Hubbard, and their four accomplices held the cellblock for two harrowing days. A state of emergency called in officers from other prisons along with the US Navy, the Coast Guard, and the Marines. The narrator on the audio guide directs visitors to the precise spot where a mortar fired through the ceiling and into the floor. Looking up, tourists can see the hole, and at their feet are the lasting scars. Although the escape was prevented, two officers and three prisoners perished. Inside a nearby cell is a poster eulogizing Officer Miller who hid the key but also died in the "Battle" (see Stuller, 1998; Wellman, 2008).

In another exhibit, curators continue to remind us of the hazards of working in Alcatraz. A large sign, "TOOLS OF THE TRADE," explains their rationale: "To prevent attacks, most guards worked without keys, guns, or handcuffs. But contrary to regulations, some guards carried hidden saps— short leather-wrapped metal clubs—in order to protect themselves or subdue a violent inmate." Photographs of a "sap or blackjack" and "leg manacles" serve as documentation of a potentially violent prison. A related poster reinforces the message on danger by informing tourists that all federal prison staff members undergo training in self-defense. So as to emphasize professionalism, the text also notes that employees learn about psychology, inmate rights, correctional methods, and the history of corrections. Contemporary photographs of correctional staff (i.e., officers, medical personnel, and educators) are intended to show a well-rounded workforce. Toward that end, a group shot of what appears to be a graduating class of recruits is captioned: "Staff composition has changed over the last decade. Women and minorities now represent over one quarter of the total staff." Apparently, curators recognize feminist gains in the federal prison system; moreover, those advances are contextualized within the wider civil rights movement. That particular message is an example of a state making claims with regard to inclusion and progressive governance.

The social world of officers, to be sure, is structured along the lines of a paramilitary organization, with a top-to-bottom chain of command. To illustrate that point, visitors are navigated into the warden's office; the large workspace has the remnants of what was once a cozy fireplace and mantle. A job description of the warden is posted, telling us that he was responsible for setting the disciplinary and administrative tone for the prison. A series of photographs maintains the importance—and authority—of the warden, beginning with Warden Johnston (c. 1930s), who is shown inspecting a formation of officers as they stand at attention. According to the text, "Johnston was allowed to hand-pick his correctional officers . . . [They] were provided with extensive training, and were considered to be the best in the Federal system." Outside the warden's office, visitors can step a few meters toward a site where the warden's mansion once stood. Like the officers who also lived on the island with their families, the warden resided within a short distance of the cellblock. Although the warden's house burned down in 1970, visitors can peer into the skeletal remains. With some imagination, tourists can visualize the mansion with its stunning view of the San Francisco skyline. A sign describing the residence shows Warden Swope with his wife celebrating Christmas (c. 1950), thereby dispelling Hollywood's portrayal of wardens as cruel tyrants.

As visitors exit through the gift shop, they are enticed to purchase an array of books and souvenirs, many of which allow them to remain connected to those who worked inside the dangerous world of Alcatraz. Among those items is a brass replica of Key 107 from the Battle of Alcatraz (at a cost of $9.95, including a complimentary postcard). Calling further attention to that enigmatic object is a large photograph of an officer standing in front of the key rack with a caption: "Missing Key Foils Escape Attempt."

CONCLUSION

In closing, we turn to the Old Melbourne Goal, where curators relay a brief narrative on local history, culture, and economics. Compared to the other prison museums that communicate messages on prisoner debt, convict labor, and state building, the theme of work at the Melbourne Gaol is pushed to the periphery. In one of the few commentaries on prison labor, a placard titled "Pentonville, Punishment and Penitence" quotes George Duncan, inspector general of Penal Institutions in Victoria (1871): "There can be no better test of a reformatory system than its success in developing and fostering habits of industry and self-control." As in the Pennsylvania system, the practice of isolating prisoners was "intended to break their spirit in order to re-form their character." Prisoners at the Melbourne Gaol (at least until the 1870s) were first placed in solitary confinement, which, of course, from an economic standpoint is counterproductive. Gradually, prisoners were allowed to mingle with other convicts, and then work in teams. Unlike the narrative at the Sydney Barracks, which boasts of the productivity of convicts, the tour at the Melbourne Gaol leaves visitors with a sense of dismay, since prison labor, as well as the entire penal regime, was considered to be an utter failure. The museum explains that overcrowding and the constant movement of inmates strained institutional order as work routines deteriorated. As mentioned previously, workshops and the stone-breaking yard did not provide enough work. By the 1880s, the very idea of reform had been abandoned; by then, local authorities regarded the Melbourne Gaol as little better than a "playground" (see Welch 2013).

By contrast, the Hong Kong Correctional Services Museum puts a positive spin on contemporary prison industries. While economics is not a major topic there, the exhibit reflects a commitment to the value of work as a rehabilitative tool. The Correctional Services Industries provides jobs to adult prisoners as required by law. Such work, according to a poster, maintains prison stability and allows inmates to contribute to society. Among the items produced by prisoners are office furniture, staff uniforms, litter containers, traffic signs, and laminated books for public libraries. Visitors are informed that "Hong Kong has developed an internationally acclaimed correctional system, which places increasing emphasis on correction and rehabilitation of offenders." Though prison museums in Philadelphia, Seoul, and Robben Island explore the misguided as well as exploitive side of convict labor, curators in Hong Kong remind us that in their culture, prison work is still dignified and socially integrative. Moving into the next chapter, we delve into the subject of science as it shapes punishment. To be examined is the manner by which prison museums approach both the positive and the negative applications of science. In many instances, curators prompt visitors to reflect on specialized penal knowledge as it informs humane incarceration as well as calculated maltreatment and torture.

SEVEN

Suffering and Science

Many postmodern inquiries into dark tourism examine the ways in which the unethical use of science and technology contributes to human rights atrocities, the classic case being Holocaust museums (Dekel, 2013; Lennon and Foley, 2010). Similarly, many prison museums consider the extent to which authorities have tapped into the scientific and technological potential for maltreatment, torture, and execution (Welch, 2009a, 2011a; see Becker and Wetzell, 2007). The Melbourne Gaol, as one example, exhibits flogging by situating corporal punishment alongside anatomy and medicine. Standing nearly eight feet high, a daunting structure known as the lashing triangle is accompanied by a poster depicting its use:

> Prisoners sentenced to a lashing [for offenses that ranged from abusing a warder to swearing] were tied face down to this frame. Their shirts were removed, a wide leather belt fastened around their waist to protect their kidneys and a narrow leather collar around their neck to stop their throat from being cut ... Prisoners were whipped with a cat-o'-nine-tails, which was soaked in salt water to minimize infection ... After a whipping the prisoner would have been taken to the prison hospital and salt rubbed onto his back ... This was to prevent infection and speed healing—although scars would remain for life.

Reading that passage, visitors learn that the practice of whipping was subject to a rather paradoxical application of science. Cautious to avoid inflicting mortal wounds, the protocol incorporated modern medicine to stave off disease. Hence, with scientific knowledge and expertise the procedure appears vaguely humane without abandoning the brutal force of corporal punishment.

Keeping a critical eye on punitive devices and the application of science, this chapter also investigates the deeper tendencies of conceptualizing criminality. Since the nineteenth century, penal practices have been, as Foucault (1977) points out, redefined by knowledge, particularly in the specialized vocabularies, rationalities, and discursive structures contained in medicine, psychiatry, and clinical treatment. Together those scientific disciplines shaped an emerging positivism, allowing criminological experts to sift through carefully collected observations and measurements. Especially compared to its classical counterpart (Beccaria), positivism realigned the criminological question. The study of crime became the study of the criminal, or what Lombroso called "criminal anthropology." The notion of "criminal man" as being fundamentally different from the rest of us was—and still is—a potent construction. Garland's analysis of science takes us even further into the realm of culture, by demonstrating how "in modern society, certain cultural themes— such as the nature of crime and criminals—have come to be articulated in what is thought of as a 'scientific' mode, that is to say as 'knowledges' or discourses which claim a special relationship to truth" (1990: 209).

Garland goes on to suggest that it is useful to think of such knowledges as specific cultural forms rather than as revealed truths standing outside of time and place. By exploring prison museums, tourists are likely to recognize the cultural forms of science in penal institutions. In many instances, curators prompt visitors to reflect upon specialized knowledge as it informs humane incarceration, on the one hand, and calculated cruelty, on the other. So as to sort out those ironies of incarceration, discussion embarks on a survey of torture devices, particularly as they adopt technological innovations for the infliction of suffering (see Welch, 2005). The next section on the "physics of hanging" examines another paradox of penal science. Designing the gallows so as to deliver a more efficient and less painful execution, reformers promoted a sense of enlightened progress. By doing so, however, they also contributed to the perceived legitimacy of the state's deathwork, thereby maintaining a cultural belief in justice, the duty of government, and the defense of the eternal good (see Foucault, 2003; Katz, 1988).

The death penalty, of course, is commonly narrated along the lines of protecting society. As described in the chapter's third section, the Melbourne Gaol exhibits the scientific approach to the identification of dangerousness. There, attention is turned to the psychiatric underpinnings of positivist criminology, delving into the subject of phrenology as it contoured capital punishment. To generate further interest, the museum puts on display a series of death masks from executed prisoners. Once the convict was pronounced dead, medical staff used plaster to replicate the shape of the convict's head. Phrenologists interested in collecting data on key personality traits, most notably, "destructiveness," then inspected the death mask. At the time, it was believed that public safety could be improved by knowing—and predicting—more about the psychological makeup of felons. The Argentine Penitentiary Museum also demonstrates the purchase of science as it guides fingerprint analysis, positivism, and related forms of measurement. Finally, a visit to Eastern State Penitentiary allows tourists to understand the scientific logic of architecture as engineered around security, surveillance, and sanitation. Joining the campaign to improve the physical and moral health of its prisoners, the institution enthusiastically embraced the need for purification.

INSTRUMENTS OF TORTURE

As mentioned previously, when the Millbank Penitentiary opened in London in 1817, authorities reserved a room to display various instruments of torture (Bennett, 1995; Evans, 1982). Today, tourists at the Clink can gaze at—and even handle—devices designed to produce excruciating pain. Indeed, the topic of suffering is ubiquitous as well as nuanced, incorporating history and culture so as to provide a thick description of torture. Consider, for instance, the infamous trials by ordeal described in a large placard: "By the time of Henry II, the system of law in England had been improved because Henry sent out his own judges from London to listen to cases throughout all England's counties. Each accused person had to go through an ordeal. There were three ordeals: fire, water, and combat." Each of those "tests of truth" was obviously rigged to ensure that a verdict of guilty would be reached (see Welch, 2011b). According to the ordeal by water, "an accused person was tied up and thrown into water. If you floated you were guilty of the crime you were accused of." The text goes on to explain that in 1215, the pope instructed priests in England not to assist in the ordeals, thereby paving the way for trials by juries. Curiously, the law allowed the accused to be tortured if they refused to go to trial before a jury, another reminder of the clear interplay between religion and governance. At a higher level of awareness, the museum's description of the ordeals raises doubts about humane progress since, instead of delivering humane reform, the procedure was aimed at inflicting more—not less—pain.

Likewise, curators at the Clink post statements explaining that certain devices were deliberately intended to breach the rule of law governing torture. As mentioned in chapter 1, a sign explains that "The Manacles" were one of the earliest forms of "enhanced interrogation," leaving the victim fastened to a wall of the dungeon for hours or days without food or water. As added punishment, high tide from the Thames River would flood the cells holding shackled prisoners. Prolonged pain and suffering were usually enough to induce compliance. A vignette highlights the testimony of Father John Gerard, who was suspended from the manacles: "All the blood seemed to rush up into my arms and hands and I thought that blood was oozing out of my fingers, but it was only a sensation caused by my flesh swelling above the irons holding them. The pain was so intense that I thought I could not possibly endure it." As a technological innovation, the manacles left no grievous marks. Therefore, without evidence of injury, the tactic was not legally registered as torture, allowing it to be used without a royal warrant. Of course, reliance on the manacles had a point of diminishing utility insofar as the victim risked going mad before confessing. Much like the ordeals, confessions brought on by the manacles should be critically understood as a form of "truth" that is culturally produced with the aid of torment (see Welch, 2011a).

Other instruments of torture were invented—or modified—to benefit from basic engineering. While most pillories were stationary wooden frames used to publicly shame offenders convicted of such minor offenses as selling rotten meat, the one installed on Southwark Street demonstrated a greater commitment to ingenuity, not to mention humiliation. Curators tell us that, according to historical records, a "rotating pillory" was designed to "house up to four criminal at the same time. When items were thrown at the criminals they would normally run to avoid being struck. The attempted avoidance of such items resulted in forcible dragging around of the others in the pillory." While visitors might visualize the almost comical spectacle of convicts spinning around the rotating pillory, another device is not so funny—the thumbscrews. A storyboard, featuring a grim illustration of that instrument of torture, activates the cultural imagination: "This small vice looking device has become world famous with the name being well publicized in stories and movies." The screws were used to crush the thumbs of thieves so as to put a stop to their crimes. In many instances, the injury became a permanent disability; sometimes, the screws contained spikes that chopped off the thumbs entirely. Tourists are reminded that thumbscrews are still used to this very day in certain parts of the world, either as punishment or as torture. So as to elicit sympathy for those unfortunate enough to be "thumbscrewed," the poster gives us "things to do":

1/ Imagine your thumbs have been crushed.
Try picking something up without using your thumbs.
2/ Now try putting the same item in your pocket.

Throughout much of the tour in the Clink, penal spectators are strategically positioned so as to get a virtual look at suffering while also being kept at a safe distance, thereby producing emotional reactions ranging from nervous laughter to gasps of horror (see Brown, 2009; Huey, 2011; Walby and Piche, 2011). The brochure advertising the Clink promotes the exhibit by offering "gruesome stories of prisoners" and a "hands-on torture chamber." Toward that end, the museum invites visitors to participate in what Stan Cohen (2001) called the atrocity triangle, whether as perpetrator, victim, or mere bystander. Tourists are navigated into a sizeable space devoted to the reenactment of suffering where they have safe contact with various tools of the torture trade (e.g., the boot, the collar). A particularly curious object is known as the Scavenger's Daughter. Invented by Sir William Skeffington, lieutenant of the Tower of London, the contraption was designed to subject the victim to excruciating "stress and duress." The Scavengers Daughter is often compared to the rack, but rather than stretching, it compresses the victim. The pressure is so extreme that it causes bleeding from the nose and ears (see chapter 1). In some ways, torturers considered the Scavenger's Daughter to be a technological improvement over the rack since it was portable. Tourists are encouraged to pick up and even try on the iron device as a means of understanding its unique geometric shape as well as of registering an eerie sensation, due in large part to its intended cruel purpose.

At the Clink, there is no shortage of "hands-on" experiences with torture instruments, which thus reinforces its visceral museum effect. Visitors are managed not only by "organized walking" but also through "organized touching" from which intended messages are communicated according to an itinerary (Bennett, 1995). In that sense, the Clink is very much a performative exhibit that transcends the ordinary "show and tell" (see Casey, 2003). With that agenda in mind, visitors are invited to test drive the ball and chain by giving them another "thing to do: pick up the chain and ball and guess how heavy it is." Because the device was invented to be portable, it retained enormous advantages. The placard explains that inmates assigned to the ball and chain were able to leave the prison and beg for money and food along Clink Street. Nonetheless, the exercise was meant to be punitive, since prisoners were not allowed to carry it but only to drag it.

The Clink's museum effect is maintained by putting on display devices so as to unnerve visitors. Recall that it is a cultural transformation that allows instruments of torture to be viewed (and even touched) by visitors as safe, since the current incarnation of the objects is not for use but rather for representation (of cruel acts in the distant past). With respect to dark tourism, instruments of torture have a sinister appeal because it is assumed that they were actually used in horrific acts (Williams, 2007). The tour of a "hands-on torture chamber" concludes with a final interactive device that invites its guests to take the role of the other. Recall the Torture Chair conveniently located near the exit. However, rather than rushing out the door, visitors amusingly take a moment to take a seat. While reading the placard, holiday smiles tend to grimace as they learn more about the painful procedure. Once the person was strapped in, the chair would be tipped forward. By way of gravity, the victim was pushed to the edge of his seat. That position—made possible through physics—rendered the victim even more vulnerable to the torturer who skillfully practiced the tongue pullers to extract a confession.

The "hands-on" lesson for penal pain is also advertised for the Hyde Park Barracks. However, unlike the Clink, the Barracks museum appears to dampen the reality of suffering by incorporating it into other—benign—activities, some of which involve "organized touching." The brochure captures that particular museum effect: "Try on a set of leg-irons, lie in a convict hammock . . . Bring your kids for dress-ups and our convicts Kids Trail" (Historic Houses Trust, n.d. a). Later in the tour, the museum shifts its tone, allowing visitors to understand how corporal punishment was used to instill harsh discipline. Moreover, the practice of flogging is described in terms of its technique and skill. Once again, the "cat-o'-nine-tails" earned its name for leaving wounds resembling cat scratches on the backs of convicts. Curators point out that there were serious efforts to maximize the stroke of the whip. Superintendent Ernest Slade bragged about his proficiency, claiming that he could make fifty lashes look like one thousand. So as to give visitors a genuine glimpse at the brutality of corporal punishment, a large colored photograph shows in detail the bloodied body of a victim who appears to have been recently whipped. As mentioned, evidence of cruelty and maltreatment at the Barracks is rather scant, as curators seem to be conscious not to turn the museum into a gruesome sideshow.

By contrast, the topic of corporal punishment at the Old Melbourne Gaol is given considerable thought. An elaborate brochure explains that life behind bars was hard: prisoners were kept in solitary confinement and breaches of discipline were met with severe punishments (Poultney, 2003). As noted at the onset of the chapter, modern notions of anatomy and medicine accompanied the lashing triangle; thus, those forms of knowledge ensured that even a brutal thrashing would not be lethal. Clearly, there is still something primitive in flogging. Lifelong scars hark back to the ancient connotation of stigma, a mark of social disgrace (see Goffman, 1963). With a thick description, the museum encourages visitors to contemplate the social significance of corporal punishment. A display case titled "Marked Men" contains the original documents of prisoners who were flogged, including their mug shot photos, hand-scripted details of their offenses, and the number of lashings they received. Curators administer a brief lesson on the extent to which the practice entered the cultural vernacular, or gallows humor:

> Heard these sayings! They originate from early times. When a whipping was often ordered as part of punishment.
>
> There is not enough room to swing a cat.
>
> Don't let the cat out of the bag.
>
> That is rubbing salt into the wound.
>
> He's a marked man.

As in the Melbourne Gaol, the physician's role in corporal punishment is openly recognized at the Old Fort in Johannesburg. Visitors are shown a poster-sized action photograph of a white officer whipping a black prisoner strapped to the lashing frame. While the image speaks to the injustice of the racist apartheid regime, a caption addresses the paradox of prison heath care: "This was the hospital wing of the Old Fort Prison Complex. It was the only place within the Old Fort where black prisoners were accommodated, although in separate wards from white prisoners. Prisoners remember the hospital wing as a place of pain. Corporal punishment was administered here, in the presence of the District Surgeon" (see chapter 8). The topic of flogging is similarly addressed at the Hong Kong Correctional Services Museum. Gazing deep into a dimly lit display case, tourists notice what appears to be an authentic cat-o'-nine tails. Curators describe the device in terms of its British origin, as it was commonly used in the Royal Navy to instill discipline. Eventually, colonial authorities subjected Chinese lawbreakers to a round of the cat-o'-nine tails, "a dreaded punishment ... that could rip and tear the skin from the back of the victim, scaring for life." A more common form of corporal punishment in colonial Hong Kong, however, was caning. The museum dwells on the minute details of instrument. The practice of caning was regulated by precise measurements. On display is a circular device used to measure the width of the "5/8 Inch Cane." According to protocol, the rattan instrument was "considered up to the required standard only if the entire cane can pass through the center of the Measuring Gauge."

Though the cane appears rather harmless as it sits idle on display, visitors should know that the lightweight rod (e.g., 3/8 inch in diameter, three feet in length) was capable of reaching a ferocious speed before striking the victim. So as to give corporal punishment an air of legitimacy under British rule, caning was stipulated in Article 16(1)(a) of the Detention Centre Regulations. The law empowered the superintendent to use caning to punish detainees for a disciplinary offense. The placard explains further that caning was abolished in accordance with the act in 1990 (numbers 191 and 192), thereby boasting a postcolonial stance (see Bosworth and Flavin, 2007).

So as to give visitors a vivid view of caning, two wooden frames are situated in the center of the gallery. Each of them was used to restrain the victim while being caned. One frame strapped the victim while standing upright. The other forced the victim into a more vulnerable posture much like being placed over a barrel. The museum effect seems directed at having visitors imagine themselves as victims of caning, particularly under imperial rule (see chapter 8).

While colonialism—as well as its resistance—serves as the political backdrop for the Seodaemun Prison History Hall, it is important to consider how methods of torture applied notions of science to inflict physical and psychological harm. The performing museum technique navigates visitors ("minds on legs") through a series of staged scenes intended to dramatize the events in the Underground Torture Chamber. In the first gallery, a dark interrogation room reenacts Water Torture. That form of mock drowning (or waterboarding) was used by the Japanese to extract confessions from the Korean patriots. With the use of mannequins, the scene features a victim suspended upside down, with hands bound behind his back. The interrogator is shown pouring water onto his face. From its inception, such "enhanced interrogation" has been portrayed (falsely) as effective and relatively harmless, creating the illusion that the injuries that incurred—both psychological and physical—are benign and reversible (Welch, 2011a). To the contrary, the medical literature indicates that brief oxygen deprivation due to waterboarding can generate neurological damage; moreover, breathing fluid into the lungs can lead to aspiration pneumonia, which can be fatal. Near-suffocation can also create severe psychological effects, including panic attacks, depression, and prolonged posttraumatic stress disorder (Bouwer and Stein, 1997; Physicians for Human Rights, 2009; Olsen et al., 2006). Of course, like other techniques described previously (e.g., the manacles), the water torture left no grievous marks, thereby erasing evidence of crimes against humanity.

As visitors step to the next scene, they peer into the "Temporary Detention Room" where the Japanese officers inflicted "psychological torture" and "mental oppression" in preparation for the interrogation. By hearing the painful shouting of those being tortured in the adjoining room, it was thought that detainees would become more compliant. To narrate the scene, three Koreans (mannequins) are shown sitting contemplatively on the floor. A short stride away, we look into an interrogation session in which two agents from the Japanese intelligence department are berating a Korean patriot. Reinforcing a sense of sited-ness, a caption informs us that those interrogations took place here and not in police stations. Further along the spectrum of suffering, the next room is titled "Fingernail Torture." The brief description reads: "A torture to induce pain by piercing a needle-like sharp skewer beneath a prisoner's fingernails." After a moment of hesitation, visitors lean sideways to view the room equipped with the instruments of torture placed on a table in front of a chair. Across the bloodstained table is a confession book. Unlike the previous exhibits, this scene has no actors; the empty space conveys loss as we fill in the blanks with mental images of past victims (see Welch, 2007, 2009a, 2009b).

In the next gallery, we are jarred back to the horrific realities of torture as curators display grotesque photographs of disfigured victims. Their desperate eyes look straight into ours. The placard explains that such "unthinkable torture" included various forms of mutilation (e.g., peeling off skin, amputation, and rupturing organs), thereby documenting a bizarre application of medical surgery meant to impose lifelong pain and suffering.

THE PHYSICS OF HANGING

With respect to anatomy, medicine, and physics, the Melbourne Gaol museum situates lethal punishment within a "sphere of cultural life" termed "science" (Garland, 1990: 209). Toward that end, the engineering of executions remains a significant theme of the tour, including an exhibit that occupies an entire wing of the prison. A huge poster reaching up to the ceiling is titled "THE SCAFFOLD." It describes how the invention was modified over time. Early scaffolds were "poorly made, failed to work properly and fell to pieces . . . Those prefabricated scaffolds were costly and inefficient . . . [The newer scaffolds were a] solid, sophisticated structure . . . based on a standard 19th century British design . . . 'A new drop' had been constructed, consisting of a platform, trap door and fixed beam above, from which the rope was suspended." The display also features an array of illustrations as well as a replica of the gallows (see figure 19). Nearby, a large board lists all 136 executions between 1842 and its closure in 1924. In modern fashion, the condemned are bureaucratically registered by date of execution, name, age, country of origin, and offense.

With even greater detail, the scaffold is presented not merely as a static structure but rather as a device requiring expert knowledge (see Foucault, 1977; Garland, 1990). Recall that a storyboard titled "The Art of Hanging" quotes from Charles Duff's *A Handbook on Hanging* (1828): "Hanging is a fine art and not a mechanical trade. Is not a man an artist who can painlessly and without brutality dispatch another man?" Despite the metaphoric use of the term *art,* the procedure was very much guided by weights and measures to deliver a perfect drop: "The art was not to bruise or cut the skin." Reading more like an engineering manual than an art critique, the poster explains: To achieve such a hanging, the rope had to be the correct length. "If the rope was too long it could wrench the head off, too short and it caused prolonged strangulation" (see chapter 1). Exact records were kept on each execution and became a stock of scientific knowledge from which hangmen could refine their technique. *The Particulars of Execution* served as the official report kept at the sheriff's office. It was written by the government medical officer and countersigned by the prison governor, who included eyewitness accounts of the hangings along with autopsy notes: "Sometimes mistakes occurred. When 27-year-old Emma Williams, 5 foot 2 inches tall (1.57 meters) and weighing 10 stone 2lbs (65 kilos), was hanged at the Melbourne Gaol in 1895, her neck was badly torn. 'The drop was a little too much for the weight,' the Governor, Mr R Burrowes, noted in his report." As noted previously, *The Particulars of Execution* included sketches and photographs of fractured vertebrae. Those illustrations speak to the role of science and anatomy in modernizing hangings. Once again, such expert knowledge had a legal component: under the Act to Regulate the Execution of Criminals (1855) death was required to be "instantaneous."

FIGURE 19. An exhibition at the Melbourne Gaol demonstrating a condemned prisoner properly restrained for execution. © retrowelch 2014

Overall, the museum effect at the Melbourne Gaol relies on the display of objects, images, and text to create a didactic ("minds on legs") lesson on the management of suffering. Once that theme is established, the narrative moves toward the significance of modernization and scientific progress. Indeed, the tale of Melbourne as told through the Gaol's museum is one that embraces expert knowledge, science, and medicine, as well as humane legal reform aimed at reducing pain, thereby delivering a more respectable hanging. With the somber tone of the tour, penal spectators are encouraged to question the rationale (and "scientific knowledge") of "humane" executions, particularly because of the intrinsically violent nature of deathwork carried out by the State (see Lennon and Foley, 2010; Welch, 2013).

At the Hong Kong Correctional Services Museum, the topic of hanging is examined from several points of view. In an upstairs exhibit titled "Mock Gallows," tourists get a look at the contraption that drops prisoners to their death. The imposing device is built to scale. With its trapdoor opened, one can look down into the first level of the museum, getting a real sense of the deep plunge. The display features several posters that describe the physics of hanging; here, the presentation has the tone of a science fair. One of the placards, "Rope Measurement for Hanging," tells us that the protocol of gauging the length of the rope came from the British in 1841, when Hong Kong was colonized (see figure 20). Initially, executions were a public spectacle on Hollywood Road near the Victoria Gaol, but by 1879 hangings were moved inside. Curators show and tell us that the rope is roughly one and a half inches in diameter, fourteen inches for neck allowance plus length of drop, and one inch difference for every two pounds. A pair of numerical columns list the "weight in clothes" corresponding to the "length of drop." For a prisoner weighing 134 pounds, the ideal length of the drop is seven feet, ten inches. In addition to the height and weight of the condemned prisoners, other measurements were registered: "The type of the knot, the size of the noose, and the length of the rope hanging in the air were determined according to the data collected." Gazing at the execution chamber, visitors notice two sandbags used to test the apparatus a few days before the execution. The sandbags also straightened "the rope so that the length of it could be of highest precision."

Under the banner "Era of the Hangman" is an elaborate narrative that places executions within the local culture, thereby casting doubt on the colonial use of hanging. Although death sentences were fairly common, they rarely came to fruition. A bar graph indicates the number of executions per

year. Between 1946 and 1966, there were a total of 122 hangings. The high water mark was 1947 and 1948, as both years had 18 executions: many of them were Japanese war criminals and collaborators who had committed atrocities during the Second World War. There were no hangings in 1963, 1964, or 1965. The reason for the lapse into disuse was political: "British governments made it plain that they would permit any appeal against the death penalty, so in practice, successive Governors commuted executions." Nonetheless, the storyboard gives tourists some ethnographic detail on the state's deathwork:

> The hangings were normally carried out at dawn ... in the "H" block at Stanley Prison. Chaplains were on hand to counsel the condemned prisoner during his last hour. He would receive a last meal, specially cooked and delivered to his cell.
> For several days beforehand, an irregular heavy thumping sound had come from behind the closed door at the end of the corridor. The man about to die knew this was the executioner dropping well-filled sandbags of approximately the condemned prisoner's weight through the trapdoor. This was to test the equipment and stretch the rope.
> The final moments came quickly; into the cell would come the hangman, to shackle the condemned prisoner with leather thongs. With the help of other staff the condemned prisoner was brought into the execution chamber, where the knotted noose was placed around his neck, while the heavy rock-hard knot was placed behind his ear. The canvas hood was then slipped over his head. At that moment, the chaplain murmured a final prayer for him. The hangman then pulled the lever, the trapdoor clanged open and the condemn prisoner dropped eight to ten feet to eternity. The knot behind his ear was pulled sharply by the prisoner's weight at the end of the drop, breaking the neck and causing instant death. A few minutes later, the prison doctor would examine the body and announce that the condemned prisoner was dead.

Despite the infrequency of executions, the chamber was routinely—or perhaps ritualistically—cleaned each and every day so that it was "technically ready for use." By the 1990s, support for the death penalty waned even further, politically and otherwise. Curators inform tourists that one of the first questions posed to the chief executive of the special administrative region was whether capital punishment would be resumed. "His answer was a firm negative." Interestingly, the condemned block and the execution chamber were demolished in 1996 to make way for the new Stanley Prison hospital. So that the colonial practice of hanging does not slip from memory, the museum displays photographs of both the interior and the exterior of the execution chamber. By doing so, the exhibit seems to be communicating a new cultural identity that embraces the cult of the individual while shunning colonial penal practices (see Bosworth and Flavin, 2007).

POSITIVISM

Prisons, as Foucault (1977) theorized in great detail, are among the key sites where power is exercised. Sharpening that observation, Foucault explained how the institutional histories of penal regimes are grounded in the complex formulation of expert knowledge. In Europe and the United States, penitentiaries during the early nineteenth century had become laboratories designed to pursue the new sciences of surveillance, control, and discipline. The emerging modern prison, according to several scholars, served as a "museum for the display and diffusion of this knowledge" (Scicluna and Knepper, 2008: 503; see Rothman, 1971; Ignatieff, 1978). Although it is tempting to dismiss the terms *laboratory* and *museum* as convenient metaphors, a close examination of the history of prison science reveals a conscious reliance on both institutions. Cesare Lombroso, for instance, adopted a decidedly clinical approach to criminal anthropology, comparing criminal skulls housed in the Anatomical and Anthropological Museums in Bologna, Pavia, Florence, and Turin. Lombroso was such an avid collector of those artifacts that he opened his own museum of psychiatry and criminology in 1884 (Lombroso, 2006; see www.museounito.it/lombroso; www.thenautilus.it/Mu_Lombroso.html). Lombroso's immensely popular work on the emerging science of criminals inspired similar collections scattered throughout Europe (Regener, 2003).

In Argentina, Lombrosian positivism—or the Italian school—also took hold in the late nineteenth century, becoming a rigorous form of legal medicine that often rivaled its European and North American counterparts. Prison clinics for the study and treatment of criminals gained added legitimacy at the National Penitentiary, where the Criminology Institute was founded in 1907. Within the penitentiary, the institute was known as the Psychology and Anthropology Office: "It was viewed as a laboratory for testing and advancing European criminological theory and as a potential producer of scientific knowledge for the international community" (Rodriguez, 2006: 165; Salvatore, 2007). Aiming to establish a worldwide reputation as a leader in scientific criminology, Argentina celebrated the work of Juan Vucetich, who devoted his career to the study and practice of fingerprinting (Rodriguez, 2004; see S. Cole, 2001). In 1916, Vucetich launched his vision of criminal identification by calling for the creation of a library, a scientific journal, and a museum to "organize the diffusion of the system" (Rodriguez, 1944: 401; quoted in Rodriguez, 2006: 241). For the next several decades, Argentine criminology and penal practices would undergo further modernization, responding to other social, political, and economic developments (Salvatore and Aguirre, 1996; Salvatore, Aguirre, and Joseph, 2001).

Beginning in 1980, visitors were invited to view those modern innovations in Argentine criminology by touring the Penitentiary Museum in Buenos Aires. Just as prisons have served as museums for the display of criminological knowledge, the Argentine Penitentiary Museum is situated inside a former prison that dates back to 1860, thereby offering tourists a pedagogical experience in which local penology is displayed alongside a narrative on nation building, as previous chapters have discussed. Recall the brochure explaining that the museum is "meant to work as a technical-cultural institution: its purpose would be to keep all materials that could witness past experiences of the penitentiary life" (museum brochure, English version: 4). The term *technical-cultural institution* reminds us that visitors are informed how to understand the emergence of penal technologies. That pedagogy on the sociology of punishment does not detach the technical from its meaning. The museum carefully narrates the significance of Argentine criminology and its role in modernizing the state.

Recognizing positivism for its profound scholarly current, Salvatore reveals how that particular expression of science became embedded in the formation of the Argentine state:

> Positivism and state-making were inextricably connected. Positivism contributed to redefining the scope of sovereignty, the instruments of power, and the hegemonic pretensions of the oligarchic state. More than a mere intellectual trend, positivism provided the ruling elite with the institutional spaces, the technologies of power, and the rhetoric needed to exercise power more effectively in the period of transition toward a more democratic republic. (2007: 254)

Between 1890 and 1940, Argentine positivists used their scientific appeal to medicalize the conception of crime and similar social problems; by doing so, they soon annexed the criminal justice apparatus, where they would experiment with certain populations, policies, and institutions. That new form of governance is what Salvatore identifies as the medico-legal state. At the forefront of the movement was José Ingenieros, who modified Lombrosian criminology, making it more suitable to a rapidly changing Argentine society.

Ingenieros challenged Lombroso's morphological, genetic, and atavistic claims about crime while emphasizing more sociological and environmental forces in order to complement a psychological approach to delinquency. Nonetheless, positivism in Argentine criminology remained very much a clinical project, relying on classification, diagnostic exams, anthropometric measurements, family histories, and psychological tests. Prisons served as laboratories for criminological research, most notably, the Instituto de Criminologia at the National Penitentiary. Ingenieros and his positivist disciples (e.g., Osvaldo Loudet) influenced a generation of physicians, lawyers, and professors to advocate key innovations for prisons: indeterminate sentences; segregation of convicts according to dangerousness; individualized treatment; and labor therapy (Salvatore, 2007; see Rodriguez, 2006).

A modern criminology based on science fits neatly into the medico-legal state by allowing political leaders to envision new forms of social control. In Argentina, the positivists advanced the social defense thesis with notions of "dangerousness" by proposing that society had the right to protect itself against individual and collective aggressors, ranging from run-of-the-mill street criminals to anarchist agitators. To be sure, positivists were not only guiding policies for criminal justice but also branching out into other spheres of social policy. By widening the definition of antisocial conduct, positivists "legitimized a new power to supervise, control, and punish behavior that, in classical penology, would not have qualified as 'crime'" (e.g., alcoholism, mental illness, prostitution) (Salvatore, 2007: 259; see Cohen, 1985; Foucault, 2003; Sozzo, 1998).

In establishing enormous sway over state policies aimed to control crime and regulate antisocial behavior, positivists generated a "new micro-physics of power, based on a scientific understanding of the populations under treatment" (Salvatore, 2007: 274). The positivist movement in Argentina during the early decades of the twentieth century thrived in large part due to its scientific rhetoric and modern sensibilities, which also had a progressive appeal spanning the political spectrum. Conservatives, liberal reformers, and socialists alike were drawn to positivism for its seemingly enlightened and humane proposals for dealing with crime, mental illness, and public hygiene, as well as for improving the welfare of women, children, and the elderly. Proponents of the medico-legal state set out to modernize Argentina according to the language of positivism, which issued a progressive grammar for governance (Salvatore, 2007; see Rodriguez, 2006).

Themes of modern medicine, research, and science figure prominently at the Argentine Penitentiary Museum. Against a wall of a room crowded with vintage objects stands a huge apothecary case displaying scores of chemical bottles and remedies dating back to the year 1898. One can recognize themes of public hygiene in the face of social pathology. Among the key actors in the Argentine medico-legal state were the positivist criminologists who embraced science to create a healthy, modern society (Rodriguez, 2006; Becker, 2007; Salvatore, 2007). That progressive campaign was not an impersonal social movement but one that was driven by charismatic leaders. The museum goes to great lengths to tell that side of the story. A major section of the exhibit is dedicated to Juan Vucetich (1864–1925), whose work on the development of (scientific) fingerprint analysis is widely celebrated in early modern Argentine history as a breakthrough in criminalistics. Adding to a thick description is a headshot of Vucetich next to his own fingerprints and the tools of the trade (i.e., table, inkpad, and rolling pin).

Upon reflecting on that segment of the tour, we are mindful of Pomian's (1990) phenomenological analysis of the museum. He contends that all collections engage in organizing an exchange between the fields of the visible and the invisible. Items on display are understood as being meaningful because they offer a glimpse into the realm of significance that itself cannot be viewed (see Rajchman, 1988). Hence, the fingerprints of Vucetich present visitors with a window to something beyond the ink on paper. That is, those patterns of spirals represent something beyond themselves, perhaps even beyond the order of nature that has been harnessed by science and positivist criminology. Similarly, Casey (2003) notes that it is the collection's formal arrangement of objects that allows visitors to see something that they cannot see, such as the past. But through the curator's mediation (the screen), the museum brings the past into the present, thereby tapping into our imagination (see Bennett, 1995).

Similarly, the room hails the research of José Ingenieros, the first director of the Instituto de Criminologia. He is known around the world for his pioneering work in modern criminology in its positivist form. There is a photograph of Ingenieros, his desk, a typewriter, apothecary bottles, and a scale. Of particular significance is a display case featuring his anthropometric calipers, which he used to measure prisoners at the National Penitentiary. The Lombrosian influence is evident, marking a shift away from Beccarria's metaphysics of crime (e.g., free will) to a study of the criminal. Furthermore, that version of modern criminology was very much a project for criminal anthropologists who directed their studies at the body, though they did not completely lose sight of environmental factors in breeding criminality (Foucault, 1977).

Returning to the Melbourne Gaol museum, we also witness an important turn in the genealogy of criminological knowledge. The vast collection of artifacts allows tourists and scholars alike to reflect on the putative advances of penal technology. Accompanying presentations on the innovations in corporal punishment and the physics of hanging is an intriguing venture into the territory of psychiatry, most notably, phrenology. As a "scientific" approach to crime, phrenology speaks to a seemingly sophisticated study of crime and how to properly respond to it (see Becker and Wetzell, 2007). After establishing that theme of the tour, attention is directed at a large storyboard titled "Phrenology and the Shape of the Skull." It explains that, beginning in the 1880s, phrenologists attempted "to determine personality types, intellect and human behaviour by examining the shape of the skull. It was used to predict criminal behavior." The poster features an illustration showing the various faculties linked to the parts of the brain, most notably, "destructiveness."

Curators, however, are quick to inject contemporary skepticism into phrenology, commenting that in the late nineteenth century its experts were consulted like palm readers and astrologers. Nevertheless, at the Melbourne Gaol phrenology inscribed itself into the protocol of executions by advocating the preparation of death masks. Following an autopsy, the victim's head was shaved to allow a wax mold to set. Once dry, the mold was cut from the head and filled with plaster. The death mask served as a replica of the victim's head for expert phrenologists to study and issue claims for penal policy: "Thus, if the death masks of enough violent criminals were collected, it should be possible to make generalizations about the shape of such heads. In this way society could be forewarned and be able to keep a closer watch on those with 'suspicious' head shapes" (Poultney, 2003: 27). Reinforcing the relationship between phrenology and the Melbourne Gaol, death masks are scattered throughout the museum (see figure 21). One particular death mask is located strategically at the center of the exhibit. The caption reads: "After examining the death mask of a certain prisoner, the expert proclaimed that he was a 'man clearly destined to a life of crime.'" That man was the legendary bushranger Ned Kelly. As we shall see in upcoming chapters, the controversy over Kelly takes many turns, including discussions on the notion of criminality and the scientific endeavor to predict it.

The theme of positivism at Alcatraz demonstrates to tourists the benevolent and enduring developments in prison science. A series of placards explains how rehabilitation emerged as well as the many ways it adjusted to

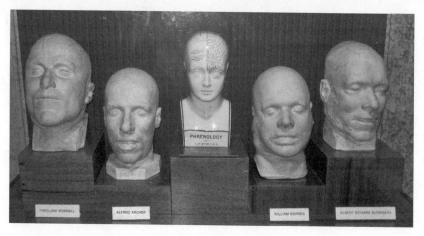

FIGURE 21. A collection at the Melbourne Gaol including several death masks that were compared to the phrenology head for determining personality traits (e.g., "destructiveness"). © retrowelch 2014

changing times. The pedagogy begins with a storyboard titled "'Scientific' Penology: Early and Mid 1900s": "Criminologists, social scientists, and prison administrators applied theories from the emerging fields of sociology and psychiatry to create healthier prison environments. They improved education, recreation, work programs, and psychological counseling. They began classifying inmates according to sex, age, criminal background, and willingness to follow rules. This led to less regimented, more reformative prisons." Similar to the Argentine Penitentiary Museum, Alcatraz narrates the emergence of "scientific" penology by way of its influential leaders in the federal government, beginning with a portrait of prison reformer Sanford Bates (c. 1930). The caption tells us that he was hired by Mabel Walker Willebrant (assistant attorney general) to reorganize the Bureau of Prisons along the lines of providing better rehabilitation programs and classification of inmates as well as upgrading staff professionalism. The exhibit carefully notes: "Resistance is encountered from the old line wardens." That statement on resistance is all the more noticeable since the narrative on rehabilitation switches gender. First Lady Eleanor Roosevelt is pictured visiting the federal women's prison at Alderson, West Virginia, in 1934. Dr. Mary B. Harris, who was the first woman to serve as the warden of a federal prison, accompanies her. Harris is credited for introducing correctional innovations, such as education programs, which became standard practice in the federal prison system. By drawing attention to Mabel Walker Willebrant, Eleanor Roosevelt, and

Dr. Mary Harris, curators seem to be celebrating early feminist accomplishments in the Federal Bureau of Prisons. Those significant gains are made in two male-dominated fields: prison governance and science. To reinforce that message, another panel displays pictures of inmates undergoing basic medical services (e.g., eye exams) and states that the US Public Health Service staffed the federal correctional institution in Springfield, Missouri.

Moving down the timeline of key developments, museumgoers are informed that in 1950 the Youth Corrections Act led to special treatment for young offenders and required that they be segregated from older inmates. In the timeline, the year 1963 marks a shift in tone as curators hint that the federal prison system began heading in more punitive directions. Attorney General Robert F. Kennedy is seen walking down a corridor at Alcatraz. The caption announces the closing of Alcatraz. Kennedy is quoted: "Let us reject the spirit of retribution and attempt to deal coolly to balance the needs of deterrence and detention with the possibilities of rehabilitation." At this point, mixed messages are sent. One panel informs visitors that in the 1960s and 1970s, the Medical Model, or "Rehabilitation Model," is given its widest application in federal prisons with the emphasis on "curing" criminal behavior through counseling, education, and individual. The montage includes prisoners posing at an award ceremony for Alcoholics Anonymous. The very next panel, however, reveals the impact of the "Nothing Works" controversy in which critics of rehabilitation (mis)represented the research by Robert Martinson (1974), concluding that prison programs were a failure. The curator's statement notes: "1970's: Studies suggest that rehabilitation comes primarily from the individual inmate and not from treatment programs. The 'Rehabilitation Model' is de-emphasized in federal prisons, but programs remain for inmates who want them."

A closer reading of Martinson's research, actually titled "What Works?: Questions and Answers about Prison Reform," did not make the sweeping claim that "nothing works." On the contrary, the report cited positive outcomes in 48 percent of the programs evaluated (Lipton, Martinson, and Wilks, 1975). By the early 1970s, there had been growing disillusionment surrounding rehabilitation, and for several years policymakers were waiting for the other shoe to drop. The publication of Martinson's article was that "other shoe," and the fact that it became known as the "nothing works" report was testimony that the chapter on liberal-oriented rehabilitation was officially coming to a close. Just as retributionists criticized rehabilitation within prisons, many progressive reformers also voiced their dissatisfaction with correctional programs. Among other things, they pointed to the criminal justice system as a source of the problem, since the heavy criminalization approach to such problems as drug addiction made matters worse, therefore insisting that the effectiveness of rehabilitation was irrelevant. Moreover, radical commentators also launched resounding attacks, proposing that rehabilitation strategies—especially court-imposed treatment—constitute another form of social control by a specialized class of experts who assume the authority to determine the fate of those caught in the criminal justice machine (see Foucault, 1977; Lynch, 2000; Welch, 2011b): "Seen in this light, rehabilitation was not merely a laudable goal that scientific research had failed thus far to achieve, but something more insidious—an ideology that explained crime in highly individualistic terms and legitimated the expansion of administrative powers used in practice to discriminate against disadvantaged groups and to achieve covert organizational goals (such as alleviating court backlogs and repressing political opposition)" (Greenberg and Humphries, 1980: 369). Without entirely dismissing warnings contained in the social control thesis, rehabilitation advocates point out that the demise of such programs was brought about by a political turn toward retribution aimed at undermining a progressive agenda. Cullen and Gendreau write: "The rejection of rehabilitation has less to do with a careful reading of empirical literature and more to do with changes in the social fabric that triggered a corresponding shift in thinking about corrections" (1989: 24).

With respect to rehabilitation, the exhibit at Alcatraz seems to strike a more conciliatory chord with the display "Entering the Second Century." There, a panel praises "Programs and Rights" by showing a "Certificate of Completion" (for Computer Literacy). Curators commend education and vocational training as an integral part of the prisoner's reentry into the community. In a group shot of prisoners in graduation regalia, complete with robes, mortarboards, and tassels, they are shown smiling for the camera. Once again, an important figure in prison administration is quoted:

> Leaning too far toward punishment or toward rehabilitation is not professionally responsible . . . It's not our job to change an inmate's way of thinking . . . It's our job to help those who want to change . . . We can't "cure" criminal behavior, but we know that some programs work for some inmates some of the time—and that's a better chance than many of them had on the street.—J. Michael Quinlan, Director, Bureau of Prisons, 1987–1992

That portion of the tour at Alcatraz concludes by calling into question the *modern* project of imprisonment, even when it is genuinely committed to rehabilitation. In large print, a sign reads, "Alternatives to Incarceration." It lists many viable examples, including halfway houses, fines, restitutions to victims, and community service.

What benefits do alternative punishments offer?

Relieve overcrowding .
Less expensive than prison
Can improve chances for inmate's readjustment to society

Tourists at Eastern State Penitentiary are also introduced to the topic of treatment, mostly in the form of medicine and psychiatry. As we shall discuss in the next section, diseases—especially tuberculosis—spread quickly in the cramped, crowded cellblocks. By the late 1800s, the prison was in need of a "state-of-the-art hospital." Laboratories, quarantine housing, and recovery wards expanded, and in 1917 all of cellblock 3 was devoted to medical care. A large map of the cellblock diagrams precisely where the specialized units were located. Chief among them was the psychiatry department. The caption tells us that by the 1960s, ESP had become known throughout Pennsylvania for its sophisticated mental health services: "Patients with severe psychiatric problems were sometimes held in rooms with thick, nearly soundproof doors." Another storyboard highlights the psychiatric staff as they introduced new therapies in the 1960s. With an obvious play on words, curators say that "the bustling hospital had a reputation for being well-run, if perhaps 'a little mad' at times." For more details, visitors can activate the audio guide and listen to the personal stories told by the staff. Officer Raymond Grady, for instance, recalls that suicide had become a serious problem in the late 1960s. It is noted that selected prisoners worked as clerks and assistants in the psychiatric unit. Charles Gindle (inmate, 1964–70) tells listeners that "one time the captain told two other fellows and me to go put a straightjacket on this fellow."

The exhibit leaves visitors with an unsettling message on "Sexuality (20th Century Issues)." A sizeable photograph shows a clinician behind his desk interviewing a prisoner whose identity is concealed as his back is against the camera. Stenciled on the folding chair is the notation "BUREAU OF IDENTIFICATION." A brief sentence explains the picture: "Like most prisons, Eastern State hired professional staff in the 20th century to address issues of both rape and consensual sex among inmates." That simple statement seems loaded with anxiety over dangerousness as well as homosexuality, both of which are depicted in highly psychiatric terms that lend them to labeling (*Civil Liberties*, 1990; *New York Times*, 1989; Plant, 1986). Within the predatory prison world, one can only imagine the negative consequences of being "identified" as a sex offender or a homosexual (see Akerstrom, 1986; Welch, 2005). As we transit to the next section, similar issues of physical, psychological, and moral hygiene are explored in the larger context of scientific methods for purification.

PURIFICATION

The notion of purification has many overlapping connotations. Consider, for instance, efforts to cleanse what is perceived to be dirty, physically and morally. Indeed, anxiety over filth is a psychological defense mechanism for guarding oneself against infection as well as vice (see Douglas, 1966). A well-informed history of the prison teaches us that the early campaign to construct healthy environments was driven by both scientific knowledge on diseases and moral initiatives in pursuit of virtue. The coupling of those ambitions was tightened along a common understanding that illness and immorality not only were related but together had the potential to spread. It is a sense of contagion, real or imagined, that is particularly worrisome. Robin Evans recounts those concerns in his aptly titled work *The Fabrication of Virtue: English Prison Architecture, 1750–1840*. In the span of twenty years, between 1775 and 1795, the English prison system underwent a wholesale rebuilding, in large part due to an outbreak of jail fever (i.e., typhus). Authorities were fully aware that the fever was capable of escaping from the prison and bringing down those who had never ventured inside its walls: "There was one example that would have been familiar to everybody. In April 1750 attendants at the Old Bailey sessions remembered being struck by a 'noisome smell' in the court. A week later, a number were taken with a highly malignant fever. Most died. The death toll included the Lord Mayor of London, two judges, an alderman, a lawyer, an under-sheriff and several of the jury, not to mention 40 others" (Evans, 1982: 95). Progressives took notice as they embarked on a dual mission to reform prisons and stamp out jail fever, enlisting along the way magistrates, lawmakers, physicians, scientists, architects, and engineers. Attention was turned to jail conditions that were crowded, dirty, and ill aired. All of those factors contributed to the likelihood of inmates being fatally infected, thus raising ethical arguments about a prison term being a prospective death sentence. In short order, prison design incorporated the construction of ventilators and the use of courtyards to circulate air and minimize pollution. Influential organizations (e.g., the Committee for Rebuilding) seized the opportunity to further connect two functions of the reformed prison: "to promote the moral health through cellularization and division of males from females, felons from debtors, and to promote the physical health by the provision of running water, drainage and open courtyard planning" (Evans, 1982: 104). In tandem, the prison would strive to earn a reputation as being clean, and therefore, respectable.

Those noble objectives, however, faced significant obstacles. Architects quickly realized that security and seclusion were not entirely compatible with health and open spaces. Faced with that dilemma, John Haviland carefully unfolded his plans for Eastern State Penitentiary. Returning to the form and function of the radial plan, we recall the ways in which Haviland reconciled the conflict between security and salubrity while not abandoning the interplay between moral psychology and medical pathology. Upon entering the institution, it becomes evident that the Gothic fortress façade insulated a more subdued practice of separate confinement. Philadelphians were keen to have the prison retain their Quaker ideals. With enthusiasm, they shared Howard's ([1929] 1777) commitment to humane prison conditions, making prisons healthy venues for the body, mind, and spirit. Guiding those religious values were secular, scientific knowledges. In 1821, the Building Commissioners invited architects to submit their proposals for what was to be the most ambitious prison in America, and perhaps the world. There were unprecedented demands, since inmates were to spend their entire sentence in solitary confinement. The cell, therefore, had to be designed to accommodate sleeping, eating, working, and religious instruction. To top it off, each cell would have its own plumbing and access to an individual exercise yard. The commissioners, mindful that American and European prisons were dreadful places, insisted that the new penitentiary be a healthy environment: "Since current theories of contagion and disease assigned an important role to 'miasmas,' or foul air, the siting of the prison and the internal arrangement of the buildings had to be carefully planned to provide the best ventilation" (Johnston, 2010: 32). Of course, as a parallel purpose, the prison had to maintain security and prevent escapes.

After bitter debate among the commissioners, the architectural job was awarded to Haviland. His background served him well in the planning stage, having apprenticed to the London prison architect James Elmes. Equally important, Haviland bonded with the Philadelphia reformers. Corresponding with the Building Commission, Haviland explained that he favored the hub-and-spoke design to improve "watching, convenience, economy, and ventilation" (1821: 19; Johnston, 1958). He did not reveal his inspiration; however, the plan was consistent with the prisons and insane asylums built in the late eighteenth century in England and Ireland. Despite his ambition, Haviland struggled in the face of the biggest public structure in the nation. No architect had ever been handed the task to house large numbers of prisoners in individual cells for the duration of their terms. The central heating of large buildings and indoor plumbing were at best rudimentary at the time. For Haviland, things did not go smoothly, and he was forced to make modifications along the way. Attempting to stabilize the heat, Haviland initially placed stoves in the tunnels under the corridors of the cellblocks; small flues were installed in the floors and the wall, which would allow hot air to permeate the interior as well as release stale air from building. The design failed and many inmates became ill from inhaling the carbon-monoxide fumes. Haviland then turned to an English system that used high-pressure hot water piped into each cell (Johnston, 2010).

The next challenge was ventilation, since the walls of the exercise yards stalled air circulation and the skylights did not provide adequate fresh air. Compounding matters, the faulty flues kept the cells damp. In 1848, a prison physician's report found that the bedding and clothing were wet with humidity. It concluded that the ventilation was defective, undermining the "importance of fresh pure air to the well-being of both mind and body" (Hill, 1853: 261). Finally, Haviland grappled with the water supply and toilet facilities. When a second tier was added to the prison, engineers built a reservoir in the prison yard along with a steam engine for pumping water. For each cell, a toilet with a cast-iron cone was attached to a waste pipe. However, the stoves located in the underground tunnels acted as heating ducts, warming the contents of the sewer pipes. As a result, noxious fumes seeped into the cells. A doctor complained that the odor would stick to the clothes of anyone merely walking through the corridors of the prison (Teeters and Shearer, 1957).

Problems with the plumbing design also violated a chief demand of Eastern State Penitentiary, namely, complete isolation. Since, at the time, it was believed that criminality was a form of contamination spread through communication, prison officials went to great lengths to prevent inmates from having any contact with one another. Despite those efforts, prisoners used the plumbing pipes to tap messages, in something not unlike Morse code. Still, it was the very nature of solitary confinement that ultimately led to the undoing of the Pennsylvania system. All the technological advances in heating, ventilation, and plumbing could not remedy the debilitating effects of total seclusion. Ironically, it seemed that ESP had become one of the insane asylums whose design it initially replicated. While the Quaker reformers were convinced that they were delivering humane redemption in its purest form, in actuality their system of confinement became widely regarded as cruel, psychologically and otherwise. Today, visitors can admire the architectural and engineering feats on display at ESP. Tour guides (and the brochure) do not hesitate to tell us that their prison had indoor plumbing even before the White House, where President Jackson relied on chamber pots. After a few hours strolling in and out of the suffocating cells, it becomes apparent that being hermetically sealed for years at a stretch would probably push most of us over the edge of sanity. At least, that is what the museum effect—through the use of authentic space—convincingly demonstrates.

CONCLUSION

Despite even genuine attempts at humane reform, prisons have been used to impose suffering on debtors and convicts as well as on political and religious dissenters. With that realization in full view, many prison museums situate spectators in front of innovative devices aimed at delivering calculated degrees of physical and psychological torment. In crafting a story line on suffering in prisons, curators usually present a chronology of penal progress that gradually abandons tactics regarded as cruel by evolving standards of decency. As discussed in this chapter, some prison exhibits also lend support to Lennon and Foley's (2010) postmodern perspective on dark tourism by calling into question certain claims of enlightened reform. Furthering that sense of skepticism, critical narratives prompt tourists to recognize the ethical dilemmas involving the application of science in penal institutions. In that historical context, specialized knowledge is closely examined, especially as it informs humane incarceration as well as facilitates maltreatment, torture, and execution.

To reiterate an earlier point, it is through themes of punishment as well as reform that science—most notably, positivist criminology—is used to articulate discourses, which claim a unique relationship to truth. However, as

Garland (1990) forcefully argues, such specialized knowledge ought not be understood as a set of verified facts standing outside of time and place; rather, we should view them as specific cultural forms. Many of the prison museums studied herein demonstrate the value of that approach by putting on display objects and images that speak to a certain belief about the strategic use of penal science. Consider once again the exhibit at the Melbourne Gaol where a close alignment of phrenology, death masks, and execution is established. Together, they reinforce a cultural theme of psychiatry, criminality, and the legitimacy of the state as it claims to protect society. As we shall discuss in greater depth in chapter 9, the Melbourne Gaol museum artfully explores the legend of Ned Kelly to question the state's reliance on specialized knowledge in pinpointing dangerousness. Moreover, curators use the Kelly gang as a cultural device to activate ethnic—and class—tensions between the predominately British settlers and the Irish who descended from transported convicts (see Hughes, 1986). That power play has all the markings of colonialism, on the one hand, and resistance, on the other, thereby polarizing tourists as they are forced to choose sides.

EIGHT

Colonialism and Resistance

Transportation, as examined in previous chapters, became the means for establishing a penal colony in Australia. Taken further, many of its advocates assumed that such an ambitious project would re-create the antipodes into a Western outpost for the British Empire (Finnane, 1997; Hughes, 1986). That twin narrative is recited at the Hyde Park Barracks in Sydney; however, the museum is careful to describe colonialism alongside its limitations as well as resistance. Turning attention to "Aboriginal Sydney," the exhibit portrays the indigenous people as visible, active, and even engaging. Aboriginals milled freely among the townsfolk and "spoke to everyone with an air of 'friendliness and equality.'" Still, there were attempts to impose order and "civilize" Aboriginals, most notably, through Governor Macquarie's Proclamation in 1816 that offered them "protection and inducements of land grants to abandon their distinctive way of life." That dream of order went largely unrealized as the Aboriginals "shunned servitude, along with European clothing and housing." They governed themselves under Aboriginal law, and held great contests in Hyde Park as late as the 1820s (see Colbung, 1979; Gelder and Jacobs, 1998).

Compared to the discussion at the Hyde Park Barracks, the topic of colonialism and resistance at the Melbourne Gaol has a darker tone. As mentioned in chapter 7, the protocol of hanging reveals efforts to modernize capital punishment. That narrative, retrospectively, is placed in the context of ethnic tensions and social control. The first executions of prisoners held at the Melbourne Gaol involved "Bob" and "Jack." Their stories are complicated for several reasons: among them, they were Aboriginal, and their hangings did not go smoothly. "Early European settlers in isolated districts," reads a placard, "lived in constant fear of an Aboriginal uprising. When five

Aborigines shot two whalers at Cape Patterson in 1841, an example was made of them." At their trial, the judge declared: "The punishment that awaits you is not one of vengeance but of terror . . . to deter similar transgressions." They were hanged publicly as several thousand people curiously watched. One observer called it an "appalling, disgusting, execrable scene": "The execution was a bungled affair. The drop did not open properly under Jack, and John Davies, the Colony's first executioner, took him back on to the scaffold while repairs were carried out. Bob and Jack died slowly, writhing convulsively while the local Aborigines looked on from a distance." Delving into the controversies over colonialism and resistance, we demonstrate how many museums studied herein use the prison as a cultural vehicle to explain the role of punishment in social control (see Jacobs, 1996; Sibley, 1995). Correspondingly, those exhibits adopt a clear pedagogy aimed at teaching visitors that in the end, virtues such as justice and equality ultimately prevail over repression and cruelty. Discussion begins with critical reflection on Hong Kong and the waning influence of British colonialism. On a similar plane, the Seodaemun Prison History Hall delivers a painful lesson on Japanese Imperialism, describing in fierce detail the independence movement and its cherished Korean figures. The next stop is Alcatraz. The Rock's history involves banishment for early native tribal leaders as well as the reclaiming of the island by members of the American Indian campaign in the 1970s. The chapter concludes with a return to South Africa, where penal institutions in Johannesburg and on Robben Island became instrumental in enforcing apartheid, only to succumb to the force of freedom.

BREAKING FROM THE BRITISH IN HONG KONG

The Hong Kong Correctional Services Museum gives visitors a good sense of its colonial past as it moved through key historical eras. Along the way, we see evidence of Hong Kong and its prison apparatus breaking from British governance, becoming increasingly independent both politically and culturally. Entering the premises, tourists are greeted by a large blue placard titled "Stanley Prison." The text, written first in Chinese and then in English, reads: "In the 1930s, the Hong Kong Government commissioned S. C. Feltham, an architect from England, to design and build a modernized prison to alleviate the overcrowding problem of Victoria Prison." With its "state-of-the-art" architecture, the new prison became recognized as "one of the most phenomenal buildings in the territory." The institution contained six cellblocks with eighty-two cells on each of its three tiers. Each cell was fitted with a window to maximize healthy ventilation. The "well-equipped" prison included a hospital block and, in the tradition of the English penitentiary, a unit for condemned prisoners, a hanging gallows, and a flogging shelf. Stepping closer to the building's entrance, one can admire the large (replica of the) Stanley Prison Bell as it sits elevated on a concrete mantle surrounded by a wreath of trimmed shrubbery. The caption explains that the original bell was cast by John Warner & Sons Ltd. in London (in 1895) and was used as a fire alarm in the Stanley Prison. So as to suggest that the bell has a living memory, it "is still polished daily to show its gleaming brass."

Inside the lobby, a large wall-sized poster lists the "Vision, Mission and Values" of the correctional service. With this introduction, curators establish a contemporary narrative about a progressive Chinese society. Visitors might notice a bit of claims making as the sign boasts that the "internationally acclaimed" correctional service helps Hong Kong be one of the safest cities in the world by protecting the public and reducing crime. Those messages on security are coupled with statements underscoring a humane, ethical, moral, decent, harmonious, and healthy environment for people in custody. Perhaps referring to Hong Kong as a postcolonial society, the poster states: "We respect the dignity of all people with emphasis on fairness and empathy." Nearby another sign boasts the slogan "Support Offender Rehabilitation for a Safer and More Inclusive Society."

Visitors might wonder why the museum goes to great lengths to describe the correctional service as committed to the humane treatment of offenders, that is, until they enter the first gallery. There the brutality of the colonial system is put on display. A placard warns us that the exhibits may be disturbing. As discussed in previous chapters, the collection includes graphic images of beheadings as well as the actual instruments of corporal punishment (e.g., canes, cat-o'-nine-tails, and the crank). Several photographs show criminals placed on public view: a large board hangs from each of their heads with a detailed description of their offense. Those photographs also reveal the expanse of the British Empire as soldiers from India are charged with supervising the Chinese offenders (see figure 22). In many instances, those images include British military officers standing in the distance, keeping an eye on both the Indians and the Chinese.

In reading the fine detail of the captions, visitors will recognize a deliberate departure from colonial punitive practices. A small placard next to the

十九世紀八十年代，兩名犯人在印籍獄吏的監管下，掛著罪狀遊街示眾。
Two criminals were displayed on the street with boards illustrating clearly their
offences under the supervision of an Indian staff in the 1880s

FIGURE 22. A photograph (c. 1880s) showing two Chinese lawbreakers secured in wooden stocks with boards describing their crimes at the Hong Kong Correctional Services Museum. British authorities recruited soldiers from India to supervise the public spectacle. © retrowelch 2014

flogging triangle explains: "In 1990, the then Corporal Punishment Ordinance (Chapter 222, Law of Hong Kong) was repealed as stipulated in Government Gazette No. 72 of 1990 issue." Hence, even in the gallery containing objects and imagery of brutality, one exits the room with a sense of progressive reform in Hong Kong (which was vacated by the British in 1997).

The adjoining corridor is lined with a series of portraits of former and present heads of the correctional service. The presentation is clearly intended to honor those who presided over the prison system; still, the "walk through history" demonstrates how the governance was transferred from the British to the local Chinese. The first photograph features Captain William Caine, who served from 1841 until 1858. His military attire, bushy mustache, and sword handle speak to the early Victorian period. Next in line is Francis

Henry May, CMG (1897–1902), whose military accomplishments are conveyed through a patch of heavy medals. Similarly, Cuthbert James Norman (1953–68) boasts a highly decorated uniform. Moreover, his portrait suggests a deeper symbol of authority and discipline, as a baton is shown tucked under his arm. Gilbert Roy Pickett, ISO (1968–72), stands out as the only administrator not pictured in military attire; rather, he sports a modest business suit, looking more like a banker than a prison warden. In the next photograph Thomas Gerald Garner, CBE, JP (1972–85), is shown in a military uniform but with a casual look, since he is not wearing a tie and his collar is wide open. CHAN Wa-shek, CBE, ISO, JP (1985–90), is noticeable for being the first Chinese in charge of the correctional service. Like Garner's, his collar is open and his demeanor is friendly. Visitor might notice that CHAN's photograph is an action shot—albeit one that is a bit contrived. He is pictured at a desk doing paper work, thereby projecting an air of confidence and competence. The presence of the British endures in the photograph of Frederic Samuel McCosh, OBE, QMP, CPM, JP (1990–95), whose military attire is decidedly formal. From 1995 onward, the heads of the correctional service are Chinese (i.e., LAI, Ming-kee, SBS, MBE, JP; NG Ching-kwok, SBS, MBE, QMP, CPM, JP; KWOK Leung-ming, SBS, CSDSM; SIM Yat-kin, CSDSM). Much like those of their early British counterparts, the uniforms of the Chinese leaders are heavily decorated.

In a series of galleries, the history of prisons in Hong Kong is chronicled in five major periods: the Victorian Era, the War Years, the Postwar Era, the Changing Era, and the Rehabilitation Era. A large poster announces that on April 30, 1841, Captain William Caine was appointed as the chief magistrate and superintendent of Gaol (Prison) and Police of Hong Kong by the Victoria Regime of the British Government. That year, the Victoria Gaol (later renamed Prison) was built as the Hong Kong population swelled to fifteen thousand. That growth was coupled with an increase in crime, gang robberies, and piracies on the high seas. Nearly five hundred prisoners were admitted to the Victoria Gaol in its first two years of operation, and by 1862, 650 convicts were under lock and key. To alleviate overcrowding at the Victoria Gaol, 280 long-term prisoners were relocated to a ship's hulk (a former sailing vessel) known as the *Royal Saxon*. So as to keep pace with the booming prison census, the colonial government opened the newly built Stanley Prison in 1937, housing fifteen hundred convicts.

Under British governance, the prison system followed an official ordinance set forth in 1853. Precisely the manner by which the institution would be run was dictated by a regularly published report known as the *Hongkong Government Gazette*. On display is an issue of the *Gazette* dated March 13, 1869. Under the banner headline is the subtitle "Published by Authority" along with the name of the colonial secretary, J. Gardiner Austin. By design, the document appears to have a direct—and legitimate—connection to the British Parliament, which presided over colonial policies. The admission data of prisoners processed into the Victoria Prison is catalogued according to "Europeans, Chinese & Colored." Likewise, their diets were determined by race. The *Gazette* lists the daily rations for each "European or White Prisoners" alongside those for "Chinese or Colored Prisoners." As evidence by those details, the white convicts were afforded better food than their non-white counterparts, such as bread, beef (or pork) without bone, and potatoes or vegetables. By contrast, Chinese and Colored prisoners were given rice, vegetables (one day per week), and salt fish. By drawing attention to nutrition according to race, curators seem to be reminding us that colonialism goes beyond matters of territory, encompassing its subjects and their bodies as well as their health (see Bosworth and Flavin, 2007). Also exhibited are vintage locks and keys used in the Victoria Prison in the late 1800s. Perhaps intended to enhance the museum effect, those objects are carefully arranged in a display case whose shadowy illumination creates a haunting presence. Similarly, a black-and-white photograph (1891) shows Hong Kong's mountain peak with English-style buildings at its foot. Despite attempts to familiarize the landscape with "dreams of England," the overall tone of the image casts the island as an exotic—even eerie—place, far away from the hustle and bustle of central London (see Taylor, 2000; Tilly, 1994).

In the section covering the War Years, visitors are shown evidence of the shifting tide of imperial rule. During the Japanese occupation of Hong Kong in World War II, Stanley prison was converted into an internment camp. A photograph from 1945 shows sixteen European prisoners of war lined up for a group shot. In nothing but shorts, their bodies are noticeably scrawny and malnourished due to unhealthy meals. The exhibit, however, strikes an optimistic chord by displaying correspondence from prisoners, particularly a cable message from Mr. T. A. Hughes (1899–1982), who was held in the Stanley Internment Camp in 1943. The telegram reads "CHINS UP CHEERIO—HUGHES." Another picture features the Liberation Flag Raising Ceremony that was held on August 31, 1945, inside the internment camp. Crowds of people fill the grounds, the windows, and the balconies as well as the tops of roofs as they celebrate the return of the Union Jack. A poster explains that by 1946 the prison system, once again operating under British authority, resumed its commitment to modern penology, including classification, segregation, and differentiated treatment programs.

The Postwar Era presented the Hong Kong prison system with more geopolitical challenges. A storyboard explains that in the wake of the establishment of the People's Republic of China in 1949, a huge mass of mainland Chinese flowed into Hong Kong. That demographic shift also brought about social and economic problems, including a steep rise in drug-related offenses. Compounding matters, disturbances broke out in October 1956; as a result, more than three thousand rioters were sent to Chatham Camp prison. Soon other prisons were opened to deal with the influx of inmates, namely, Chimawan Prison (1956) and Tai Lam (1958). Amid widespread disorder, however, those institutions were not designed to be punitive per se. As shown in a photograph, the prisoners at Chimawan were assigned to public works, such as afforestation, road making, and other projects for the benefit of the local community. At Tai Lam, an ambitious drug-addiction treatment center was unveiled. Elsewhere, training centers for young offenders were set up. Then in 1967, a major riot resulted in mass arrests, sending an additional 1,779 citizens to prison: "Once again, the prison service was responsible for undertaking the uphill task of accommodating a massive group of prisoners to enable the safety of community not to be disturbed." In terms of administrative leadership, the gallery includes pictures of both Chinese and European officers (i.e., Mr. WU Chun-Keung, Mr. Zajic, and Mr. McDonald). Also on display are some interesting objects that give visitors some clues to surveillance. For instance, each cell was equipped with a "supervising door hole cover" that allowed the guards to keep an eye on the prisoners. Similarly, their correspondence was monitored. Inside a glass case is an authentic "Prisoners' Letters Register" (1947–48). The logbook shows handwritten entries that record which prisoner received mail and the name and address of the person who sent it.

The exhibit then visits Hong Kong's Changing Era. At the onset, curators describe how conflict elsewhere adversely affects the city and its prison system:

The civil war of Vietnam taken place during the 1960s and 1970s had created astounding impact on Hong Kong. For the next two decades, around 203,000 Vietnamese refugees and boat people abandoned their homeland and swamped into Hong Kong. New camps run by the Prisons Department/

Correctional Services Department were opened to accommodate such huge amount of foreign population. The sudden strain imposed enormous demand as prison staff had to be redeployed from normal duties to cope with the continued influx of boat people.

In 1973, another riot broke out: this time inside Stanley Prison. An actual news clip describes the event. Below the banner headline, "New Violence in Stanley: Armed Squads Quell Rioters," the story tells us that all 2,391 prisoners were placed under lock down as jail sirens activated patrols of officers—armed with batons and shields—who shot tear gas and scaled the cellblock with a long fireman's ladder. Action photographs that verify the commotion accompany the text. The lengthy article includes quotations from a convict spokesman who stated their demands:

Better TV facilities, with longer hours of viewing.

Better food.

Abandonment by prison authorities of new search system aimed at finding smuggled narcotics.

Prison officials blamed the riot on "young violent criminals on the cell block . . . [who] always wanted to make trouble and think up excuses."

In the aftermath, the entire department's administration was restructured. Among the new policies was a detailed inmate classification system that still exists today. Moreover, prison leadership stepped up its commitment to drug rehabilitation, vocational training, prison industries, nursing, and after-care service. To carry out those programs, the prison system recruited correctional professionals and specialists. Documenting those moves, the museum has on display a *1982 Legal Supplement to the Hong Kong Government Gazette (Published by Authority)* announcing a change of title for the Hong Kong Prisons Department, renamed the Hong Kong Correctional Services Department.

The last installment in this section of the tour focuses on the Rehabilitation Era. Here visitors are given another round of rhetoric on the importance of humane treatment for prisoners. A placard is quick to point out that in 1981, "Prison Rules" banned corporal punishment as well as the practice of imposing food rations as a form of discipline . . . The old days of plain rice and water were over. Also there was the liberalization of restrictions on how many letters an inmate could receive and send. Nonetheless, the exhibit recognizes that prison staff—even with rehabilitation as its thrust—should "not lose sight of the basic responsibility of keeping dangerous prisoners under secure custody." A display case holds two items of interest. Underscoring the theme of surveillance, the first object is a servise recorder. Looking like a large stopwatch, the device is used to facilitate the "head count" of prisoners. The caption states: "Patrol staff shall visit the area under his charge, peg the servise recorder by using the pegging pin once an interval at the specific time. Note: The Day Orderly Officer will certify the Servise Recorder card after checking." As a remnant of the Victorian era, the other object is a large crown-shaped emblem of "Her Majesty's Prisons" from the old headquarter at Arbuthnot Road.

Moving into the next gallery, "Inside Prisons," visitors are introduced to an eclectic collection of images and objects so as to provide a glimpse of Hong Kong's penal world. Still, much of the early stage of the exhibit maintains themes of reform reaching back to mid-nineteenth-century Britain. According to a poster: "In the past, the work of a prisoner was mostly pointless and non-productive. It was aimed at instilling discipline, work habits and obedience, as outlined by the 1865 Prison Act in England." The text emphasizes that over time, work became a method to develop skills that may lead convicts to useful careers upon release. Beyond that rather brief description, the gallery relies on a series of action photographs to reinforce notions of transformation. In the first picture, several convicts are seen breaking rocks under the watchful eye of a prison guard. The caption explains that such punishment was abolished in 1992. The next image shows inmates at Pik Uk Correctional Institution learning how to repair television sets. Standing at attention just a few steps away is a Chinese prison guard, thereby suggesting that even vocational training demands strict surveillance. Interestingly, on the wall in the background is a display titled "Guilds of London," perhaps a holdover from the colonial regime. Next is a curious photograph of a British prison officer standing over a Chinese convict working at a sewing machine. Rather than conveying themes of rehabilitation, the image might strike some viewers as being authoritarian, since the officer seems to be holding a set of large keys in one hand while the other is pointing at the inmate. Moreover, the prisoner is not even wearing a shirt. Altogether, the scene looks more like an Asian sweatshop than a modern correctional institution.

The room contains other objects that, albeit retrospectively, suggest control. Perhaps catching visitors by surprise is an "Electro-Convulsive Therapy Apparatus" that was employed in the 1960s in Siu Lam Psychiatric Centre. Although the caption explains that the equipment delivered treatment for prisoners suffering from severe depressive disorder, the actual machine appears reminiscent of the controversial British movie *A Clockwork Orange* (1971). In that film, an inmate is subjected to a horrific form of behavioral conditioning. Looking closer at the device on display, one will notice the daunting "waveform" knobs and various flip switches on the "DUOPULSE E.C.T. APPARATUS (made in England, Etron LTD)." Placed next to the Electro-Convulsive Therapy Apparatus is a logbook from the Psychiatric Centre with handwritten entries (in English) by the medical officer alongside an "Application for Transfer Order" certifying the inmate to be mentally disordered. In tandem, those items speak to the power of expert knowledge in the social control of a marginalized population (see Foucault, 1973, 1980a). The narrative of "Inside Prisons" concludes with more upbeat messages on the importance of prisoner reform. Still, one cannot help but detect the lingering influences of the strict colonial regime. A four-panel montage features photographs of obedient inmates. Each image is identified by a single key word: Supervision, Discipline, Guidance, Order.

Tourists at the museum are then navigated toward a stairwell that is decorated with an enormous photograph. The group shot includes staff at the Victoria Prison (1880). Seated front and center—as symbols of power—are the British administrators (one civilian, two military). Behind them, standing on the steps of the prison, are rows of British officers and custodial personnel. In the far back are Indian officers, thereby giving even greater significance to the reach of the British Empire. The picture also includes Chinese men dressed in traditional clothing. But unlike the British and Indian officers who represent colonial authority, the Chinese seem more like servants; indeed, some of them are sitting on the ground with their legs crossed. Once upstairs, visitors are given more evidence of colonialism and cultural identities, most noticeably in an exhibition on prison staff uniforms. In another "walk through history," we gaze at a series of quasi-military outfits dating back to the mid-twentieth century. Inside glass cabinets, life-size mannequins pose somewhat aloofly, thereby enhancing their sense of importance. That slight distance seems to allow visitors to get close to those symbols of colonial power without having actual contact. In terms of ethnicity, each of the mannequins (male and female) has a distinctly "Western" look, with one exception. In the corner, there is a mannequin dressed in Indian military attire. At first glance, the ensemble of mannequins looks more like one in an upscale department store; however, at a deeper level of interpretation, they are not mere fashion models, but rather models of sophisticated colonial rule.

Those three-dimensional objects give way to flat—one-dimensional—photographs of Chinese officers wearing contemporary prison staff uniforms. Still, there is something more authentic about those images. Taken further, those current depictions of the Hong Kong prison personnel seem to reject the pretense of colonial power.

The tour concludes with exhibitions on staff events and overseas cooperation. As opposed to a hierarchical trajectory of power embodied in colonialism, there is an effort to show the new Hong Kong correctional system as part of a larger campaign for community service. In numerous brightly colored photographs, correctional administrators and staff are seen participating in an array of activities (e.g., blood donation drives, volunteer programs for the elderly, the Special Olympics, and other charitable events). The Hong Kong Correctional Service also boasts its membership in regional organizations. A large plaque is dedicated to the 23rd Asian and Pacific Conference of Correctional Administrators (2003). The Hong Kong emblem joins a lengthy list of other delegates, including Australia, China, Japan, and Vietnam. Compared to the early days of harsh colonial rule, contemporary Hong Kong projects a spirit of equality and cooperation. At least, that is the impression that visitors might form as a result of touring the Hong Kong Correctional Services Museum.

KOREAN FIGHTERS FOR INDEPENDENCE

As its raison d'être, the Seodaemun Prison History Hall probes the dialectics of imperialism and resistance. In this very place, according to the brochure, independence activists were jailed and martyred. Visitors are quickly met with a series of storyboards that reinforce the museum's overall theme, beginning with the one titled "A Symbol of Oppression and Terror, Seodaemun Prison." It explains that the institution was initially operated by the Japanese to suppress Korean patriotism; later, under Korean rule, the prison held pro-democracy activists who challenged the despotic regime. A poster shows an illustration of the city gate (at Street No. 101 of Hyeonjeo-dong) in front of the Seodaemun Prison. The caption informs us that "Japanese imperialists installed a large-size prison around that area as a tool for ruling the colony." By the 1930s, the prison was greatly expanded due to a rapid influx of Korean resistance fighters. Visitors can gaze at a detailed model of the prison with its spoke-and-hub design, reminiscent of Haviland's blueprint for Eastern State

Penitentiary in Philadelphia (see chapter 4). Two-tone photographs of inmates accompany a placard labeled "Huge prison, Colony." It goes on to explain that the "Japanese imperialists" established so many prisons in the main cities on the Korean peninsula that it transformed the country into one big prison. A map dotted with prison sites helps us visualize the span of the colonial project. That imagery is also used in a montage titled "Invasive Inroads of Imperialism," as pictures reveal the wide-scale destruction of the Korean cities.

The tour segues into three consecutive galleries collectively named the National Resistance Hall. A red poster with the heading "National Resistance Independence Movement" captures key events. We learn that despite the forcible annexation of Korea by the Japanese in 1910, the Korean people never relinquished. The movement spawned a steady stream of attacks, many of which were orchestrated by the "Righteous Army's War of Resistance." Along with a group shot of Korean soldiers (wearing uniforms resembling Taekwondo), a poster notes: "The Righteous Army in the Joseon dynasty was raised in many places across the country to fight against a series of Japanese invasions. Their loyal spirit was inherited by the independence activists as an ideological background, and motive rushing forward for the restoration of sovereignty." A "Map for Nationwide Uprisings of the Righteous Army" pinpoints the strategic coordinates throughout the Korean peninsula. In a carefully lit display case, an original "Report on the Arrest of Generals of Righteous Armies" gives visitors a glimpse into the record keeping of the movement. To commemorate the "martyred" generals of the Righteous Army, there are several portraits of those executed by Japanese forces (see chapter 9). Visitors are then drawn to another cabinet containing a sword, perhaps symbolizing the honor of battle. Next to the sword, another object seems to speak to the ingenuity of resistance: it is also a sword but it is disguised in a sheath shaped in the form of a cane. Together, both weapons represent the importance of overt as well as covert rebellion against the Japanese occupiers.

Along those lines of inquiry, the exhibit investigates matters of espionage and repression. For instance, in 1910 the Japanese rulers concocted charges that a Korean brigade was plotting to assassinate the governor-general, thereby leading to the arrest of more than 160 Korean patriots. The event became known as the Anak Incident. Among those detained were members of the Sinmin-hoe (New People Society). Soon thereafter, the Japanese targeted the Sinmin-hoe as alleged conspirators, imprisoning another 105 patri-

FIGURE 23. A hood used by the Japanese occupiers to cover the head of a Korean political prisoner (Seodaemun Prison History Hall, Seoul). © retrowelch 2014

ots at Seodaemun Prison. The controversy is remembered as the 105 Person Incident. Staged in the center of the gallery is a tall display case standing nearly seven feet tall. It contains a hood used to cover the head of a prisoner (see figure 23). Without any caption, curators seem to be telling us that the hood represents attempts to silence and cover up the resistance. Nearby another cabinet holds two pairs of handcuffs and a set of shackles, thereby maintaining themes of coercion and even slavery. In the background, a wall is decorated with photographs of Korean patriots. As they stare blankly into our eyes, we can only imagine the horrific treatment they suffered at the hands of the Japanese occupiers. Next, a storyboard features a brightly colored illustration showing an explosion with bodies being thrown from the blast. The caption states: "The 'Heroic Struggle' was adopted as a strategic methodology to push forward the recovery of Korea's national sovereignty. Their tactic was to target Japanese figures and pro-Japanese Koreans with violence. As a result, the Japanese imperialists suffered some heavy blows." Violent resistance is underscored in another poster titled "Anti-Japanese Associations." It explains that the Korean independence activists organized locally and abroad, collecting funds to support the struggle, including attacks on Japanese police and military. Those groups also planned and carried out assassinations.

Widespread resistance culminated in general strikes. In 1929, more than three thousand laborers launched the nation's largest anti-Japanese protest, paralyzing the city of Wonsan for eighty days. The storyboard tells us that the full-scale strike proved to be successful against the "Japanese capitalists." Another related exhibit commemorates the Joseon Communist Party's Rehabilitation Movement. Carefully partitioned, the display stands apart from the rest of the gallery, looking more like a shrine. The headline draws attention to an organization named "Gyeongseong Troika." That group formed in 1933 as an effort to rebuild the Joseon Communist Party, which had been dissolved in 1928. The collective of students, workers, and farmers banded together to defeat Japanese rule. "However, the imperialists chased, arrested and sent about 120 people to Seodaemun Prison in 1934."

Visitors at Seodaemun Prison History Hall are likely to discover a significant theme threaded through this portion of the tour, namely, the promotion—and subsequent repression—of Korean culture. A placard introduces us to the Suyangdongu-hoe (Character-Building Friends Society), which was founded in 1926. The group was committed to "social and cultural improvement," only to be targeted by the Japanese police in 1937. Although the courts cleared those suspected of espionage in 1940, the four-year trial kept many of them in prison, where they were tortured. Some died during their imprisonment. Other activists resorted to shortwave broadcasting to dispense prodemocracy propaganda, including the "Voice of America." In 1942, the Japanese detected the transmissions and detained another 150 Koreans. Similarly, a monthly Korean Christian magazine *(Seongseo-Joseon)* founded in 1927 and published in Japan was shut down for printing an article criticizing the Japanese government. Also in 1942, the Japanese imperialists arrested thirty-three Korean Hangeul scholars belonging to the Joseon-eohakhoe (Korean

Language Society) for distributing Korean script with the aim to encourage national and ethnic identity. Indeed, dating back to 1910, resistance fighters were committed to preserving the Korean language as the occupiers moved to liquidate the local culture and replace it with Japanese traditions. A large placard titled "Ideological Conversion Education for Prisoners" informs us that "the Japanese carefully elaborated and implemented custom-made schemes fit for each individual in an attempt to convert Koreans to imperialism. Those who were better behaved were given lighter sentences by the Japanese." Photographs show the conversion programs taking place in classrooms and huge auditoriums as well as in the prison yard with thousands of inmates arranged in rows and columns. Totalitarianism in action might be the prevailing impression.

This portion of the tour does not, however, conclude on a defeated note. On the contrary, the exhibit celebrates the resistance as a successful prodemocracy movement. A final message informs visitors: "After 36 years of hardship Korea was liberated on August 15, 1945. Koreans came to power and took over the government. Seodaemun Prison was a symbol of the 80-year journey to freedom. Now, the site has been reborn and Seodaemun Prison History Hall [echoes] to the world the invaluable importance of freedom and peace."

AMERICAN INDIANS AT ALCATRAZ

As mentioned previously in our discussion on the banishment, Alcatraz—much like Robben Island—exiled indigenous people, namely, members of the Hopi, Apache, and Modoc tribes, during the Indian wars of the mid- to late nineteenth century (Golden Gate National Parks Conservancy, 1996). Today, visitors to the Rock have an opportunity to learn more about the struggles of the American Indians. Eagerly waiting to deboard the ferry, we scan an imposing sign covering the front of the barracks:

UNITED STATES PENITENTIARY
ALCATRAZ ISLAND AREA 12 ACRES
1 1/2 MILES TO TRANSPORT DOCK
ONLY GOVERNMENT BOATS PERMITTED
OTHERS MUST KEEP OFF 200 YARDS
NO ONE ALLOWED ASHORE
WITHOUT A PASS

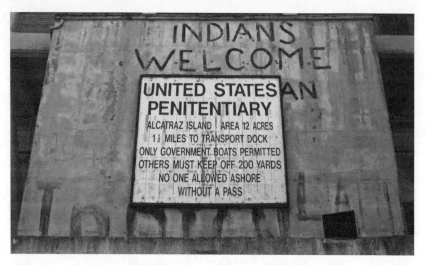

FIGURE 24. An official government sign scrawled with Native American graffiti (c. late 1960s) greeting visitors stepping onto Alcatraz Island. © retrowelch 2014

In the background of the warning is large red graffiti: "INDIANS WELCOME" (see figure 24). The message dates back to the late 1960s when Native Americans reclaimed the island, six years after the Federal Bureau of Prisons closed the prison. In the face of more than a century of governmental silence on the plight of the American Indians, curators at Alcatraz invite tourists to engage in some worthwhile conversation on the subject. Still standing on the dock, we view a photograph (c. 1969) of a teepee with the San Francisco skyline in the distance. The caption quotes Richard Oakes (Mohawk), Indian Occupation spokesman: "It would be fitting and symbolic that ships from all over the world entering the Golden Gate would first see Indian land, and thus be reminded of the true history of this nation."

Once inside the exhibit hall, visitors step into a gallery titled "We Hold the Rock: The Indian Occupation of Alcatraz, 1969–1971." An entire wall is covered with a group shot photograph (c. 1970) of American Indians crowded inside the main corridor of the former penitentiary. The picture seems to capture a moment of both newfound solidarity and defiance. Again, the words of Richard Oakes are superimposed: "This is the beginning of our fight for justice and self-determination." Visitors are welcome to sit on a bench and watch four different videos that describe the American Indian Movement as it unfolded at Alcatraz. Deepening the scholarly narrative, a detailed storyboard chronicles the main developments in the occupation of Alcatraz. It reminds us that when seventy-nine young Indian men, women, and children arrived on the island on November 20, 1969, they took a firm stand against "broken treaties, broken promises, and broken lives suffered by America's native people since the arrival of European explorers in the fifteenth century." Those occupiers were soon joined by hundreds more who held the Rock for nineteen months in a nonviolent act that quickly sparked a national dialogue on the rights of indigenous people. The exhibit reaches out to tourists, urging them to "experience the occupation through the eyes of those who were there."

With a pedagogical format, the poster begins with a section titled "Before the Occupation." When the Europeans reached North America in the fifteenth century, the land was populated by a wide variety of tribal groups with languages, traditions, stories, and practices. As more and more Europeans arrived, competition for land and resources resulted in the native people being "overpowered and forced to conform to the needs of larger society." Sharing a contemporary perspective, the text quotes Wilma Mankiller (Cherokee): "We're still doing ceremonies and having dances we've had since the beginning of time. After all that's happened to us, it really is a revolutionary act for our people to step out on the ceremonial grounds and dance." That uplifting message deflates a bit as we read the next passage on Indian boarding schools. In bold print, the poster quotes the bigoted words of Richard H. Pratt, captain, US Army: "The only good Indian is a dead one ... Kill the Indian in him and save the man." Pratt was also the first superintendent of the Carlisle Boarding School (Pennsylvania), where Indian youths were forced to abandon their native identity. The official program used government agents to remove children (some as young as five) from their families, often without consent. From then, the youth were denied tribal affiliations and not allowed to speak their native language or follow their religious rituals. It was not uncommon for the youth to go two years between visits from their families. A pair of photographs that show three Indian youth establishes a before-and-after effect. The first photograph shows the children in traditional Indian dress (with feathers in their long hair). The next picture has them posing as "Europeanized" school boys with Western suits and short, cropped hair.

Similarly, the topic of land rights is raised but also with an unfavorable tone. We are reminded that due to westward expansion, Indians were moved from their ancestral homelands and settled on reservations. Then in the

1950s, the government began breaking up those reservations in an attempt to seize the land. That "urbanization" initiative relocated more than one hundred thousand Native Americans to large cities (e.g., Cleveland, Dallas, Denver, Phoenix, and San Francisco): "The government basically said 'We are going to get out of the Indian business.' By 1969, 106 reservations, rancherias, and bands of Indians had already been terminated," explained Adam Fortunate Eagle (Red Lake Chippewa). It was in those cities, ironically, that members of the Indian diaspora found one another, forming communities and organizations that would align with African-American, Chicano, and Asian groups. That "Third World Coalition," LaNada Boyer (Shoshone-Bannock) boasts, went on strike at the University of California, Berkeley, in 1968.

When the penitentiary at Alcatraz closed in 1963, the federal government classified the land as "surplus," leaving it under the management of the General Services Administration. For years, the city of San Francisco deliberated over plans to reinvent the island, including a proposal to create a commercial theme park to celebrate space exploration. Bay Area Indians, such as Adam Fortunate Eagle, noticed "that little spot in the water" with all those buildings standing empty: "And we have nothing." Predating the major occupation of 1969, other symbolic acts served to link the "surplus" Alcatraz with the history of the indigenous people. In 1964, five Sioux Indians boarded a charter boat and landed on the island. They claimed the land under a Sioux treaty from 1868 that entitled Indians to take possession of land unused by the federal authorities. After making their point, they returned to the mainland. Similar protests put Alcatraz in the backdrop of the struggle for Native American land—and cultural—rights. The full-scale occupation took hold on November 20, 1969, lasting for nineteen months. The group, calling itself the Indians All Tribes, continued to invoke history to communicate the enduring story of the native people. Leaders of the intertribal cooperation offered to buy Alcatraz from the federal government for twenty-four dollars (in beads, colored cloth, and other trade goods), thereby drawing a parallel to the purchase of Manhattan Island (New York City) in 1626. Their rhetoric was intended to raise awareness of the Indian reservations. For instance, in "The Proclamation to the Great White Father and All His People," the group stated that Alcatraz reminded them of the reservations because "it is isolated from modern facilities, the soil is rocky and unproductive, and the land does not support game" (Golden Gate National Parks Conservancy, 1996: n.p.).

Others weighed in on the controversy: "Alcatraz was perfect for Indians, since it already had the hallmarks of reservation land: no health care, no modern plumbing, no schools, no industry or jobs and very poor soil" (McHugh, 2007: 48). The charismatic Richard Oakes proclaimed that "Alcatraz is not an island but an idea" (48). In turn, the media coverage and public opinion were favorable to the American Indian Movement at Alcatraz. Celebrities, including Marlon Brando, Jane Fonda, and rock band Creedence Clearwater Revival, joined the cause.

But like many progressive campaigns, attention eventually turned elsewhere. The occupation struggled to raise the funds and buy the supplies needed to sustain the island's Indian community. Infighting, vandalism, and the theft of island infrastructure by less idealistic members contributed to the demise of the community. Then in what is described as a one-two-three punch, Alcatraz ceased to be a viable refuge for American Indians and their values. First, the government towed away the island's water supply. Next fires swept through the warden's house, the lighthouse keeper's quarters, and other structures: the occupiers and the government blamed each other for the blaze. Then two tankers collided in the Golden Gate strait, spilling oil into the bay. Many speculated that if the lighthouse had still been fully functioning, the collision of the freighters might have been averted (McHugh, 2007: 48). By then, the general optimism that had initially spawned a utopian alternative to an otherwise exploitive American culture was exhausted. On June 10, 1971, federal agents cleared Alcatraz of any remaining activists. In spirit with the movement, Adam Fortunate Eagle in his book *Alcatraz! Alcatraz!* reminisced that the lasting effect of the occupation was an upsurge in Indian pride throughout the nation.

Perhaps prophetically, Richard Oakes initially proposed in 1969 that Alcatraz be converted into a museum (for Native American culture). Not too far off the mark, throngs of tourists visit the island daily. While the former prison is still the major draw, visitors can gain deeper insight into the history of colonization and the resistance it creates. Located on the edge of the island is the original water tower, which underwent renovation to restore its original form. A large poster outlines the Alcatraz Historic Water Tower Stabilization project. Among its goals was to document and restore Native American graffiti. In 2012, the National Park Service unveiled the rebuilt water tower with bold red letters reading, "Peace and Freedom. Welcome. Home of the Free Indian Land" (Wollan, 2012). Those symbols of defiance promise to give visitors an added level of awareness of the island's complicated story (see Loo and Strange, 2000).*

STRUGGLE AGAINST APARTHEID

As observed in chapter 4, the story of colonialism and resistance is embodied at the Old Fort in Johannesburg, which was built by the Boer Zuid Afrikaansche Republiek in 1882. The military installation also served as a jail aimed at controlling not only the nonwhite population but also the *uitlanders* (foreigners, mostly English-speaking immigrants) that were considered to be a threat to the Boer government. Although the Boers survived the Jameson Raid by the British in 1896, they would later surrender in 1900. Shortly thereafter, the Old Fort became a prison complex for enforcing a racially segregated society. With the exception of Nelson Mandela, the Old Fort held white (male) prisoners as their black counterparts were confined to Number 4, the notorious section of the compound.

From the beginning, the Old Fort held political prisoners. Accordingly, they often demanded their legal rights, thereby presenting a formidable resistance to the prison authorities. By way of photographs, visitors are introduced to four famous prisoners, each of whom represented a unique threat to the establishment. First, we meet General Christiaan de Wet (1914), a Boer hero who was detained for leading the rebellion against South Africa's entry into World War I on the side of the British. In the picture, he is seated comfortably while holding a rifle in his right hand. Next is the leader of the Foster Gang, Robert Foster (1914), who was imprisoned for murder and robbery. Sporting a flashy coat and tie, Foster appears to be mugging for the photographer with a cocky grin. Dressed in more modest gentlemen's clothing is C. C. Stassen (1922), sentenced to the Old Fort prison for murder during the white Mineworker's Strike. Finally, shown working behind his desk—stacked with papers—is South African Communist Party member Joe Slovo (1960), who was detained during the state of emergency.

Of course, along the themes of resistance, the presence of Nelson Mandela looms large at the Old Fort. Much like the other prisoners just mentioned,

---

* Although the official narrative about American Indians at Alcatraz keeps focus on their attempts to reclaim the island, informed visitors might consider how the native people are currently subjected to paternalism ("for their own good") and harsh "justice" by the criminal justice system (Archambeault, 2003; Nielson, 2000; Zatz, Lujan, and Snyder-Joy, 1991).

Mandela is pictured in civilian clothes, in particular a striped pullover sweater. His bearded face suggests a casual demeanor. However, the image is dated 1962 when he was in hiding from the apartheid regime and therefore disguised as a chauffeur. A more recent photograph of Mandela shows him clean-shaven; his white hair gives off the aura of an elder statesman. The storyboard condenses an otherwise lengthy chronicle of his life. Among the high points, we are reminded that Mandela "is one of history's most extraordinary individuals ... a global icon of freedom and reconciliation." At the Old Fort is Mandela's recollection of the systemic humiliation of the "bleak, castle-like structure located on a hill in the heart of the city." Upon admission, he and the other prisoners were taken to an outdoor quadrangle and "ordered to strip completely and line up against the wall. We were forced to stand there for more than an hour, shivering in the breeze and feeling awkward—priests, professors, doctors, lawyers, businessmen, men of middle or old age, who had been accustomed to being treated with deference and respect."

Mandela's unswerving commitment to the struggle for a democratic South Africa is admired by his supporters but was reviled by the rulers of the apartheid government. As a result, he became the longest-serving political prisoner at Robben Island (and in other prisons): "On 11 June 1964, Mandela and seven of his fellow Rivonia trialists were sentenced to life imprisonment for sabotage and treason. At 1 AM the following morning, they were herded from their cell in Pretoria Central Prison onto a small plane and flown to Robben Island ... He negotiated his way out of captivity and, on 11 February 1990, he walked through the gates of the prison as a free man to assume his role as 'President-in-Waiting.'" As we shall discuss in even greater detail in the next chapter on memorialization, the narrative on Mandela—along with other antiapartheid activists—commemorates his contributions to the founding of a new, democratic South Africa. Before moving to those uplifting messages, we remain at the Old Fort museum where curators issue graphic evidence of repression, corporal punishment, and humiliation.

Though the Old Fort portion of the tour is organized around its Boer and later British architecture, there are a few items that reveal its brutal past. A large action photograph shows a white prison officer in full swing with a whip. His target is a black prisoner strapped to the flogging triangle. Upon closer inspection, viewers can detect open wounds on the shirtless back of the prisoner. With that image in mind, visitors make their way to the remote end of the prison compound known simply as Number Four. By way of a placard,

"Black People and Prison," we learn that Number Four was a part of a system of maintaining racial discrimination during the apartheid era, when "going to prison was part of everyday life for black people." Most of those behind bars were "pass violators" who were thrown together with thieves, rapists, and murderers. In 1960, one in eight members of the black population had been convicted, turning "innocent people into criminals. Some became political activists in prison." The exhibit reflects on the words of Oliver Tambo, former president of the African National Congress: "Racism, one of the great evils of our time, bedevils human relations, between individuals, within and between nations and across the continents. It brutalizes entire peoples, destroys persons, warps the process of thought and injects into human society a foul air of tension, mutual antagonism and hatred." Dating back to 1902, Number Four, known then as the Native Jail, had always been overcrowded; by 1953, more than twenty-two hundred prisoners were confined to a prison built for nine hundred. Stepping into a dark concrete room, we get a sense of its previous incarnation as a densely punitive space where dozens of prisoners slept along its floor. "Power and Punishment" headlines a sign that reads: "Number 4 was designed to punish, not rehabilitate. For the prison to function, it relied on violence. Warders used violence to maintain control. Prisoners used violence to gain power." Much like apartheid itself, the communal cells were governed by a strict hierarchy of cell bosses whose social power and status determined where other inmates slept—usually head to toe "like sardines." In a predatory manner, the cell bosses deputized their "lieutenants," authorizing them to resort to intimidation and violence against the more vulnerable prisoners, robbing them of their blankets and personal belongings. Being a political prisoner had its advantages. From a poster titled "Resistance and Resilience," we learn that because political prisoners were usually arrested (and imprisoned) in groups, they possessed a strong sense of solidarity that kept the cell bosses at bay.

Located outside are the latrines where the white warders stared at the squatting prisoners as they defecated the "long drop." Compounding the humiliation, prisoners recall, was the ubiquity of filth. In the words of Alex La Guma (political prisoner, 1956), "Filth. The mats are filthy, the utensils are filthy, the convicts' clothes are filthy. The latrines overflowed and made a stench." A related placard labeled "Strip" quotes a prisoner who remembered: "We took off our clothes and stood naked in the yard . . . The warders mocked us for the nakedness they had ordered." Curators point out that nakedness has deep cultural connotations, quoting a political prisoner: "For us, the children of the Basotho nation, we respect elderly people. A man can never undress in front of me." Switching to the point of view of a black warder, visitors gain even more insight into the ways in which degradation was racially embedded. For instance, body cavity searches demonstrated the extent to which blacks shamed one another: "Some of these people grew up with me and as a warder I did not like to make them open their anus. Sometimes it was old man in his 50s, a respectable somebody. White warders wouldn't have done it to their own people. But it was a duty that we were forced to do." Another panel of text describes punishment as a means to enforce power. At their disposal, the guards could order prisoners to wear leg irons for indefinite periods as well as assign them up to seven days of solitary confinement, twenty-one days of hard labor, and twenty-five lashings. Incidentally, the lashing frame was in operation until the mid-1980s. Over time, beatings became more arbitrary, injecting another level of fear and intimidation into an already tense atmosphere.

While much of the tour concentrates on the cruelty inside Number Four, attention also shifts to the brutality unfolding in the black townships. A sizeable collection of photographs, posters, and news clips is displayed in the courtyard of the prison. A picture as recent as 1988 shows three black teenagers posing for the camera without their shirts so as to reveal their wounded and scarred bodies (and faces) after being beaten by the police in Johannesburg. At the center of another photograph is a small child crying in agony after being sprayed by police tear gas. A graph titled "Statistics of Repression: Police Violence against Children, 1984–86" provides the following figures: three hundred killed, one thousand wounded, eleven thousand detained without trial, eighteen thousand arrested on charges arising out of protest, 173,000 held awaiting trial in police cells. The montage includes an illustration of a child inside a bull's eye, with a caption that reads: "Our children need peace, not bullets" (see chapter 10). Scenes of huge antiapartheid protests are scattered throughout the exhibit. Adding to the dense theme of resistance is a panel describing the Working for a Just Peace campaign that challenged the policy of compulsory conscription into the armed services. A somber photograph shows more than twenty young white men at a press conference standing in front of the campaign's banner; it states simply: "WE WON'T FIGHT IN THE SADF" (South African Defense Force). Nearby, a similar message quotes the End Conscription Campaign booklet, *Stop the Call Up,* from 1985: "Young men who refuse to serve are faced with the choice of a life of exile or possible six years in prison."

Resistance to racial colonization and injustice is also explored in a large exhibit on Mahatma Gandhi, who was imprisoned at Number Four for seven months and ten days between 1908 and 1913. His offense: leading the Passive Resistance Movement against pass laws for Asians and refusing to carry a pass. To be discussed in depth in the next chapter, Gandhi's dedication to civil disobedience is commemorated by displaying his personal belongings as well as his thoughtful words, such as "I have a call I must answer. I must deliver my message to my people. This humiliation has sunk too deep in me to remain without an outlet. I, at least, must act up to the light that has dawned on me." At this stage of the tour, our guide escorts us to the other end of the prison complex to visit the Women's Jail. There we see more evidence of South Africa's domination of women of color alongside the efforts to resist it.

As noted previously, the architecture of the Women's Jail—with its light-filled atrium—seems more subtle than that of Number Four, but its exercise of power and control was just as violent. That subjugation is narrated within a historical context as a placard dubbed "Coming to the City" recounts "the hardships and resistance" of thousands of black women who migrated to Johannesburg after gold was discovered in 1886. While their husbands worked in the mines, women remained in the homesteads, but eventually they began to seek work in the city. Still, employment options were limited usually to domestic service in the homes of white families. Others preferred to be self-employed in the realm of cooking, dressmaking, beer brewing, and even sexual services. In the city, those women faced a hostile and alien environment. Their very movement was restricted by a host of bewildering laws, after-dark curfews, and vagrancy statutes. Many experienced a sense of isolation and vulnerability due to low-wage work and being denied the right to join a trade union. Black women were kept under suspicion by the government, which allowed police to harass them in the streets as well as raid their homes: "Without meaning to, it was easy to break the law if you're black."

The museum at the Women's Jail organizes the tour around a series of objects on display in the atrium. Among them is the "pass book"—one of the iconic instruments and symbols of racial discrimination. A caption informs us that pass book laws were used to control black people, dictating where they could live, work, and travel. Technically, all South African citizens were required to carry their pass books at all times; however, the police selectively targeted nonwhites for inspection.* In the 1930s and 1940s, pass offenses tripled, prompting the government to legislate for more restrictions, including the Native Laws Amendment Act (1948) and the misleadingly titled Native Abolition of Passes Act (1952) aimed at "idle or undesirable natives" who could be expelled at any time. The old passes were soon replaced with a new ninety-six-page brown (or green) reference book containing extensive details related to employment, taxes, and so on. The pass book ordinances were met with resistance almost from the beginning, with black women protesting in 1913. In 1956, more than twenty thousand black women marched with signed petitions to repeal the pass book laws. Two years later, demonstrations in the city center were violently dispersed by the police, prompting even more protests. Thoko Ngoma of the Federation of South African Women (1958) recalls: "We had a procession, walking and shouting and telling all women, please let's not go to work tomorrow. Let's go to the Fort, to Number Four—once we leave here we must never expect to come back. Tomorrow we are going to sleep at Number Four." The next day, four thousand women joined the march as it moved toward the Women's Jail. Thousands were arrested, filling the jail beyond capacity. The apartheid regime responded by extending another round of pass ordinances. Arrests became routine for the next several decades as young black women were socialized to expect such harassment. "My grandmother had taught us to say goodbye every time we left home, because we never knew if we would come back or not. We used to say, 'If you don't see me, check for me at Number Four,'" said Nolundi Ntamo, a pass offender in 1980 and then repeatedly.

In the aftermath of the student uprisings in 1976, the government considered political prisoners to be particularly menacing. Under the Terrorism Act, antiapartheid activists were detained, interrogated, tortured, and placed in isolation cells furnished with two buckets: one for the toilet and the other for water. Those cells, known as "Isolasie Selle" or "Khulukuds," are on display at the Women's Jail where visitors can enter their space, which resembles a form of cold storage. Mmaguata A. Molefe, a political prisoner in 1976, is

---

* Some visitors (particularly from the United States) might see parallels between South Africa's "pass book" and the history of the "slave pass" in America's South (see Parenti, 2004). Moreover, in contemporary America, there is the "driving while black" phenomenon in which African Americans are disproportionately subjected to being stopped by police. That practice is widely regarded as inherently discriminatory and racist (see Cole, 2001; Harcourt, 2007; Russell, 2002).

shown photographed as she stood outside the cell door when she visited the jail in 2003. She tells us about her ordeal: "It was important that you didn't give up. I was thirty days pregnant when they started interrogating me. At two months I miscarried but I was never taken for treatment. You had to be strong. I became violent to them because I knew they could do whatever. I was not going to go down begging on my knees because they wanted you to incriminate yourself and other people." The use of the isolation cells extended to other prisoners held at the Women's Jail, including those who violated pass book laws as well as other codes of conduct. Consider, for instance, the story of Yvonne Ntonto Mhlauli, who was incarcerated at the Women's Jail in 1981 for violating the Immorality Amendment Act No. 21 (1950), which prohibited whites from having intercourse not only with blacks but also with Chinese, Indians, and coloreds. Yvonne moved to Hilbrow (a cosmopolitan "whites only" section of "Jo-Burg" that was becoming more mixed with blacks) in pursuit of a career in acting and modeling. A policeman charged her with holding hands with a man. Yvonne was sent to jail, the man was never charged. At this portion of the tour, the guide goes on to explain that even though whites were rarely charged under the Immorality Amendment Act, at times the police might force them to swallow fish oil as informal punishment.

By way of a poster, the museum's critique of apartheid draws attention to an array of cultural matters. Visitors are reminded that racial power was channeled through language, and Afrikaans—the language of the political rulers—was the language of the jail. Rules governing the spoken word applied not only to prisoners but also to black wardresses, as both were punished if they did not speak Afrikaans. Moreover, black wardresses were commonly demeaned by their white counterparts. For example, black wardresses were addressed as "vagaash," an Afrikaans term that in Zulu translates to "vahashe" or that in English means "visitor." White wardresses, by contrast, were called "nona," or "little miss," as a sign of respect. Reflecting on that discriminatory custom, curators add that those terms deprived black wardresses of their identity, dignity, and sense of belonging. Situated on the upper level of the atrium, another object is used to tell a similar story about racial inequality. An ordinary chair joins the exhibit with a placard explaining its significance. Under jail instructions, black wardresses were not allowed to sit during their entire shift. They had to remain vigilant, walking with their hands behind their backs while being expected to curtsy to their white colleagues. Linda Xamesi, a black wardress in 1974, remembers: "You were not allowed to sit down . . . We would stand from 7 AM to 7 PM. We would get some assistance from the political prisoners who were locked in isolation—people like Sis Debs, Winnie and others. They gave us chairs to sit on because they felt sympathy for us" (see Super, 2010, 2011a, 2011b).

Continuing the tour, visitors are likely to notice a personal statement written on a large window. It reads: "My son was born here and it has affected him forever"—Assienah Mnisi, prisoner, 1973. The message serves as a reminder of how apartheid—as a form of colonialism—maligned nonwhites, transferring stigma from one generation to the next. The museum, however, maintains a sense of hope. An exhibit displays posters from the days of protest, including one titled "End White Rule! Democratic Elections for a Constituent Assembly Now!" As we segue into a discussion on Robben Island in the next chapter, the struggle for racial equality continues to be recognized. Moreover, that prodemocracy movement is celebrated in a unique cultural style known as memorialization (Bennett, 1995; Williams, 2007).

CONCLUSION

A tour of the Clink, as mentioned in chapter 5, entails the story of the Gordon Riots, which consumed London in 1780 when Protestants railed against the Catholic Relief Act, which extended liberties to Catholics. Initially, the mob targeted Catholics—mostly the Irish—as well as their churches and property. But then the disturbances swirled into a more diffused riot aimed at government authority. In its wake were London's prisons, many of which were burned and destroyed. Interestingly, widespread unrest prompted municipal leaders to quickly guard the city's main cultural institution, namely, the British Museum. The staff was sworn in as special constables while troops set up camp in the museum's gardens. Chelsea pensioners, armed with muskets and swords, occupied the museum with enough provisions for a three-day siege. On the roof, volunteers had gathered large stones to be hurled at the vandals should they breach the outer defense. Although the museum survived unscathed, concerted efforts to protect it from attack demonstrate the extent to which the institution was regarded as an important heritage site (see Miller, 1974).

As we reflect on the significance of cultural sites within the realm of dark tourism, it is fitting to summarize the changing role of the prison. In Hong Kong, Korea, Alcatraz, and South Africa, we learned how the prison was used as an instrument of colonial control over the indigenous people. Next, the prison became an arena—and symbol—of resistance whereby the prevailing regimes of power were challenged and ultimately defeated. Finally, the prison was transformed into a museum, becoming a cultural vehicle that communicates both of those historical narratives. The following chapter shows that many prison museums have been awarded special cultural status since they stand as the very sites where colonial authority was eventually overthrown by activists committed to independence and self-determination. Visitors are not only subjected to lessons on colonialism and resistance but also incorporated into the exhibit and its intended tribute. That is, their very presence—or pilgrimage—inside the prison museum adds to the commemoration of key historical figures and social movements. Much like in the rush to protect the British Museum amid the Gordon Riots, prison museums benefit from the diligence of curators, conservationists, and descendants of prodemocracy fighters. Admittedly, there remains an important distinction. While the British Museum serves as a depository of prized artifacts gathered in distant territories within the British Empire, prison museums are often organized around a critique of colonialism and the resistance it incites (see Welch, forthcoming).

NINE

Memorialization

As tourists walk deep inside the highly partitioned section of the Old Fort prison museum in Johannesburg, they discover an intriguing exhibit commemorating Nelson Mandela. The display, titled "466/64—Prisoner in the Garden," makes reference to Mandela as the 466th prisoner admitted to Robben Island in 1964. Chronicling Mandela's imprisonment on the island, as well as in the Old Fort, Pollsmoor, and Victor Verster prisons, the display offers a first glimpse of the hidden gems retrieved from government files and those in his own collection. The archive, a poster explains, is the first step in the long and exciting process of recovering and celebrating Mandela's life and work; the archive is bequeathed to all citizens of South Africa and to the world for posterity. Entering the gallery, we are greeted by large wooden trunks stacked on a floor covered in sand so as to transport us to the rugged terrain of Robben Island. The mysterious boxes, we soon learn, hold important documents concerning Mandela's career as a political prisoner. Carefully lit glass cases contain some of those precious items. For example, a lengthy handwritten letter is identified as a copy of the one sent to Major Van Vuuren, the commissioner of prisons, protesting the withdrawal of his study privileges after authorities uncovered Mandela's memoir secretly stashed in the prisoner's garden.

The archive resembles a buried treasure, and visitors can read for themselves a portion of the draft that was kept inside a Cadbury's Bourneville Cocoa canister. It includes commentary from Mandela's close comrades on the island, thereby allowing us to understand that the writing was, at least in part, a collaborative project (see Mandela, 1994). In 2003, Mandela returned to the Old Fort. Upon reflection, he spoke: "You must know your past and the cruelty that was committed to your people. But don't keep this too much in mind because we are here to build a new South Africa. That is what you must commit yourself to. You remember what has happened in the past so that, in future, you can avoid it." Along with objects and images, curators construct a space conducive to somber memorialization. A few well-chosen words help visitors connect metaphorically with the prisoner's garden, since the exhibit is "the seed out of which an interactive centre will grow, dealing with the philosophy of reconciliation that is Nelson Mandela's legacy to the world."

In his instructive book *Memorial Museums,* Paul Williams recognizes the trend of "museumification," in which public space and institutions have undergone symbolic transformation. In many instances, such cultural reinvention relies on strategies of interpretive drama to enhance memorialization, a curatorial practice designed to activate solemn remembrance (see Casey, 2003). Continuing our survey of select prison museums, we consider the various techniques used to convert a former prison into a heritage site, which, among other things, intends to promote respect for certain prisoners whose great personal sacrifice contributed to noble causes, including the struggle for racial equality, freedom, and political independence. Toward that end, analysis is organized around four styles of dramatization, namely, hybridity, authenticity, minimalism, and absence. As we shall see, those dramatic maneuvers allow curators to blend the physical and semiotic elements of the former prison. Along the way, we remain mindful of Durkheimian concepts involving the sacred and the mythological as well the Foucaultian view that museums exercise a unique form of cultural power aimed at improving those who visit their galleries (Bennett, 1995). Together, those perspectives refine our understanding of how prison museums aspire to promote civility, introspection, and reverence.

HYBRIDITY

Williams (2007) is quick to point out that former prisons are the most common institutional spaces converted into memorial museums. Moreover, such memorialization is best exemplified in honoring political prisoners, especially in the face of unjust regimes. Indeed, those institutions are particularly communicative along the lines of conveying political persecution: "Knowing life as a political prisoner is obviously a difficult projection for those who have never suffered. Once a prohibitive space is made accommodating as a tourist facility, other forms of identification (personal objects, photographs, and recorded testimony) are added to make the suffering of prisoners more readily available, giving the prison greater historical context and emotional texture" (Williams, 2007: 90). Robben Island's transformation from a forbidden place to a tourist destination is geared toward making the former prison more accessible to those interested in the plight of political prisoners. While the site embodies the struggle of Nelson Mandela, we are reminded that thousands of other activists were banished there. Many of them were incarcerated merely for being a member of a banned organization (e.g., the African National Congress). Helping visitors connect with the island's past purpose, former political prisoners serve as tour guides who share personal—and collective—memories of persecution at the hands of the apartheid rulers.

As a hybrid space, Robben Island initially offers tourists a split experience as they enter not only a former prison but also a heritage site. However, that dual awareness is complicated by the realization that the island, in fact, possesses a natural beauty that transcends the otherwise sober mood. Admiring Table Mountain as it sits majestically at the back of the harbor, one might feel mixed emotions, since the former prohibitive space is surrounded by an active tide inhabited by aquatic life such as whales, seals, and even penguins. In many ways, the rich ecology delivers a soothing sensation, offsetting the island's reputation for political—and racist—cruelty. Of course, Mandela's cell is often a central hub where visitors pay tribute to the struggle (see figure 25). Still, the pilgrimage to Robben Island is a holistic event, incorporating nature, narratives on imprisonment, and finally victory over injustice. The entire trip is worthwhile because it affords visitors an opportunity to participate in memorialization, not in gloom but with hope. With cameras snapping at all angles, tourists capture their own moment on the island ("I was here"). Some of those photographs feature themselves posing with the ex–political prisoner/tour guide as they both smile in a shared gesture of solidarity (Coombes, 2003; Shearing and Kempa, 2004).

On the other end of the emotional spectrum, some prison museums retain the suffering of past atrocities while also using memorialization as a form of catharsis. Williams (2007) informs us that former prisons can give voice to the—normally silent—"body in pain" that is often the hallmark of all forms of the trauma of political violence. Therefore, exhibition space becomes a metonymic manifestation of traumatic memory (Coombes, 2000; Pecoil, 2004). As mentioned in previous chapters, the Seodaemun Prison History Hall is situated inside the Administration Building, the very site where

FIGURE 25. The iconic cell of Nelson Mandela (Robben Island, South Africa). © retrowelch 2014

Korean patriots were interrogated and tortured by Japanese Imperialists. After first being directed into the basement where those atrocities actually occurred, visitors are then directed to the second floor. Among the exhibitions commemorating the Korean resistance is a large room that spatially departs from the other galleries because it stands empty. Paradoxically, that emptiness is crowded with identification photographs covering the walls. Visitors tend to move closer to the pictures, looking into the eyes of the political prisoners. One might imagine that those prisoners are somehow trying to tell us about their incarceration or, worse, mistreatment, torture, and execution. Retreating to the middle of the room, however, does not give visitors refuge from the pain. Rather, we find ourselves surrounded by hundreds of staring faces, turning us into the center of attention. One returns the gaze but not in the form of a blank stare but instead as an act of sympathy.

Similarly, grief—as an emotional anchor—surrounds related memorials. An impressive painting (by artist Yun Yeo Hwan, from 2007) pays earnest tribute to Yoo Kwan Sun, one of Korea's revered "Patriotic Martyrs" (see figure 26). The portrait shows Yoo dressed in a formal white robe. She sits motionless, holding the Korean national flag partially furled on a stick. Her greatness is

柳 유
寬 관
順 순

烈 열
士 사

Patriotic Martyr
Yoo, Kwan-sun

FIGURE 26. A portrait of Yoo Kwan Sun, "Patriotic Martyr" (Seodaemun Prison History Hall, Seoul). © retrowelch 2014

conveyed by the manner in which she courageously faces the audience without making direct eye contact. That degree of distance is not cold; rather, one detects pride as well as sorrow—not for herself but for her fallen patriots. Located across the footpath from the Administration Building of the prison complex, visitors can examine the simple brick structure that housed the underground dungeons built in 1916 by the Japanese to confine female political prisoners. It is here that Yoo died in 1920 after enduring torture. Museum curators discovered those solitary cells in 1992, restoring them in an effort to memorialize the trauma of the women who suffered in those very spaces.

At Number Four in Johannesburg, the City Heritage group assembled a multidimensional exhibition titled "Gandhi: Prisoner of Conscience— Commemorating the Centenary of Satyagraha, 1906–2006." It was inaugurated on October 2, 2006: the 137th anniversary of the birth of the Mahatma. A vast collection of objects and images animates an old dilapidated wing of the prison complex. The room's authenticity goes unquestioned due in part to the flaking brickwork. However, this is not a dingy space at all. The overhead track lighting invites visitors to spend time gazing at various items of interest. A timeline of Gandhi's defiance navigates us—"minds on legs"— down the length of the gallery. Pastel banners and Plexiglas placards resurrect Gandhi's noble words of resistance: "Let the accusations of breaking the law fall on us. Let us cheerfully suffer imprisonment. There is nothing wrong in that. If the government sends us to gaol, I shall be the first to court imprisonment. And if any Indian is put to trouble because of his refusal to register, I will appear in his case free of charge." Curators are keen to inscribe Gandhi's activism within a larger universe of civil disobedience. Inside a display case, a document quotes Henry David Thoreau: "Under a government which imprisons unjustly, the true place for a just man is prison." Museum studies scholars insist that personal objects contribute enormously to memorialization, since those items help form connections between the visitor and the subject of tribute (Casey, 2003; Williams, 2007). Not only does their inclusion contribute to the overall cultural value of the exhibit, but the techniques of display also affirm their semiotic power. Consider, for instance, something as mundane as a pair of sandals (see chapter 2). Given the context, we presume that they once belonged to Gandhi. Still, the footwear's specialness is reinforced by being displayed inside a thick transparent case situated alone on the floor of the gallery, far away from any other objects or images that otherwise might compete for attention. Enhancing a museum effect that prompts visitors to create an imaginary relationship with the world-renowned dissenter, the sandals are placed straight ahead so that we might visualize Gandhi facing—even bonding with—us.

At Robben Island, the tour guide—and former political prisoner—keeps the cluster of eager tourists scampering throughout the prison compound. At times it is hard to keep up with the group as we maneuver down and around a maze of corridors. Once back inside the cellblock, visitors notice a series of small signs memorializing the political prisoners (and their years of confinement): for example, Junior Nkosi (1964–76), Sedick Isaacs (1964–78), and Johnson Miambo (1963–83). It should be noted that while former prisons strive to re-create the incarceration experience, there is something unnatural, even contrived, in the way certain objects are assembled, since they never would have coexisted in the course of punishment. Nevertheless, visitors tend to suspend their belief in accuracy and real order, thereby absorbing the historical—and moral—lesson at hand (Williams, 2007). Leaning inside the cells, we witness how the otherwise unnatural exhibition tells a story about life as a political prisoner. Take, for instance, an empty red and brown cement bag with bold black lettering. As it sits inside a display case, we sense that it possesses a certain meaning. Nearby a storyboard relies on the testimony of a former political prisoner to narrate its significance:

> We started education on the island with cement bag paper. Those prisoners who built the harbour and the new prison stole empty cement bags for our education inside the cells. We used the cement bag paper to make books. Sometimes the criminals who worked for the warders smuggled in paper or lead pencils in exchange for tobacco.
>
> After years of complaining, they allowed us to buy stationery. Johnson Miambo would divide the stationery and would break a pencil into four pieces, one for each section.
>
> After Colonel Willemse arrived he told [the warders]: "You cannot deal with these political prisoners by using force against them. They are cleverer than you. You must study."
>
> Things started to change because of Willemse. We started teaching the warders who were doing the same subject as ourselves. Even that Delport, the cruel fellow of the quarry.
>
> So the foundation of education on Robben Island was brown paper cement bags. You finished your Standard Ten and then moved into C section—that became the University of Robben Island.

So, through a curatorial technique, visitors learn about an important aspect of life on Robben Island. Moreover, that particular object—a cement bag—serves as a transmitter of culture and, in doing so, commemorates the value of education and self-improvement behind prison walls (see Foucault, 1986b).

Prison-based memorial museums stand apart from conventional prison museums with respect to how the prisoners are portrayed. At Alcatraz and Eastern State Penitentiary, tourists are drawn to the cells of infamous gangsters, such as Al Capone. Without much narration, one rests comfortably with the notion that incarceration in a maximum-security unit is probably the best place for those public enemies. Visitors at former prisons transformed into memorial sites, however, "do not passively accede to the authority of the state by conceiving inmates as malevolent, as per the normal societal conception, but instead, in cases of political persecution, view them as blameless victims of a malevolent state" (Williams, 2007: 90). Consequently, political prisoners are narrated not as cautionary tales; rather, in cases such as Yoo Kwan Sun, they are admired as heroic martyrs. Indeed, their personal sacrifices strengthen sacred devotion and enhance their mythological prestige (see Durkheim, 2008 [1915]).

AUTHENTICITY

Hybridity serves as an effective form of memorialization in large part due to its sited-ness, which, of course, underscores the overarching sense of authenticity. While prison museums are correctly judged to be genuine because they exist inside former prisons, many of those sites are granted sacred meaning when it becomes known that certain persons were executed there. At the Seodaemun prison, visitors are presented with the historically accurate narrative that behind those very walls many Korean patriots were put to death. That objective truth is linked to the subjective truth that designates specific spaces as hallowed ground. In the far corner of the prison compound sits the Execution Building. We recognize that it is a sacred site due to several visual cues. First, a wide containment wall surrounds the death house. Second, the partition itself is decorated with an engraving of the "yin and yang" symbol that represents complementary forces interacting to form a dynamic system. (The South Korean flag, or Taegukgi, also features the "yin and yang" emblem.) Finally, although visitors are allowed to enter the (forbidden) space through an ornate archway, a sign informs them that taking photographs is strictly prohibited. Attention is also drawn to a tall tree standing nearby. A metal placard titled "Wailing Poplar" states: "This tree was planted in 1923 at the time when the execution building was constructed. It was said that patriots in the course of being dragged to the execution hall grabbed this tree and wailed with deep resentment for their unachieved independence." For the benefit of those who would like to capture the image of the Execution Building, a picture of the structure is posted some thirty meters from the actual site. Visitors are allowed to photograph the picture, and many do.

What tourists cannot view, however, is the cellar of the Execution Building where the bodies of the executed patriots were dropped and later retrieved. So as to complete the instructional narrative on the execution protocol, a mock "dead-body pickup room" is on display at the National Resistance Hall. The brick structure—built to scale—invites visitors to step into the dimly lit space and witness the mechanics of hanging. Looking up, we see the opened floorboard of the gallows through which the condemned patriot would fall. Despite a brief lesson on the engineering of execution, the emotional tone of the exhibit remains solemn. A plaque reminds us: "Many independence activists during the Japanese occupation, as well as many innocent people who demanded democratization after liberation, died here." As a sacred memorial, the interior of the room features individual photographs of eighteen men and women who were executed by the Japanese. By design, the display of the execution house and the "dead-body pickup room" is treated with reverence. The sacred ambiance was enhanced even further in 1992 when a hidden underground passageway was discovered. The Corpse Removal Exit is a tunnel through which the Japanese would secretly slip out some of the dead bodies after execution, especially if the victim showed signs of torture (see figure 27). The gate of the tunnel remains open, allowing tourists to gaze deep into the abyss. Adding to its forbidden status, a chain is drawn across the entrance with a sign that reads "No Trespassing" (see Foucault, 1986a).

The Melbourne Gaol museum similarly examines the topic of execution and the disposal of bodies in ways that perpetuate myth as well as veneration. Since the Melbourne Gaol is the original site of those events, authenticity goes unquestioned. As discussed in the previous chapter, the hanging of (in)famous bushranger Ned Kelly remains a vibrant subject of Australian conversation. Indeed, polarizing views range from honoring Kelly to despising him. The museum at the Melbourne Gaol delves into the controversy by way of several exhibits exploring his life and, just as importantly, his death. Consider, for instance, the elaborate set of storyboards collectively titled "Ned Kelly: Beyond the Grave." The first image is an illustration of Kelly's

FIGURE 27. Corpse Removal Exit through which Japanese occupiers disposed of executed Korean prisoners. The tunnel was discovered in 1992 (Seodaemun Prison History Hall, Seoul). © retrowelch 2014

execution at the Gaol (the credit reads: "The last scene of the Kelly drama; the prisoner proceeding to the scaffold," courtesy La Trobe Picture Collection, State Library of Victoria). He is shown with a hood partially covering his head as the hangman prepares the noose. Uniformed personnel of the Gaol join three members of the clergy. Kelly stands out for several reasons. As the condemned prisoner, he is the center of attention. Moreover,

Kelly is noticeably taller and more muscular than the others, reflecting his actual—and symbolic—stature. Visitors will recognize in the picture the very location of the Gaol where the hanging took place—not far from the exhibit. Hence, sited-ness has a gravitating effect on the story of Kelly's execution. The next panel states a few more facts:

11 November 1880

Execution of Ned Kelly
    The body remains hanging for 30 minutes and is then wheeled across the hospital yard to the dead house
        Some form of post mortem examination is most probably performed
        A death mask is made [see chapter 7 for details on death masks]
        The body is buried in the Gaol burial yard

Curators inform us that in 1864 a law passed making the bodies of executed prisoners the property of the state, thus requiring them to be buried on the grounds of the Gaol. The only identifiers were the initials of the prisoner and the execution date inscribed in the wall above the grave (see chapter 5). The timeline jumps to 1924 when the Melbourne Gaol is closed, setting aside the land for educational and legal uses. In 1929, the bodies of the executed prisoners were exhumed, including the one marked "EK" (presumed to be Edward "Ned" Kelly even though there were other prisoners with the same initials). When the steam shovel broke open the coffin, workers and onlookers rushed to souvenir bones. The skull was then recovered by Mr. H. Lee. So as to authenticate the narrative, the text is accompanied by a photograph of the excavation site dated 1929. In the early 1930s, Kelly's skull was delivered to Sir Colin McKenzie, founder of the Australian Institute of Anatomy in Canberra, where it remained (and was displayed) until 1972. That year, the Old Melbourne Gaol opens as a museum where Kelly's skull, death mask, and other artifacts were exhibited. The storyboard features a photograph of the death mask placed carefully next to the skull, creating a bizarre sense of "before and after."

A new twist in the story of the Kelly skull unfolded in 1978 when it was stolen from an unbroken display case. Adding to the mystery is the fact that there were no signs of a break-in. "Despite many circulating rumours, it wasn't until the late 1990s that it became widely known that the skull stolen from the Gaol in 1978 was being hidden on a farm in Western Australia's Kimberly region. Self-styled 'custodian' of the skull, Tom Baxter, said that he wanted the skull returned to Kelly's descendants. His demands raised questions about both the authenticity and the 'ownership' of the skull." A large color photograph shows Baxter with the skull in 2000. The image combines Baxter's friendly demeanor with what appears to be archaeologically authentic human remains. Nine years later, Baxter donated the skull to the Victorian Institute of Forensic Medicine where it is subjected to a CT scan for comparisons with Kelly's death mask and photographs. Forensic scientists extracted DNA for possible investigations in the future along with performing laser mapping, clay reconstruction, and synchroton analysis. In 2010, the Victorian attorney general appealed to the public for assistance in identifying the skull (as well as in the recovery of other remains taken from the gravesite). Less than a month later, a souvenir tooth taken by Alex Talbot in 1929 was brought forward by his grandson. Enhancing the sense of authenticity, the tooth is accompanied by a photograph from the 1920s of Mr. Talbot holding the skull. The final panel titled "November 2010" brings us up to date. DNA analysis continued and if an uncontaminated specimen can be extracted it will be compared to the DNA of a living descendant of Ned Kelly. The passage keeps our suspense, concluding, "Watch this space . . . "

In 2011, Leigh Olver, an art teacher who descended from Ned Kelly's mother, donated blood for analysis. Scientists compared his mitochondrial DNA with that of the skull. The Forensic Institute then announced the results: "It appears that after all this time, after being abducted more than once, placed on display for the world to see, hidden for decades, cherished, handled, sought after and tested, the skull is not Ned Kelly's. 'Mr. Olver's DNA and the DNA from the skull do not match,' said Fiona Leahy, a historian and legal adviser at the institute" (Kenneally, 2011: 3). However, all is not lost. Investigators discovered a match between the Olver DNA and a fragment of another skull dug up at Pentridge Prison (where the prisoner remains were reburied): "So while most of Kelly's skull is still missing, the rest of him appears to have been found" (Kenneally, 2011: 3). Adding to the enduring mystery is the speculation that the skull that underwent examination could belong to the notorious British serial killer Frederick Deeming, who died in 1892. (It is widely believed that Deeming was Jack the Ripper—see chapter 10.) The Forensic Institute continued seeking a maternal relative to test the DNA (Kenneally, 2011: 3).

Without much formal explanation, we know—almost intuitively—that graves are sacred sites (see chapter 5). The process of burying suggests a final resting place; therefore, digging up skeletons and reburying them not only disrupt the finality of death but also demand another round of grief, ceremony, and memorialization. Williams points out that "reburial in a public memorial space reflects a desire that the unnatural and historically significant nature of their deaths is socially recognized" (2007: 82; Feldmen, 2003). That sense of cosmic reordering appears to be pursued by Tom Baxter, who held on to the skull for over three decades, promising to return it if the government gave Kelly a proper Catholic burial (see chapter 5). The unsettled debate over Kelly's reburial persists: "What of Kelly's skeleton? Should it be returned to the extended family? Or should there be a public grave? Many Australians regard Kelly as a national hero. Countless books and movies tell the story of his life. But others see him as a villain. 'You can't just bury the man,' Mr. Olver said. 'Someone is going to dig him up again in half an hour'" (Kenneally, 2011: 3; see Norden, 2010).

In relation to the phenomenon of memorialization, visitors at the Melbourne Gaol prepared a vigil on the 130th anniversary of the execution of Ned Kelly. A floral display was set at the gallows section of the Gaol where Ned was hanged. A handwritten note proclaims:

11–11–2010

On this anniversary of your execution Ned, which took place 130 years ago, we remember you!
    In the words of the historian Ian Jones: "We would be justified in saying that Ned Kelly, the man, was infinitely greater than his legend, a man of greater nobility and moral courage than anything we have even hinted at in the past."
    We salute your courage Ned and understand your life and the injustices you and your class faced. May all Australians study your story.*

Correspondingly, fresh flowers and memorial notes were on display at the base of the exhibit on Ellen Kelly. One message reads:

11–11–2010

On the 130th anniversary of her son's death we Australian women think with deep sympathy of the enormous loss and grief of Ellen Kelly (Quinn) suffered in this prison on the occasion of Ned's unjust and unnecessary execution.

* Peter Norden delivered the 2010 John Barry Memorial Lecture at University of Melbourne. The presentation, "Ned Kelly, John Barry and the Role of Social Activism on Criminal Justice Reform," which took place on November 11, coincided with the 130th anniversary of the execution of Kelly. The brochure for the event pictures Norden holding a replica of the Kelly death mask.

We hope that no other Australian mother in the future will ever have to suffer Ellen's trauma.

We salute her as a spirited, resourceful pioneer of Victoria. No wonder Ned and all her children and descendants loved and love her so much.

We salute you Ellen!

MINIMALISM

Though memorialism has traditionally been expressed through imposing architecture and tributary statues, a subtle move toward minimalism has taken hold. Williams observes, "There has emerged a distrust of majestic state monuments. In reaction to both right- and left-wing monumental statist aesthetics, a more skeptical visual language of size, scale, line, color, and weight has come to dominate new artist-competition style memorial projects" (2007: 94). While aspiring to evoke a sense of the sacred, minimalism quietly borrows from modern art to erect shapes and scenes that encourage contemplation. In the yard of Seodaemun Prison History Hall, visitors are drawn to the "Bowl of Korean Spirit" (or "Bowl of National Soul," created by Lim Seung O, in 2010). The huge metal rice bowl is tucked partially into the earth. So as to demonstrate that the "bowl" represents something meaningful, the artwork is surrounded by a platform of cobblestones. The "reverence monument" relies on a series of concentric circles, perhaps tapping into a subconscious interpretation of eternity. Without any edges, it pays a smooth—solemn— homage to "patriotic martyrs who died in Seodaemun Prison for their devotion to the independence movement to remind people of their noble sacrifices," according to a nearby plaque that is also shaped in the form of a circle. A companion book for visitors adds: "It symbolizes their will for freedom and peace that is the basis for Korea's future. 165 names of independence activists are carved [into the bowl] and more will be added" (Seodaemun Prison History Hall, 2010: 126).

Although it is tempting to destroy institutions where terrible events have occurred, such demolition risks playing into what Jean Baudrillard (1983) famously warned: forgetting the extermination is part of the extermination (see McAtackney, 2013, 2014). Planners of the memorial at Constitution Hill in Johannesburg seem to have it both ways—and more. In the center of the prison compound stand the remnants of the Awaiting Trial Block (ATB) that operated for nearly one hundred years. A sign tells us: "The cells here held black male awaiting-trial prisoners. The building represented the nature of the jail complex—a place where black men and women returned repeatedly, arrested for short periods with no access to the law, simply because of the colour of their skin." While the ATB was torn down in 2001, four stairwells were retained as "a haunting reminder of the horrific experiences of many black South Africans." Those remnants do not fail to attract attention as they reach up four stories; still, there is something exposed about their presence. They preserve the painful memory of apartheid's cruel regime. It has been noted that minimalist monument designers, much like their modern art peers, strive to have their works not become so much "*about* things in the world" but rather "*be* things in the world" (Hubbard, 1987: 113). Toward that end, the bricks of the ATB are integrated into the Constitutional Court chamber as well as the Visitor Centre. Hence, the physical—and emotional— past is embedded into living institutions (see Segal, 2006; Segal and van den Berg, 2006).

To create beacons of hope and forgiveness, designers of minimalist memorials have resorted to what has become known as a standard symbolization of atrocity, including pools of water, beams of light, and, most commonly, the eternal flame (see Brown, 2004; Coombes, 2000; Williams, 2007). Constitution Hill is no exception to that trend. Near the ATB, visitors face the "Flame of Democracy" as they read the Preamble to the Constitution of the Republic of South Africa 1996. Here, not only is the opening passage of the Constitution literally written in stone but it also enshrines social justice and fundamental human rights as well as the healing of the divisions of the past. That secular document, however, concludes with an appeal to the divine: "May God protect our people." Revealingly, those words are translated into the other official languages of South Africa, a reminder of a broader consensus and inclusion.

An underlying logic of minimalism drives artists not only to do more with less but, in doing so, to activate some deeper sensation in those who take a moment to consider the meaning of the artwork. From that standpoint, minimalism in memorialization is often associated with the avant-garde because it provides a refuge from overtly political or nationalist themes. Among the architects leading that style of memorialization are Maya Lin (e.g., Vietnam Veterans Memorial in Washington, DC) and Daniel Libeskind (e.g., Jewish Museum in Berlin and the Imperial War Museum in North Manchester). In their own way, each of them has introduced the "void" into an expanding repertoire of minimalistic techniques. The "void" takes aim at the sensory mode but strategically moves the visitor away from any particular emotion, whether that is anger or sadness (Williams, 2007). Inside the Hyde Park Barracks in Sydney, one might recognize that sort of minimalism as curators shift attention from the plight of those confined there to the institution itself. On the third level, visitors are greeted by the enigmatic "Ghost Stair." A sign explains: "The grey base represents the void of the original stairway; the opening was the entry for the original stairs. The steel handrail traces the line of the original handrail, a section of which remains in the wall where it was cut off in about 1887." While seemingly suggesting that architecture has a life—or an afterlife—the Ghost Stair evokes an otherworldly sixth sense (see chapter 5). However, rather than leaving the story line dangling, curators are pleased to report that the top flight of the existing northern stairway has been authentically restored to the original Francis Greenway design. Adding to that closure, the lower flights, replaced in 1887, remain intact.

At Eastern State Penitentiary, eleven site-specific installations give artists free reign to incorporate the existing cells into their own cultural vision. While some projects engage visitors with various multimediated messages about incarceration, others are more subdued. In one of those minimalist works, artist Jordan Griska revamps a cell into what he calls "Separate System." While the title draws on the strict Quaker regime of solitary confinement, Griska deliberately exaggerates the prison's bleak and uniform living space by encasing the entire cell in sheet steel. Looking more like a metal container than a prison cell, it captures society's steely indifference to those confined there. On the other end of the sensate spectrum is an installation named "Cozy," a creation by Karen Schmidt. Unlike in the harsh interior of Griska's piece, Schmidt literally hand-knit every square inch of the cell, giving it an ironic warmth. As minimal as the presentation seems, it is actually quite busy considering that there is a total of 419,879 stitches (the bed alone comprises nearly forty-two thousand stitches). Knitting, Schmidt explains, is time materialized: "The stitches are like tick marks that an inmate might scratch into the cell wall to mark the days." As a spatial technique, she distances the viewer from the cell by barring entry, thereby producing a sense of longing. Under the surface, there is a deeper story that inspired the project. Speaking through the audio guide, Schmidt tells us that she learned about an inmate who escaped by scaling the wall with yarn. In 1861, George Black stole enough yarn from the penitentiary's dye shop to climb to his freedom—albeit temporarily, since he was recaptured. Linking Black metaphorically to the materials contained in "Cozy," the artist used more than twenty-five thousand yards of yarn to spin together an almost fairly-tale story about escape.

Scholars remind us that public parks share with museums and prisons an important historical function: that is, serving as spaces of nineteenth-century reform (Bennett, 1995; Williams, 2007). Parks surrounded by bucolic beauty stood as an antidote to the vice of street culture; hence, those who step into the manicured lawns of the commons would be immersing themselves into the Romantic tradition of divinity. Similarly, museums and prisons were conceived not as mere paragons of order, but as venues for virtuous transformation and improvement. Visitors at the Seodaemun Prison museum are likely to experience the cultural power of its reconfigured prison grounds. Instead of resembling the rough terrain of its past, the yard is meticulously groomed, presumably by a professional landscape architect. Even with its park benches and curvy footpaths, the scenery does not suggest a cheerful picnic mood. Rather, its minimalism and wide-open space—dotted by former cellblocks—prompt remembrance and commemoration of those confined there decades ago under much different circumstances. In large part due to its sited-ness, such reflection tends to resonate well after the visit, thereby improving us as civilized beings (see Foucault, 1986b).

ABSENCE

Absence marks the fourth in a series of dramatic styles involving memorialization. From the start, however, we encounter an obvious paradox. How does a curator recognize absence without actually filling in the void? Perhaps one way is to provide enough context to allow viewers to use their own imagination, memory, or even false memory to complete the picture. For purposes of memorialization, the most conventional use of absence is the rider-less horse in state funerals (see Williams, 2007). In that instance, the emotional register is grief and sorrow. Still, absence can be understood as a neutral phenomenon that relies on a curator's agenda, narrative, and screen to produce the appropriate mood. Empty cells in prison museums, by their very nature, are examples of absence; but how visitors fill in the blank depends on an array of other contextual information. At Robben Island, all of the cells are vacant, but upon encountering the one once occupied by Mandela—even though it is not specifically identified as his—we imagine him lying on his unfurled sleeping mat. But we don't do this as a way of reincarcerating him. Rather, our imagination—or false memory—runs in the direction of commemoration, even applauding his courage and perseverance.

Compared to other styles of dramatization, techniques of absence are arguably the most phenomenological, since absence requires that curators furnish enough "nothingness" so that the audience can bear witness to the past. On the top level of the Hyde Park Barracks, curators keep a large room empty with the exception of several silhouettes standing near the windows. Walking along a stretch of hardwood floor, we notice a poster titled "Characters." It reads: "The confused & confounding din of so many voices may well be imagined." The visually sparse exhibit is designed by artist Heather Dorrough, who uses cutout profiles to project the mood and gesture of Barracks men according to the recorded details of size, shape, crime, and punishment. The otherwise empty space is filled with "a crowd of voices, episodes, sounds & silences [as they] jostle with each other for attention & identity." Dorrough recognizes the significance of absence and memorialization by informing us that the sounds "evoke the patterns & presence of lost human experience."

Similarly, at Constitution Hill, the Awaiting Trial Block memorial has a plaque simply named "Songs" to commemorate the melodies of prisoners who sang to comfort and entertain one another. Their music maintained their solidarity while defying the authorities. Curators invite tourists to visit the invisible past by pressing a button to listen to the songs of political prisoners. By activating audio tracks, curators at the Hyde Park Barracks and Constitution Hill transform a vacant—and static—area into a performing space. In the absence of motion, the sounds, voices, and music animate the exhibit, thereby giving it a sense of life—then and now. It should be noted that the use of recordings to collapse time and space, however, risks compromising the intent of the curatorial agenda, since we associate drama with manipulation. That is particularly the case when an exhibit delivers highly nationalistic and propagandist messages (see Casey, 2003; Williams, 2007). Nevertheless, when executed effectively, the use of sound can reinvent absence into a dynamic environment.

Collections of artifacts, including the presence of such items as an inmate's game board, often trigger a cognitive response on the part of penal tourists, who, for instance, might wonder what it would be like to play checkers inside a prison (e.g., Alcatraz). On the other end of the experiential spectrum, the use of absence can prompt a sensate reaction. Consider a visit to Eastern State Penitentiary during the "Winter Adventure Tours" (December through March). As the initial attraction to its grand architecture begins to fade, tourists realize that there is no central heating. The corridors, and especially the cells, are stone cold. The chill is deepened by gloomy cells that beg for occasional sunshine through the skylight. We not only witness the prison but also feel its alienating interior. That visceral effect gives the space an even stronger affective power. While literally shivering in the cold, visitors feel what it is like to be emotionally isolated and perhaps forgotten. Within the collective memory, the presence of prisoners is erased and replaced by absence: hence, out of sight, out of mind. Particularly after the demise of reform and rehabilitation, prisons—as neglected institutions and human warehouses—turn convicts into voids within voids.

Another ingenious use of absence parallels the notion of *simulacra*. By way of Baudrillard (1994), the concept refers to copies of things that no longer have an original (or never had one to begin with). At the Argentine Penitentiary Museum, an entire exhibit is devoted to the National Penitentiary. Archival photographs authenticate—and even commemorate—that architectural marvel, along with a large model boasting its impressive radial design. The actual existence of that institution is merely imaginary, since it was demolished in 1961. Even in its absence, however, the National Penitentiary continues to serve as a cultural monument to Argentine penology. With conspicuously draped Argentine flags used to accent the state's pageantry, the secular exhibit merges with the sacred. As mentioned previously, a placard cites the poetics from the famous novel *La Vuelta de Martin Fierro*. In that passage, the penitentiary is depicted as a form of justice as well as a venerated site that baptizes prisoners, thereby unifying Durkheimian observations on spiritual cleansing with transcendent redemption (see chapter 5).

As Gresham Sykes chronicled in *Society of Captives* (1958), incarceration is intended to impose emotional and psychological hardship. Those "pains of imprisonment" involve an array of deprivations: liberty, personal belongings, family contact, and so on. Indeed, many of those punishments are minute, incremental, and even petty. Again, Foucault (1977) noted that such disciplinary regimes typify a microeconomy of perpetual penality. At the Women's Jail in Johannesburg, curators memorialize the prisoners by incorporating absence into a narrative on petty deprivations. In one of the courtyards, attention is drawn to a boxlike metal sculpture inscribed accordingly: "An apple tree once stood here. Ex-prisoners tell stories of watching the apples grow and waiting for them to ripen. They would identify a certain apple for themselves and fights would break out if another prisoner took their apple. Wardresses would punish the prisoners by confiscating the apples when they were ripe." Of course, a sense of loss takes on a greater toll when accompanied by banishment to a faraway land. While the penal colony in Australia easily comes to mind as the quintessential practice of transportation, visitors at the Argentine Penitentiary Museum are introduced to Tierra del Fuego, which is located at the southern tip of the continent. There, in the town of Ushuaia, a rugged prison camp operated from 1902 to 1947. Vintage photographs show convicts (and guards) in a frigid, isolated, dreary landscape—perhaps the ultimate "nothingness." Like the National Penitentiary, the Argentine version of a Siberian penal colony no longer exists. Despite its absence, however, the history of such banishment and seclusion persists in the collective memory.

MAPPING MEMORY

Before closing this discussion on memorialization, it is fitting that we turn some thought to memory. While the two concepts are closely related, there are important distinctions, particularly in the context of museums. In response to feminist and postcolonial critiques, the mission of many museums has been reconsidered. Rather than simply serving as disciplinary spaces of academic history, they have become "places of memory, exemplifying the postmodern shift from authoritative master discourses" to the horizontal, practice-related notions of community (Andermann and Arnold-de Simine, 2012: 3). While commemoration is not left by the wayside, there is an effort to invite remembrance. Still, attempts to locate memory are elusive. Neurophysiologists contend that personal memory is based not on information retrieval but rather on reimagining; consequently, it is selective and often unreliable (Loftus, 1995). Advocates of a remembrance culture do not dispute that limitation, and they therefore suggest that the emphasis be placed on emotional investment rather than on historical knowledge. Toward that end, it is argued that descriptive information on atrocities alone does not prevent future mass violence, "but instead a degree of imaginative empathy is being called for in order to ensure moral responsibility" (Arnold-de Simine, 2012: 15). At the core of that movement is the highly contested concept of "collective memory," which, just like "traditional historiography," is actively constructed with the aid of signs, symbols, texts, images, ceremonies, places, and monuments—as well as museums (Assmann, 2004).

As a subset of memorial museums, "memory museums" set out to capture and transmit stories, particularly those of victims of mass suffering. Though artifacts contribute to a larger narrative about the past, curators of memory museums insist that personal testimonies should become the objects of the exhibition. Consider, for instance, "Mapping Memories: Former Prisoners Tell Their Stories" at Constitution Hill heritage precinct in Johannesburg. Organizers brought back former prisoners who were confined to the Women's Jail and the (all-male) Number Four, giving them an opportunity to share memories made fragile by the passage of time. The thrust of the project was to facilitate autographic mapping and remapping by former prisoners of the literal and psychic spaces within the jail complex. Curators preface the workshop by noting the significance of the jail's sited-ness, since it is one of the oldest buildings in the city. Moreover, it held virtually every important political leader in South African history as well as thousands of ordinary South Africans caught in the web of colonial and apartheid oppression (Segal and van den Berg, 2006). It seems that from the beginning the jail was destined to be forgotten, since much of its history had not been formally recorded or archived. A register of prisoners did not exist; moreover, prisoners were prohibited from keeping diaries. Curators managed to find some groups of political prisoners, but "many were reluctant to dredge up the extremely painful memories that jails evoke. Some refused to participate because of the horror of their experiences" (Segal and van den Berg, 2006: 1). Those who did join the workshop contributed enormously to the project; furthermore, their stories (and portrait photographs) became a central part of the narrative shaping the tour of Constitution Hill.

Curators introduced an array of techniques to prompt and document memories, including drawing, painting, and sculpture. Together those activities "gave both connection and distance, connection because these were memories closely known and distance because the act of learning a new language diverted attention from what was being said to how it was said" (Segal and van den Berg, 2006: 4). Indeed, it was the acquisition of a new medium that served as a buffer between traumatic experience and its confrontation. Accordingly, workshop leaders set out to assist the healing process by enabling the former prisoners to avoid some of their raw emotions. With a higher sense of purpose, "Mapping Memory" intended to contribute to a human rights culture in South Africa.

In one of the exercises, former prisoners were asked to walk through the jail and plant red flags in the spaces that triggered their best and worst memories of their incarceration. The procedure allowed former prisoners to reacquaint themselves with the physical layout of the jail. Such locomotion ("minds on legs" or even "hearts on legs") also prompted them to connect with the sitedness of their emotions. Adding greater dimension to the experience of rediscovering those sites, former prisoners were instructed to take photographs of their flags. With an instant camera in hand, they could reframe and capture the space as they saw fit, perhaps enabling them to reclaim ownership over their memories. Finally, the flags remained throughout the jail, thus serving as visual icons for visitors (or "secondary witnesses").

Testimonies of the former prisoners were compiled, posted, and published (Segal and van den Berg, 2006). In the following passages, we see that their disclosures matched common themes of imprisonment, especially under the apartheid regime. A sentiment expressed in many of the memories was solidarity with other prisoners and ingenuity in circumventing the barriers of communication. Joyce Dipale recalled:

> My best memory is when I woke up the following day after being brought here and I saw I was with my comrades. I was with the youngsters, Baby Tjawa, Nomsa Maseku. We communicated with the prisoners on the other side of the wall using the "aeroplane" method. We used to throw fruit, pads and messages in packets over the wall that separated us from our other comrades ... We could also shout to each other over the wall and find out how we were doing.

Some political prisoners felt privileged to be in the company of famous activists, thereby reinforcing a sense of purpose and commitment to the cause: "It was at the Fort when I met fellow Africans from different members of the PAC. I was also excited to meet the leadership, which of course included the 'Prof,' Robert Sobukwe," said Joseph Gogo Khoza. Likewise, Edward Sonnyboy Bhengu remembers in detail the political developments unfolding during his incarceration: "This is when I was detained in 1963 under the Detention without Trial Act. It was after the passing of the Sobukwe clause in Parliament. We were arrested for belonging to the terrorist organization uPogo, which was the military wing of the PAC. We were detained at Number Four under the 90 days Detention Act and later the 180 days Detention Act." Nonetheless, he has fond memories of being detained with others: "I was entertaining. I used to crack jokes ... and kept my inmates very happy."

Given the harsh conditions at the Women's Jail, prisoners were elated to learn that they were being transferred to the new institution nicknamed "Sun City" because, by contrast, it seemed like a resort:

My best memory was when we were moved to Sun City—Diepkloof Prison—
because we were told that we were going to sleep in beds and be able to watch TV.
We were also told that we were going to eat better food compared to that junk at
the Women's Jail in Number Four. The day we were moving to Diepkloof Prison
I was dancing and jumping all the way to the *gumba gumba*. I was so happy for a
while I even forgot that I was still a prisoner (Yvonne Ntonto Mhlauli).

Unsurprisingly, being released was the best moment for many inmates. In the
words of Bella Dlamini: "I put my happiest flag at the front door because this is
where I had been in jail for two years. It was terrible to have been in this place."

On the other end of the emotional spectrum, former prisoners were asked
to remember the worst aspects of their detention: "My worst memory is of all
of the nights that my baby would be crying and the other inmates would shout
and swear at me saying *'Thulisa umntwana sigwetyiwe thina, sifuna ukulala'*
(Keep your baby quiet, we are sentenced prisoners and we do not need a crying
baby, we need sleep)," recalled Assienah Mnisi. Prisoners at the Women's Jail
were subject to demeaning institutional rules; for instance, as a show of proper
respect to authority, they were required to walk with their hands behind their
back. Punishments for violating those petty rules were swift. As one of her
saddest moments, Yvonne Ntonto Mhlauli told the workshop: "On my way to
the visitor's room. I was stopped by the wardress, Swanepoel. She said that I
could not go and see my visitor because my hands were not at the back of me.
I was punished immediately and instead of going to see my friends I was sent
to isolation—*drie maaltye* (three meals) for ten days."

Of course, memories of violence are understandably traumatic, a concern
that museum planners openly acknowledge (Andermann, 2012; Brown,
2004; Coombes, 2000). Again, painful memories are attached to actual
spaces, becoming trauma sites that "exist factually as *material testimonies* of
the violence and horror that took place there" (Violi, 2012: 37). Curators,
therefore, are faced with an ethical question: how can a victim be asked to
recall past suffering without appropriating or even exploiting their experiences (Violi, 2012)? That dilemma is not easily resolved. Blending victimiza-
tion with Foucault's (1986a) notion of "forbidden spaces" (heterotopia),
Patricia Alarm relayed the following incident: "My worst memory was when
I was beaten up on the stairs going into section three. I was beaten up because
I stood up for a new inmate who stepped into the *mbendeni* (the haunted
area) where we prisoners were not allowed. They broke my arm. I will never
forget that." In a similar vein, "my worst memory was the first time when I
saw a dead person," said Zolile William Mgweba. He added: "It was Bheki

my friend who was killed trying to save me. The other memory that I cannot forget was at night I was sodomized by the cell boss."

A sense of place within a trauma site also has important consequences for the *positioning* of visitors:

> Independently of how much remains of the past, and how carefully it is preserved, visitors know they are in the very place where terrible events occurred, and this knowledge contributes to a complex, multifaceted perception of it. Visitors not only see something of this terrible past, they also imagine that which cannot be seen. The emotional intensity and pathemic effect characteristic of experiences of visiting trauma sites depend crucially on the evocative power of indexical traces to activate the imagination of the visitors. Visible and invisible aspects of visitor experience become inextricably intertwined. Traces, in virtue of their indexical "authenticity," are at one and the same time visible documentations of the past and powerful activators of imaginary forms of reconstruction. (Violi, 2012: 39)

Interestingly, some of the worst memories of former political prisoner did not involve their own incarceration but rather atrocities occurring in the community: "My worst memory was when the detailed report of the aftermath of our campaign in Sharpeville came through. The thought of so many unarmed civilians being mowed down by the system made me even more committed to the struggle" (Joseph Gogo Khoza).

The exhibition on "Mapping Memory" was ceremoniously opened on Women's Day (August 9, 2006) to coincide with the fiftieth anniversary of the women's march to Pretoria. The campaign to remember and memorialize the site is mobilized by a women's forum known as Sizoya Sibuye (SiSi). One of its chief aims is "to make Number Four as famous as Robben Island, because it seems that the world at large forgets that many women played an important part in achieving democracy for our country" (Segal and van den Berg, 2006: 8; see Brown, 2004; Coombes, 2003). In the courtyard of the Women's Jail museum, visitors can read an engraving on a stone monument:

WOMEN IN THE
FIRST NATIONAL ASSEMBLY OF
THE FIRST REPUBLIC OF SOUTH AFRICA
1994–1999
Women's Development Foundation Celebrating
Women's Contribution to a Non-Sexist, Non-Racial
And Democratic South Africa
May Their Legacy Inspire Generations to Come

To reiterate, memorials are places for reverent commemoration and passive contemplation. Museums, by comparison, are educational institutions dedicated to critical interpretation and historical contextualization. The two commonly coalesce in an attempt to add a moral framework to the narrative as well as more detailed explanations to commemorative acts (Williams, 2007). Along the way, there is a changing aesthetic of remembrance that refuses to gravitate toward a place of "wreath dumping" (Young, 1992). Instead, there is a preference for "counter-monuments" that startle visitors, forcing them to think about what the memorial stands for. By design, "counter-monuments" extend "the challenge to speak about what is deemed unspeakable and visualize what is deemed unimaginable" (Arnold-de Simine, 2012: 20).

CONCLUSION

Recent scholarship recognizes that memorial museums run counter to a cultural sensibility that preserves the glorious and destroys the dreadful, especially when it is associated with tragedy, atrocity, and death on a mass scale. Toward that aim, museum planners realize that in order to encourage remembrance, visitors need a concrete locus for their attention. As Pierre Nora phrased it, history is attached to events while memory is attached to sites (see Engelhardt, 2002). Such genuine sited-ness activates memory in the first order for those who were there and imagination for those who follow. Together they generate collective memory that unfolds within a spatial framework (Halbwachs, 1992): "It is, arguably, a sense of place—rather than objects or images—that gives form to our memories, and provides the coordinates for the imaginative reconstruction of the 'memories' of those who visit memorial sites but never knew the event first-hand" (Williams, 2007: 102).

Tourists making their way to such sites as Constitution Hill, Robben Island, or Seodaemun Prison History Hall will likely conform to the ritual component of visitation. There the exhibits are not designed as a morbid theme park; rather, the tour—or pilgrimage—is steeped in Durkheimian sacredness and Foucaultian normalization. In tandem, a sense of reverence is instilled while civilizing those who might benefit from the historical lessons on cruelty, racism, and domination (see Bennett, 1995). At memorial prison museums, the sensate experience is analogous to churchgoing since, once inside the institution, the total environment delivers not only didactic messages on justice but also uplifting poetics on the eternal good of mankind: "Both memorial museums and churches make concrete the notion of sacred ground and bring people together (as a congregation perhaps) under a single topic of communion" (Williams, 2007: 98). In many instances, those sacred themes are heightened by evidence of sacrifice. While much of the memorialization is directed at prisoners, especially political activists, there are also tributes to correctional officers who died in the line of duty. As discussed in chapter 6, the "Battle of Alcatraz" (1946) involved a foiled escape that, according to the front page of the *San Francisco Chronicle,* left "One Guard Killed, 16 Injured." In a nearby cell, the empty space is occupied by a large poster commemorating the deceased. Along with his photograph, the caption reads: "In Memorium: During the May 1946 escape attempt, Officer William A. Miller was one of several correctional officers held hostage in this cell. He was mortally wounded when he hid the key that the inmates needed to complete their escape. His quick thinking, bravery, and attention to duty prevented the escape from succeeding, and he will never be forgotten." Similarly, the Hong Kong Correctional Services Museum honors fallen officers. A series of pictures includes the dignified portraits of Ms. TANG Po-wan (killed by female prisoners while on duty at Tai Lam Centre for Women on April 12, 1971) and Mr. SO Sui-bo (killed by inmates while on duty at the Cape Collinson Training Centre on November 17, 1958). The homage to John Stimson, interestingly, offers greater detail than his obituary. A native of Banff, Scotland, Stimson was forty years old when he was murdered in 1868 at the Victoria Gaol. On the day of his death, the storyboard explains, Stimson had reported Loo A On to the superintendent for laziness and insubordination. Loo was punished with ten strokes from a rattan cane and was deprived of dinner. Later that day, Loo struck Stimson with a hammer, severely fracturing his skull. A second blow hit his leg. The memorial to Stimson seems a bit ambiguous. Did Stimson's zeal for discipline bring about his own death? The final passage, nonetheless, gives closure to the event. Loo was found guilty and executed publicly near the Gaol entrance.

TEN

Cultural Power

Winding down this carceral travelogue of sorts, it is fitting that we offer some concluding thoughts on cultural power as it pertains to penal tourism. In doing so, further consideration is given to what might attract visitors to prison museums. Once there, curators must craft their narratives in order to fulfill the institutional mission, whether that is to inform, educate, or even civilize tourists. Efforts to answer those questions benefit from added meditation on Durkheim, as well as Foucault, thereby sharpening a cultural sociology of punishment. Thus far, much of the Durkheimian interpretation has relied on a constellation of socioreligious concepts, including the mythological, the cult of the individual, and the sacred. Moving forward, this chapter explores more aspects of the sacred as they relate to death as well as the sacred victim. Discussion then revisits the pull of punishment and the many ways it affects those visiting prison museums, giving them a sense of hands-on power. Finally, we exit through the gift shop, where further evidence of cultural power manifests in consumption by travelers, tourists, and posttourists.

THE SACRED VICTIM

The dark side of penal tourism, to be sure, is fueled by an interest in death, especially murder (see Stone, 2006; Stone and Sharpley, 2008). The act of taking life is especially immoral when it involves defenseless victims, most notably, children. The child victim radiates a brazen violation of sacred purity. While at the Women's Jail in Johannesburg, visitors are keen to visit an exhibit on Daisy de Melker, who, according to a placard, was born in

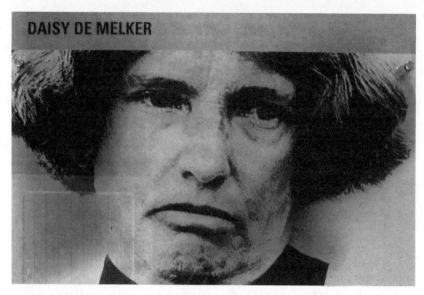

DAISY DE MELKER

FIGURE 28. Daisy de Melker, who was hanged in 1932 upon being convicted of murdering her son Rhodes (Women's Jail, Johannesburg, South Africa). © retrowelch 2014

Grahamstown in 1886 into family of eleven brothers and sisters. Daisy married three times. Her first husband was William Alfred Cowle, with whom she had five children. Four of them died in childhood, and later William succumbed to an unexpected illness. She then married Robert Sproat, who died less than two years later. When her only surviving son, Rhodes Cecil Cowle, died suddenly, Sproat's brother approached the police. Authorities exhumed the bodies of her husbands and son and charged Daisy with homicide. Prosecutors could not prove that she killed her husbands, but they did convict her of the murder of her son Rhodes. On December 30, 1932, she became the second woman to be hanged for murder in South Africa. Resembling cabinets of curiosity, the display features two glass cases containing apothecary jars labeled "poison." A large close-up photograph of her grimacing face seems to suggest wickedness and guilt. The caption adds: "Her ghost is said to haunt the jail" (see figure 28).

Before departing from the prison museum in Johannesburg, tourists are likely to revisit the tragic theme of the child victim. A large display is dedicated to Hector Pietersen. At the age of thirteen, he was fatally shot by police while participating in a protest in Soweto in 1976. A poster provides some background about the demonstration: "In 1955, Bantu Education was introduced. From the outset it was badly financed and teachers were paid very low wages." By the 1970s, students began to revolt against the apartheid educational system requiring that pupils be taught in Afrikaans rather than in any one of the tribal languages. Curtis Nkondo described Bantu Education as *"E tshwana le phate ea mahlatsa ha e tshela sefahlehong sa ngwana wa motho e motsho"* (It's like vomit poured from an old skin onto the face of an African child). An exhibit features the iconic photograph of a dying Hector being carried by eighteen-year-old Mbuyisa Makhubo alongside Hector's sister, Antoinette Sithole, whose outstretched hand conveys the sacrilege of the killing. Together, the three of them appear to form a holy trinity. The text goes on to note that Makhubo, fearing for his life, went into hiding before fleeing to Botswana. His last letter home was sent from Nigeria in June 1978. It is believed that the South African security forces—known locally as the "white devils"—tracked him down and killed him. In Soweto, the precise location of Hector's death and the nearby Hector Pietersen Museum continue to draw large crowds of solemn tourists.

With the *sacred* child in the background, the story of Emma Williams draws on the theme of the "bad mother." In 1893, Emma and her husband arrived in Melbourne from Tasmania, but things quickly began to unravel. Amid the Australian Depression, she struggled to find work. Soon after becoming pregnant, her husband died of typhoid. Emma tried to give her son to an orphanage but to no avail. Her problems deepened as she resorted to prostitution to survive. In 1895, the body of a small boy was found in the Port Melbourne lagoon with a stone tied round his neck. Emma was arrested. Her pimp, William Martin, reported to the police that Emma complained that the child was a nuisance and she refused to care for him. Emma said, "There was always grumbling in the house as the child would cry after me and this was a bother." Emma was found guilty but the execution was delayed when she claimed—albeit falsely—to be pregnant. Local activists against the death penalty unsuccessfully rallied on her behalf. At the age of twenty-seven, Emma was hanged. It seems the entire colony was condemned. The *Champion* newspaper editorialized that the case of Emma Williams would "exhibit Victoria to the world as the very lowest and most degraded of all civilized communities." The blown-up version of her police mug shot that is on display shows Emma staring coldly into the lens, leaving visitors without much sympathy.

The extensive coverage of murder and execution at the Melbourne Gaol can be a bit overwhelming. So it is understandable that some visitors might not immediately recognize the name Frederick Bailey Deeming. As the story goes, Deeming is seriously considered to be the notorious serial killer Jack the Ripper. Curators provide a chronology of Deeming's whereabouts, noting that he traveled extensively around the globe. When he and his second wife, Emily, arrived in Melbourne from England, he rented a cottage in Windsor under the name of Mr. Drewin. On at least one occasion, he purchased tools and cement. When John Stamford, the owner of the house, noticed a "disagreeable smell," he contacted the police. Emily's body was dug out of its cement casing under the hearthstone. Further investigations in England led to the discovery of the bodies of his first wife, Marie, and their four children, which were buried under their home in Liverpool. In 1892, Deeming was arrested in Western Australia while masquerading as the dashing Baron Swanson. His lawyer, the future Prime Minister Alfred Deakin, argued the insanity defense. The jury was not persuaded, and Deeming was hanged on May 23, 1892. Still, the mystique of Jack the Ripper endures.

The narrative on murder and executions turns critical attention to the wrongly convicted, thereby embracing the sanctity of innocence—and even the truth. Upon entering what is labeled "The Condemned Cell," a placard explains that in this very site, Colin Ross spent his last two months after being sentenced to death for the murder of schoolgirl Alma Tirtschke. Despite strenuously protesting his conviction, he was hanged in the Melbourne Gaol on April 24, 1922. A handwritten "Innocence Note" is on display: "Dear Friends, outside, a few words from Colin Ross who is going to hang an innocent man. I appeal to the people of Australia to see that I get justice. My life as been sworned [sic] by the police and wicked people. I ask you this because if they will do it to me they will do the same to you. Take this to some paper office for me please. I am an innocent man." Curators then resort to locomotion to direct visitors to the top floor of the Gaol (cell 9) to learn "more about this remarkable story." So, we walk—"minds on legs"—up the octagonal staircase in search of the rest of the Colin Ross saga. That portion of the exhibit includes several panels. A poster titled "The Crime" tells us that attacks on children were so rare that when the brutal rape and murder of Alma hit the headlines, it shocked the nation. Amid the media frenzy, police scrambled to make a quick arrest. Twelve days after the crime, Ross— who ran a wine saloon—was detained: "A local prostitute with a grudge against Ross told police she had seen Alma in the saloon." A series of separate photographs of Alma, Ross, and the detectives serves to authenticate the narrative. At the trial, prosecutors relied on an early form of forensics whereby government experts claimed that samples of Alma's hair were found in blankets from Ross's home. The defense team was denied permission to arrange independent tests. Nearby a poster titled "Hanging" quotes Ross: "I am now face to face with my Maker, and I swear by Almighty God that I am an innocent man." The execution was botched because a four-stranded rope was used for the first time. It failed to deliver a proper snap, leaving Ross dangling for nearly twenty minutes. Notes from the medical officer, also on display, document the execution, which amounted to a slow strangulation. The four-stranded rope was never used again.

Evoking the transcendent, another placard prophetically titled "Time Will Tell" includes pages from Ross's bible, mostly from Psalms. Verse 11—which says that "False Witnesses did rise up"—is marked "Against Colin." He also underlined the passage "they have spoken against me with a lying tongue," where Ross added, "Time will tell." The exhibit also includes an eleven-minute documentary, "The Hanged Man's Shadow—Australian Story," based on the work of Kevin and Linda Morgan. A six-minute clip from that film aired nationally on the Australian Broadcasting Corporation on April 13, 2000. A sign simply states: "On 27 May 2008 the Governor of Victoria granted Colin Ross a posthumous pardon." For tourists interested in further exploring the left sacred, the Melbourne Gaol offers a "Hangman's Night Tour": "Experience Australia's most haunted building by candlelight . . . if you dare!" Similarly, "Ghost Hunts" give opportunities to take part in a "real life paranormal investigation" inside Victoria's oldest prison.

HANDS-ON POWER

Since we are wrapping things up, let us take a moment to revisit some of the book's main discoveries, especially with respect to cultural power. By entering prison museums, tourists are exposed to various agendas, techniques, and messages. Recall from the opening chapter that former prisons tend to invert the Disney experience by plunging tourists into the bleak topics of pain, suffering, and misery. In an exercise of cultural power, prison museums confine visitors to a space far removed from "the happiest place on earth" (Williams, 2007: 99). Drawing on the psychological pull that actual *sited-ness* produces, curators seek to educate their audience about penal history, architecture, religion, politics, economics, science, and so on. By having safe contact with the prison and its various devices, visitors further internalize their experience of the visit.

Much like with the interactive strategy employed at the Clink (i.e., "things to do"), the tour of Eastern State Penitentiary is committed to "hands-on history" by incorporating each of the components of the museum effect, namely, objects, images, and space. The exhibit titled "TOWERCAM!" (note the exclamation point) demonstrates how a prison museum breaks from its static foundation and embraces the dynamics of surveillance. Before actually participating in some hands-on panopticism, we learn a bit more about the genealogy of the guard tower. A large poster, "Towers over Time," chronicles the emergence of ESP's *architecture parlante,* pointing out that initially the guard towers were "mostly for show," delivering a Gothic statement about the horrors of incarceration. However, "with every prisoner living alone, in the new Separate Confinement system, there wasn't much to see from above." The semiotics was eventually eclipsed by the instrumental turn in penal architecture. Accompanied by vintage photographs, the text explains that when the Separate Confinement regime was abandoned in 1913, inmates spent considerable time in the yard. The guard in the tower not only had to keep watch over hundreds of prisoners but more importantly had to make sure they did not escape. In the 1920s, the warden, a veteran of World War I, imported his military background into ESP by outfitting the new towers with Krag repeating rifles and Thompson submachine guns. The institution and its surveillance apparatus, during the 1950s, took on a more modern— even industrial—veneer. Steel and brick replaced the wooden structure, making it fireproof. Additionally, the towers benefited from bulletproof glass on their trap doors, searchlights, and even toilets: "They were designed to withstand a riot below."

While keeping attention on the physical elements of surveillance, curators address its psychological aspects. However, rather than dwelling on the standard line of panoptic analysis that focuses on those being watched, the exhibit explores the watchers. "Everlasting Alertness . . . " is written in red bold print across the heading of a storyboard. It notes that the guards who manned the towers "found the job demanding in ways they didn't expect." Visitors are asked: "Would You Want This Job?" The very question seems to suggest "no," since we learn that most officers did not want to work in the towers; hence, the job was generally assigned to the rookies. Many of them quit or were fired without ever being reassigned to the cellblock. While stationed in the tower, they had to call their commanding officer every fifteen minutes to "report in" (a reminder that they themselves were subject to monitoring). It was an isolating experience due to not having much direct human contact. A photograph shows a cramped space furnished with a small sink, toilet, and firearms. Their occupational stress was compounded by the realization that they could be tested at any time. Said one tower officer, "I was more restricted than the inmates." Visitors are instructed to press the red button on a video machine to watch interviews with former guards.

The "hands-on" experience extends to the "Tower Cam" that positions tourists in front of a large electronic screen showing the prison yard. A joystick allows them to take the role of the tower guard and move the camera in every direction as well as zoom in on their subjects (see figure 29). With the aid of technology, we experience surveillance from the source of power. Moreover, each component of Bentham's panoptic scheme is evident in the exhibit, namely, economics, geometry, and theology. As discussed in previous chapters, the panopticon was intended to reduce the number of guards needed to provide adequate supervision of the prisoners; in practice, even a single watcher held enormous authority over everyone in his visual field. Of course, that economic advantage was made possible by the circular shape of the panopticon. Similarly, the guard tower at ESP is located in the center of the prison yard. With the joystick, "Tower Cam" re-creates the "pan" (everything) and "optics" (see) by providing 360 degrees of vision. (As a subtle reminder of the significance of the circle, a pure white wooden bench located inside the exhibit is completely round.) Finally, Bentham's notion of the omniscient deity figured prominently in his design of the "ultimate penitentiary." Through continuous, visible, and unverifiable inspection of inmates, Bentham theorized that prisoners would internalize the gaze of the guard, thereby becoming their own self-monitor. By being able to move—and zoom—the camera, visitors are given a unique opportunity to experience that godlike power (see Bentham, 1995, 2008 [1787]; Foucault, 1977, 1996; Smith 2011; Welch 2011d).

Cultural power is activated in other exhibits as well. As described previously, the Clink prison museum invites tourists to actually handle instruments of torture, including the Scavenger's Daughter, the Spanish Boot, and so forth. By doing so, visitors have safe contact with those devices, perhaps even imagining what it might be like to inflict pain and suffering on unwilling subjects. Curators, however, manage the experience by encouraging visitors to "take the role of the other." Recall the spiked collar, a gruesome torture device that cuts into the neck, creating open wounds that get infected

FIGURE 29. The TowerCam giving visitors a "hands-on" experience with panopticism (Eastern State Penitentiary, Philadelphia). © retrowelch 2014

by the lead, resulting in lead poisoning. By way of "organized touching," visitors are invited to feel the weight of the collar and visualize it locked tight around their neck. That form of safe contact gives tourists a tangible experience without feeling its negative consequences. Such distancing is a common phenomenological technique in prison museums (see Brown, 2009; Casey, 2003). Further afield, the notion of distancing is examined in other ways. On display is a long pole known as the "thief catcher," which was used by the "Charlies" (watchmen deputized by King Charles II) in the 1700s and early 1800s. Its length created much needed distance between the Charlies and the criminals, who typically drew knives and swords. While maintaining the theme of danger, the poster explains that the Charlies used their expertise to eradicate menace from society: "A good shot would be at the jugular with the upward point directly under their chin. Now immobilised the thief would be brought to 'The Clink.'" So as to contemporize the narrative, curators engage visitors with the following quiz: "What do modern policemen wear today to protect them from guns and knives?" Not only does that question transport tourists to the present, but in doing so, they are also encouraged to consider the safety of the police.

While prison museums exercise their own brand of cultural power to educate and sensitize visitors to controversial issues (e.g., torture and the death penalty), some go even further to illuminate the role of cultural power in society at large. In Johannesburg, an exhibit at Number Four offers another round of critique on apartheid with respect to culture and social control. A collage of photographs and commentary informs us that in the 1960s, a political vacuum emerged when the South African government crushed the opposition in the wake of the Sharpeville Massacre as well as the banning of such groups as the African National Congress. Filling the void, a youth-driven Black Consciousness movement took hold. Among its luminaries was Steve Bantu Biko, who called for "the decolonialization of black people's minds." A poster quotes statements from Biko's *I Write What I Like* (1978):

At the heart of black consciousness is the realisation by blacks that the most potent weapon in the hands of the oppressor is the mind of the oppressed. If one is free at heart, no man-made chains can bind one to servitude but if one's mind is so manipulated and controlled by the oppressor then there will be nothing the oppressed can do to scare his powerful master . . .

The first step therefore is to make the black man come to himself; to pump back life into his empty shell; to infuse him with pride and dignity, to remind him of his complicity in the crime of allowing himself to be misused and therefore letting evil reign supreme in the country of his birth.

The campaign for Black Consciousness gained considerable momentum in schools, church organizations, and workshops. Biko famously proclaimed: "Whites must be made to realise that they are only human, not superior. Same with blacks. They must be made to realise that they are also human, and not inferior." People took notice, including members of the white establishment. Biko was targeted, banned, and eventually taken into police custody, where he mysteriously died. The minister of justice, Jimmy Kruger, announced to the Nationalist Party Congress that Biko died as a result of a hunger strike, adding sarcastically, "I am not glad and I am not sorry about Mr Biko. His death leaves me cold." Amid swirling accusations that the police murdered Biko, Kruger admitted that Biko in fact died of brain damage. Again, Kruger mocked the inquest: "A man can damage his brain in many ways. I have also felt like banging my head against a brick wall many times, but realising now, with the Biko autopsy, that may be fatal, I haven't done it." Several pictures show Biko, his burial plot, and the headstone that memorializes his death:

Bantu Stephen Biko
Honorary President
Black People's Convention
Born 18–12–1946
Died 12–9-1977
One Azania One Nation

An action photograph shows a huge crowd (of twenty thousand) gathering to mourn. Unsurprisingly, police tried to undermine the cultural pull of Biko's death by installing roadblocks at his funeral—but not with much success. Biko's story resonates not only in South Africa but also globally, in part due to the movie *Cry Freedom* (1987). Adding to his legendary status, Biko is played by the big screen stalwart Denzel Washington.

Indeed, prison museums have the capacity to transmit cultural themes along the lines of national, ethnic, and personal identities. At the Hyde Park Barracks, a unique exhibit leaves some visitors with a sense that they themselves are connected to Australia's penal history. A boldly titled storyboard asks, "WHO DO YOU THINK YOU ARE?" It explains to the readers: "Long after the convict era ended, the stigma attached to having a convict ancestry remained. The 'stain' of convict heritage was something to be hidden rather than celebrated. Whole branches dropped from family trees when they found to contain a convict" (see Hughes, 1986). The poster goes on to mention that the 1970s were a turning point, inviting a new openness in understanding Australia's convict past. Curators emphasize that over the last few decades, "finding a convict in the roots of one's family tree has become a badge of honour ... It is estimated that one in ten Australians has a convict ancestor." A related storyboard reinforces the theme of identity by suggesting: "Ask someone in your family if you have a convict ancestor." A photo of a family reunion (the Smalls) is accompanied by a caption noting that since 1971 the descendants of the First Fleeters gather annually. The museum also encourages tourists to explore a Convict Database in which they can seek their own family origins. By typing surnames into the search engine, visitors can match their family with ships, voyages, and dates of arrival. Through state-of-the-art information technology, that simple interactive exercise streamlines the pull of punishment.

EXIT THROUGH THE GIFT SHOP

Nearing the end of this book, we take a critical look at what has become a staple of the museum industry, namely, the gift shop. Though prison museums are not removed from the commercial forces of tourism, it would be a missed opportunity to depict their stores as run-of-the-mill consumerism. Consider, as just one thick description, the gift shop at Alcatraz, a sprawling series of densely packed rooms. With its neatly arranged objects and images, the space delivers its own museum effect, thereby reinforcing the experience of the previous tour. Much like in the cellblocks, visitors cannot help but notice the bars on the windows while being inundated with a vast range of products, most of which repeat the mantra "escape." The most visible conveyers of that theme are movie posters. While some films are based on actual events, such as *Escape from Alcatraz* (featuring Clint Eastwood), others are wildly fictitious. A B-movie dating back to the 1950s titled *Alcatraz Island: The Prison Fortress All Gangland Dreads!* promotes the story by stating: "When no other jail can hold them—they send them to 'The Rock.'" An image of a gorgeous femme fatale is accompanied by a subplot: "They'd even bust out of Alcatraz to get a dame like her."

The sheer volume of retail is marveling. It is clear that the gift shop has something for everyone, including travelers and tourists, as well as posttourists.

In search of a deeper understanding of the history of incarceration at Alcatraz and the plight of the indigenous people, travelers are drawn to a wide selection of serious books, including *Pow Wow Rising: The National Indian Youth Council and the Origins of Native Activism* and *Restorative Justice: A Bestselling Book by One of the Founders of the Movement.* Similarly, travelers interested in penal architecture might be attracted to the many vintage photographs, most notably, the impressive aerial shots of the Rock.

Tourists, of course, will not be disappointed as they make their way through the mall-like aisles of Alcatraz memorabilia, thereby reinforcing their highly focused visit to the former penitentiary. After spending hours roaming the maximum-security unit and having their picture taken behind bars, they can now add to their tourist wardrobe. Nothing signals "tourist" more effectively than colorful T-shirts and baseball caps. Here tourists can load up on shirts blazoned with clever slogans:

Escape From Alcatraz . . . I Gotta Get Out
Alcatraz on the Rocks
3000 Rooms—All Inside
Your Home Away from Home
A Convict Hilton Hotel
10 Minute Swim from San Francisco, Calif.

So that the tourist can further boast about the trip to Alcatraz, many of the T-shirts feature lettering not only on the front but also on the back:

REGULATION #5
You are entitled to food, clothing,
shelter and medical attention
anything else you get is a privilege.

For those interested in more authentic attire, inmate uniform shirts and caps are also available; however, the fact that they have an Alcatraz insignia clearly shows that they are not really for prisoners but rather for tourists. For post-tourists who treat the entire trip to Alcatraz as a game, they might be amused to find—you guessed it—jigsaw puzzles. With one thousand pieces, the entire family can sit for hours at the dining room table and reminisce about their "day in captivity." (Durkheim would be proud of such solidarity and family unity.)

The point of this commentary is that the gift shop also has cultural power capable of projecting potent messages. From the standpoint of Foucaultian penology, one will notice the wording on the magnets available for purchase:

Regulation #23
If you make GROUNDLESS COMPLAINTS
for the purpose of creating dissatisfaction
and/or stirring up trouble . . . you will be
subject to DISCIPLINARY ACTION

Regulation #30
CELLHOUSE RULES
Loud talking, shouting,
whistling, singing, or
other unnecessary noises
are not permitted

It does not take a lot of imagination to visualize those magnets being placed on the kitchen fridge, thereby delivering firm—albeit humorous—statements on the importance of discipline, order, and good behavior in the home. Similarly, tourists and posttourists alike might laugh aloud at the sight of Alcatraz Soap ($4.95). The packaging reads, "Shower Reg. #29: You are expected to bathe in a reasonable length of time." Chuckling is likely to morph into nervous laughter about prison rape and the fear of dropping the soap in the shower. A comforting reminder that "your purchase supports the parks," however, offsets that tension. Indeed, there are multiple calls for "doing good." The gift shop does not simply engage visitors with crass consumption; there remains a not so subtle attempt to enlist them into the altruistic campaign to preserve Alcatraz as a national treasure. A poster is boldly titled:

BUY A ROCK, SAVE THE ROCK

Alcatraz is undergoing a major renovation, including stabilization of the historic cellhouse, that will preserve the island's history for future generations. This work will generate several tons of rubble—demolition debris—considered to be the unavoidable by-product of preservation. Most of it must be removed from the island, and you can help.

Save the rock by purchasing a piece of its history. This will keep it out of local landfills and will also help defray some of the costs of this multi-year restoration project. The ongoing story of repair, replacement, and preservation on Alcatraz island continues.

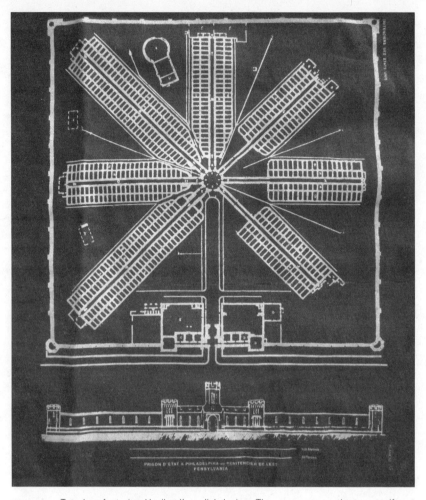

FIGURE 30. Tote bag featuring Haviland's radial design. These are among the smart gifts at Eastern State Penitentiary (Philadelphia). © retrowelch 2014

This plea for help suggests that a purchased rock will not become another meaningless "pet rock." Rather, it serves to symbolically connect the visitor to Alcatraz. Likewise, other gift shops, such as those at Eastern State Penitentiary, Robben Island, and Seodaemun Prison, also strive to promote prison museums as important heritage sites without airbrushing their controversial pasts. Of course, the preservation of former prisons would not be possible without visitors—whether they be travelers, tourists, or posttourists (see figure 30).

CLOSING THOUGHTS

As Foucault (1977) noted, early prisons were open to the public with the aim of displaying and diffusing the emerging sciences of penology. Moreover, such modern thinking, according to a Durkheimian perspective, was "an imaginative innovation whose evolution responds to the deep cultural imperative for order" (Smith, 2008: 89). However, just as prisons have strived to purify their inmates, so too have they struggled to cleanse themselves, since there has always been something shameful about incarceration. Even during the late Victorian period, prisons were blamed for declining property values; but it seems that such an undesirable landmark delivered a blow to the real estate markets through symbolic contagion rather than any rational assessment of danger (Pratt, 2002; Smith, 2008). Nonetheless, the public has retained its curiosity about the prison, as represented in the media and, of course, penal tourism, an experience that gives people safe contact with forbidden spaces.

While each of the ten museums examined in this project tells a unique story about the role of the prison within its own culture and history, there remains a unifying theme. Despite all the political and financial investment toward making modern prisons "work," they ultimately concede to failure. That pattern is remarkable across time and cultures. Former prisons are ruins, evidence of the death of an institution as well as its ambition. Prison museums, however, bring those abandoned places back to life. Although shells of their former selves, prison museums benefit from their sited-ness in ways that prompt us to reflect on punishment—past and present. With all the evidence staring us in the face regarding the failure (or at least severe limitations) of incarceration, prisons persist as conspicuous cogs in the larger machinery of punishment. From that standpoint, penal tourism is hardly cathartic, since visitors are likely to leave the exhibit pondering the postmodern futility—and inhumanity—of imprisonment.

REFERENCES

Akerstrom, M. 1986 "Outcasts in Prison: The Cases of Informers and Sex Offenders." *Deviant Behavior* 7:1–12.

Alexander, J. 2005 "The Inner Development of Durkheim's Sociological Theory." In *The Cambridge Companion to Durkheim,* edited by J. Alexander and P. Smith, 136–59. New York: Cambridge University Press.

Alford, C. F. 2000. "What Would It Matter if Everything Foucault Said about Prisons Was Wrong?" *Theory and Society* 29:125–46.

Alpers, S. 1991. "The Museum as a Way of Seeing." In *Exhibiting Cultures: The Poetics and Politics of Museum Display,* edited by I. Karp and S. Lavine, 25–32. Washington: Smithsonian Institution Press.

Alpert, H. 1939. *Emile Durkheim and His Sociology.* New York: Columbia University Press.

Andermann, J. 2012. "Returning to the Site of Horror." *Theory, Culture & Society* 29 (1): 76–98.

Andermann, J., and S. Arnold-de Simine. 2012. "Introduction: Memory, Community and the New Museum." *Theory, Culture & Society* 29 (1): 1–13.

Anonymous. 1701. *Hanging Is Not Enough.* London: Longman.

Archambeault, W. 2003. "Soar Like an Eagle, Dive Like a Loon: Human Diversity and Social Justice in the Native American Prison Experience." In *Convict Criminology,* edited by J. I. Ross and S. Richards. Belmont, CA: Wadsworth.

Argentine Prison Museum n.d. Brochure: English version.

Arnold, K. 2006. *Cabinets for the Curious.* Dartmouth: Ashgate.

Arnold-de Simine, S. 2012. "Memory Museum and Museum Text." *Theory, Culture & Society* 29 (1): 14–35.

Assmann, A. 2004. "Four Formats of Memory." In *The Fragile Tradition: The German Cultural Imagination since 1500.* Vol. 1, *Cultural Memory and Historical Consciousness,* edited by C. Emden and D. Midgley, 19–37. Oxford: Peter Lang.

———. 2006. "Memory, Individual and Collective." In *The Oxford Handbook of Contextual Political Analysis,* edited by R. E. Goodin and C. Tilly, 210–24. Oxford: Oxford University Press.

Barnes, H., and N. Teeters. 1946. *New Horizons in Criminology*. 3rd ed. New York: Prentice-Hall.

Bataille, G. 1973. *Oeuvres Completes*. Paris: Gallimard.

———. 1986. *Erotism: Death and Sensuality*. Translated by Mary Dalwood. San Francisco: City Light.

Baudrillard, J. 1983. *Simulations*. New York: Semiotext(e).

———. 1994. *Simulacra and Simulation: The Body in Theory*. Ann Arbor: University of Michigan Press.

Beaumont, G., and A. de Tocqueville. 1964 (1833). *On the Penitentiary System in the United States*. Philadelphia: Carey, Lea, and Blanchard.

Becker, P. 2007. "The Criminologists' Gaze at the Underworld." In *Criminals and Their Scientists*, edited by P. Becker and R. Wetzell, 105–33. New York: Cambridge University Press.

Becker, P., and R. Wetzell. 2007. *Criminals and Their Scientists*. New York: Cambridge University Press.

Beidelman, T. O. 1974. *W. Robertson Smith and the Sociological Study of Religion*. Chicago: University of Chicago Press.

Bellah, R. 1967. "Civil Religion in America." *Daedalus* 117 (3): 97–118.

———. 2005. "Durkheim and Ritual." In *The Cambridge Companion to Durkheim*, edited by J. Alexander and P. Smith, 183–210. New York: Cambridge University Press.

Bender, John. 1987. *Imagining the Penitentiary: Fiction and the Architecture of the Mind in Eighteenth-Century England*. Chicago: University of Chicago Press.

Bennett, T. 1995. *The Birth of the Museum: History, Theory, Politics*. London: Routledge.

———. 1998. "Speaking to the Eyes: Museums, Legibility, and the Social Order." In *The Politics of Display: Museums, Science, Culture*, edited by S. Macdonald, 25–35. London: Routledge.

Bentham, J. 1995. *The Panopticon Writings*. Edited by M. Bozovic. New York: Verso.

———. 2008 (1787). *Panopticon; or, The Inspection-House*. London: Dodo Press.

Biko, S. 1978. *I Write What I Like*. Chicago: University of Chicago Press.

Blondel, J. F. 1771–77. *Cours d'Architecture*. 6 vols. Paris: Desaint.

Bosworth, M., and J. Flavin. 2007. *Race, Gender and Punishment: From Colonialism to the War on Terror*. New Brunswick, NJ: Rutgers University Press.

Bouwer, C., and D. J. Stein. 1997. "Association of Panic Disorder with a History of Traumatic Suffocation." *American Journal of Psychiatry* 154:1566–79.

Brown, M. 2009. *The Culture of Punishment*. New York: New York University Press.

Brown, T. 2004. "Trauma, Museums and the Future of Pedagogy." *Third Text* 18 (4): 247–59.

Bruggeman, S. 2012. "Reforming the Carceral Past: Eastern State Penitentiary and the Challenge of the Twenty-First Century Prison Museum." *Radical History Review* 113:171–86.

Bryson, N. 1988 "The Gaze in the Expanded Field." In *Vision and Visuality*, edited by H. Foster, 87–108. Seattle: Bay Press.

Buckingham, J. S. 1849 *National Evils and Practical Remedies, with the Plan for a Model Town*. London. Facsimile edition by Augustus M. Kelley, Clifton, 1973.

Burke, P. 1989. "History as Social Memory." In *Memory, History, Culture and the Mind*, edited by in T. Butler, 97–113. Oxford: Blackwell.

Burkhart, A., and S. Medlik. 1981. *Tourism, Past, Present and Future*. London: Heinemann.

Caimari, L. 1997. "Whose Criminals Are These? Church, State and *Patronatos* and the Rehabilitation of Female Convicts (Buenos Aires, 1890–1940)." *Americas* 54 (2): 185–208.

———. 2001. "Remembering Freedom: Life as Seen from the Prison Cell (Buenos Aires Province, 1930–1950)." In *Crime and Punishment in Latin America*, edited by R. Salvatore, C. Aguirre, and G. Joseph, 391–414. Durham: Duke University Press.

———. 2004. *Apenas un Delincuente: Crimen, Castigo y Cultura en la Argentina, 1880–1955*. Buenos Aires: Siglo Veintiuno.

Cameron, D. 1972. "The Museum: A Temple or the Forum." *Journal of World History* 14 (1): 197–201.

Carrabine, E. 2000. "Discourse, Governmentality and Translation: Towards a Social Theory of Imprisonment." *Theoretical Criminology* 4 (3): 309–31.

———. 2004. *Power, Discourse and Resistance: A Genealogy of the Strangeways Prison Riot*. Dartmouth: Ashgate.

———. 2012. "Just Images: Aesthetics, Ethics and Visual Criminology." *British Journal of Criminology* 52:463–89.

Carroll, J. 1980. *Sceptical Sociology*. London: Routledge & Kegan Paul.

Casella, E., and C. Fredericksen. 2004. "Legacy of the Fatal Shore: The Heritage and Archaeology of Confinement in Post-Colonial Australia." *Journal of Social Archaeology* 4 (1): 100–125.

Casey, V. 2003. "The Museum Effect: Gazing from Object to Performance in the Contemporary Cultural-Historical Museum." *Archives and Museum Informatics, Europe: Cultural Institutions and Digital Technology* (conference proceedings). Paris: Ecole du Louvre, September 8–12.

Certeau, M. de. 1984. *The Practice of Everyday Life*. Translated by Steven Randall. Berkeley: University of California Press.

Civil Liberties. 1990. "Red Tags for Gays Scrapped." *Civil Liberties* 369:7.

Claassen, J. 2010. *Remembering South Africa*. Cape Town: Struik Travel & Heritage.

Cohen, S. 1985. *Visions of Social Control*. Cambridge: Polity.

———. 2001. *States of Denial*. Cambridge: Polity.

Cohen, S., and L. Taylor. 1976. *Escape Attempts: The Theory and Practice of Resistance to Everyday Life*. London: Hammondsworth.

Colbung, K. 1979. "On Being Aboriginal: A Personal Statement." In *Aborigines of the West: Their Past and Present*, edited by R. Berndt and C. Berndt, 100–105. Perth: University of Western Australia Press.

Cole, D. 2001. *No Equal Justice*. New York: New Press.

Cole, H. 1884. *Fifty Years of Public Work of Sir Henry Cole, K. C. B., Accounted for in His Deeds, Speeches and Writings.* 2 vols. London: George Bell & Sons.

Cole, S. 2001. *Suspect Identities.* Cambridge, MA: Harvard University Press.

Colombo, G. 2000. *La Scienza Infelici: Il Museo di Anthropologia Criminale di Cesare Lombroso.* Turin: Bollati Boringhieri.

Constitution Hill. n.d. Visitors Brochure.

Coombes, A. 2000. "The Art of Memory." *Third Text* 52:45–52.

———. 2003. *History after Apartheid.* Durham: Duke University Press.

Cooper, C., J. Fletcher, D. Gilbert, and S. Wanhill. 1993. *Tourism Principles and Practice.* London: Pitman.

Coser, L. 1977. *Masters of Sociological Thought.* New York: Harcourt Brace Jovanovich.

Creazzo, G. 2007. *El Positivismo Criminológico Italiano en la Argentina.* Buenos Aires: Ediar.

Crimp, D. 1993. *On the Museum's Ruins.* Cambridge, MA: MIT Press.

Cullen, F. T., and P. Gendreau. 1989. "The Effectiveness of Correctional Rehabilitation." In *The American Prison: Issues in Research and Policy,* edited by L. Goodstein and D. L. MacKenzie. New York: Plenum.

Dekel, I. 2013. *Mediation at the Holocaust Memorial in Berlin.* London: Palgrave Macmillan.

Del Olmo, R. 1981. *América Latina y su Criminología.* Mexico City: Siglo XXI Editores.

———. 1992. *Criminología Argentina: Apuntes para su Reconstrucción Histórica.* Depalma: Buenos Aires.

———. 1999. "The Development of Criminology in Latin America." *Social Justice* 26 (2): 19–45.

Dewar, M., and C. Fredericksen. 2003. "Prison Heritage, Public History and Archaeology at Fannie Bay Gaol, Northern Australia." *International Journal of Heritage Studies* 9 (1): 45–63.

Dickens, C. 1842. *American Notes for General Circulation.* London: Chapman and Hall.

Dolan, F. X. 2007. *Eastern State Penitentiary.* Charleston, SC: Arcadia.

Douglas, M. 1966. *Purity and Danger.* London: Routledge, Kegan Paul.

Duncan, M. G. 1996. *Romantic Outlaws and Beloved Prisons.* New York: New York University Press.

Dunn, R., and M. Dunn. 1982. *The Papers of William Penn.* Vol. 2, *1680–1684.* Philadelphia: University of Pennsylvania Press.

Durkheim, E. 1958 (1895). *The Rules of Sociological Method.* Translated by S. A. Soloway and J. H. Mueller. Glencoe, IL: Free Press.

———. 1961. *Moral Education.* New York: Free Press.

———. 1983. "The Evolution of Punishment." In *Durkheim and the Law,* edited by S. Lukes and A. Scull, 102–32. London: Palgrave Macmillan.

———. 2008 (1915). *The Elementary Forms of the Religious Life.* Translated by C. Cosman. New York: Oxford University Press.

———. 2012 (1933). *Division of Labor in Society*. Translated by G. Simpson. Mansfield Centre, CT: Martino.

Durkheim, E., and M. Mauss. 1963 (1903). *Primitive Classification*. Translated by R. Needham. Chicago: University of Chicago Press.

Dussel, E. 1995. *The Invention of the Americas: Eclipse of "the Other" and the Myth of Modernity*. New York: Continuum.

Dwight, L. 1826. *First Annual Report*. Boston: Boston Prison Discipline Society.

Eagle, A. F. 1992. *Alcatraz! Alcatraz! The Indian Occupation of 1969–1971*. Berkeley: Heyday.

Eitner, L. 1978. "Cages, Prisoners, and Captives in Eighteenth-Century Art." In *Images of Romanticism: Verbal and Visual Affinities*, edited K. Kroeber and W. Walling. New Haven: Yale University Press.

Elias, N. 2005. *The Civilizing Process*. Oxford: Blackwell.

Engelhardt, I. 2002. *A Topography of Memory*. Brussels: Peter Lang.

Ernst, W. 2000. "Archi(ve)textures of Museology." In *Museums and Memory*, edited by S. Crane, 17–34. Stanford: Stanford University Press.

Esslinger, M. 2003. *Alcatraz: A Definitive History of the Penitentiary Years*. Carmel, CA: Ocean View.

Evans, Robin. 1982. *The Fabrication of Virtue*. Cambridge: Cambridge University Press.

Feitlowitz, M. 1998. *A Lexicon of Terror: Argentina and the Legacies of Torture*. New York: Oxford University Press.

Feldmen, Allen. 2003. "Political Terror and the Technologies of Memory." *Radical History Review* 85:58–73.

Ferrell, J., K. Hayward, W. Morrison, and M. Presdee. 2004. *Cultural Criminology Unleashed*. London: Glasshouse.

Ferrell, J., and M. Hamm. 1998. *Ethnography at the Edge*. Boston: Northeastern University Press.

Finnane, M. 1997. *Punishment in Australian Society*. Oxford: Oxford University Press.

Flower, W. H. 1898. *Essays on Museums and Other Subjects Connected with Natural History*. London: Macmillan.

Foucault, M. 1965. *Madness and Civilization*. Translated by Richard Howard. New York: Random House.

———. 1973. *The Birth of the Clinic*. London: Tavistock.

———. 1975. *Pierre Riviere, Having Slaughtered My Mother, My Sister, and My Brother: A Case of Parricide in the 19th Century*. Translated by Frank Jellinek. New York: Pantheon.

———. 1977. *Discipline and Punish*. New York: Vintage.

———. 1977 (1963). "A Preface to Transgression." In *Language, Counter-Memory, Practice,* edited by Donald Bouchard. Ithaca: Cornell University Press. Reprinted and translated from the original published in *Critique* (1963): 751–70.

———. 1978. *The History of Sexuality*. Vol. 1, *The Will to Knowledge*. Translated by Robert Hurley. London: Penguin.

———. 1980a. *Power/Knowledge*. Edited by C. Gordon. New York: Pantheon.

———. 1980b. "Prison Talk." In *Power/Knowledge,* edited by C. Gordon. New York: Pantheon.

———. 1986a. "Of Other Spaces." *Diacritics* 16 (1): 22–27.

———. 1986b. *The History of Sexuality.* Vol. 3, *The Care of the Self.* New York: Pantheon.

———. 1988. "The Dangerous Individual." In *Politics, Philosophy, Culture: Interviews and Other Writings, 1977–1984,* edited by L. D. Kritzman. London: Routledge.

———. 1991. "Governmentality." In *The Foucault Effect: Studies of Governmentality,* edited by G. Burchell, C. Gordon, and P. Miller. Chicago: University of Chicago Press.

———. 1996. "The Eye of Power." In *Foucault Live: Collected Interviews, 1961–1984,* edited by S. Lotringer, 226–40. New York: Semiotext(e).

———. 2003. *Society Must Be Defended: Lectures at the College de France, 1975–76.* Translated by D. Macey. New York: Palgrave Macmillan.

———. 2008. *The Birth of Biopolitics: Lectures at the College de France, 1978–79.* Edited by M. Senellart. Translated by G. Burchell. New York: Palgrave Macmillan.

———. 2009. "Alternatives to the Prison: Dissemination or Decline of Social Control." *Theory, Culture, & Society* 26 (6): 12–24.

Fried, M. 1980 *Absorption and Theatricality.* Berkeley: University of California Press.

Frommer's. 2009. *Melbourne: Day by Day.* Melbourne: Wiley.

Garland, D. 1990. *Punishment and Modern Society: A Study in Social Theory.* Chicago: University of Chicago Press.

———. 2005. "Penal Excess and Surplus Meaning." *Law & Society Review* 39:793–834.

———. 2006. "Concepts of Culture in the Sociology of Punishment." *Theoretical Criminology* 10 (4): 419–47.

———. 2009. "A Culturalist Theory of Punishment." *Punishment & Society* 11 (2): 259–68.

Garuba, H. 2007. "A Second Life: Museums, Mimesis, and the Narratives of the Tour Guides of Robben Island." In *Desire Lines: Space, Memory and Identity the Post-Apartheid City,* edited by N. Murray, N. Shepherd, and M. Hall, 129–44. London: Routledge.

Geertz, C. 2000 (1973). *The Interpretation of Cultures.* London: Hutchinson.

Gelder, K., and J. Jacobs. 1998. *Uncanny Australia: Sacredness and Identity in a Post-Colonial Nation.* Melbourne: University of Melbourne Press.

Godfrey, B., and D. Cox. 2008. "'The Last Fleet': Crime, Reformation, and Punishment in Western Australia after 1868." *Australian and New Zealand Journal of Criminology* 41 (2): 236–58.

Goffman, E. 1963. *Stigma.* Englewood Cliffs, NJ: Prentice-Hall.

———. 1967. *Interaction Ritual.* Chicago: Aldine.

Golden Gate National Parks Conservancy. 1996. *Discover Alcatraz: A Tour of the Rock*. San Francisco: Golden Gate National Parks Conservancy.

———. 1997. *Discover Alcatraz Escapes: A Tour of the Attempts*. San Francisco: Golden Gate National Parks Conservancy.

Goode, G. B. 1895. *The Principles of Museum Administration*. York: Coultas & Volans.

Goodman, D. 1990. "Fear of Circuses: Founding of the National Museum of Victoria." *Continuum* 3 (1): 19–39.

Goodwin, J. 1963. *Alcatraz: 1863–1963*. Garden City, NY: Doubleday.

Greenberg, D. F., and D. Humphries. 1980. "The Co-Option of Fixed Sentencing Reform." *Crime and Delinquency* 26:206–25.

Greenberg, D., and V. West. 2001. "State Prison Populations and their Growth, 1971–1991." *Criminology* 39 (3): 615–54.

Greenwood, T. 1888. *Museums and Art Galleries*. London: Simpkin, Marshall.

Gregory, D. 2004. *The Colonial Present*. Oxford: Blackwell.

Guy, D. 1990. *Sex and Danger in Buenos Aires: Prostitution, Family, and Nation in Argentina*. Lincoln: University of Nebraska Press.

———. 2001. "Girls in Prison: The Role of the Buenos Aires Casa Correccional de Mujeres as an Institution for Child Rescue, 1880–1940." In *Crime and Punishment in Latin America,* edited by R. D. Salvatore, C. Aguirre, and G. Joseph, 369–90. Durham: Duke University Press.

Halbwachs, M. 1992. *On Collective Memory*. Chicago: University of Chicago Press.

Hall, B. 1829. *Travels in North America in the Years 1827–1828*. Edinburgh.

Harcourt, B. 2007. *Against Prediction: Profiling, Policing, and Punishing in an Actuarial Age*. Chicago: University of Chicago Press.

Harkin, M. 1998. "Durkheim, Emile." In *Encyclopedia of Semiotics,* edited by P. Bouissac, 205–7. New York: Oxford University Press.

Harvey, D. 1990. *The Condition of Postmodernity*. Oxford: Blackwell.

Haviland, J. 1821. "Explanation of a Design for a Penitentiary, July 2: Daybook I." *Haviland Papers*.

Hayward, K. 2012. "Five Spaces of Cultural Criminology." *British Journal of Criminology* 52:411–62.

Hayward, K., and J. Young. 2004. "Cultural Criminology: Some Notes on the Script." *Theoretical Criminology* 8 (3): 259–74.

Hertz, R. 1960. *Death and the Right Hand*. Translated by Rod Neeham and Claudia Neeham. Glencoe, IL: Free Press.

Hill, F. 1853. *Crime: Its Amount, Causes, and Remedies*. London: John Murray.

Hirst, J. 2008. "An Oddity from the Start." *Monthly* 36 (July): 1–9.

Historic Houses Trust. n.d. a *Hyde Park Barracks Museum* [brochure]. Sydney: Historic Houses Trust.

———. n.d. b. *Convict Sydney* [promotional card]. Sydney: Historic Houses Trust.

Howard, D. L. 1958. *John Howard: Prison Reformer*. New York: Archer House.

Howard, J. 1929 (1777). *State of Prisons*. New York: E. P. Dutton.

———. 1973 (1787). *Prisons and Lazarettos*. Glen Ridge, NJ: Patterson Smith.

————. 2012. *The State of the Prisons in England and Wales.* Memphis, TN: General Books.

Hubbard, W. 1987. "A Meaning for Monuments." In *The Public Face of Architecture: Civic Culture and Public Space,* edited by N. Glazer and M. Lilla. New York: Free Press.

Hubert, H. 2004. "Introduction to Daniel Chantepie de la Saussaye." In *Manuel d'Histoire des Religions,* translated by Henri Hubert. Paris: Armand Colin.

Huey, L. 2011. "Crime behind the Glass: Exploring the Sublime in Crime at the Vienna Kriminalmuseum." *Theoretical Criminology* 15 (4): 382–99.

Hughes, R. 1986. *The Fatal Shore: The Epic of Australia's Founding.* New York: Knopf.

Hurley, K. 1996. *The Gothic Body.* Cambridge: Cambridge University Press.

Huyssen, A. 1995. *Twilight Memories: Marking Time in a Culture of Amnesia.* New York: Routledge.

Ignatieff, M. 1978. *A Just Measure of Pain.* New York: Pantheon.

Impey, O., and A. MacGregor, eds. 2001. *The Origins of Museums: The Cabinet of Curiosities in Sixteenth- and Seventeenth-Century Europe.* 2nd ed. Cornwall, UK: House of Stratus.

Irwin, J. 1985. *The Jail.* Berkeley: University of California Press.

Jacobs, J. M. 1996. "Urban Dreamings the Aboriginal Sacred in the City." In *Edge of Empire Postcolonialism and the City,* edited by J. Jacobs, 103–31. London: Routledge, London.

James, D. 1994. *Resistance and Integration: Peronism and the Argentine Working Class, 1946–1979.* New York: Cambridge University Press.

Johnston, N. 1958. *The Development of the Radial Prisons: A Case Study in Cultural Diffusion.* Ph.D. dissertation. University of Pennsylvania.

————. 1978. *The Human Cage: A Brief History of Prison Architecture.* New York: Walker.

————. 2000. *Forms of Constraint: A History of Prison Architecture.* Urbana: University of Illinois Press.

————. 2010. *Eastern State Penitentiary: Crucible of Good Intentions.* Philadelphia: Philadelphia Museum of Art.

Kahan, P. 2011. *Eastern State Penitentiary: A History.* Charleston, SC: History Press.

Kann, M. 2005. *Punishment, Prisons, and Patriarchy.* New York: New York University Press.

Karp, I., and S. Lavine. 1991. *Exhibiting Cultures: The Poetics and Politics of Museum Display.* Washington, DC: Smithsonian Institution Press.

Katz, J. 1988. *Seductions of Crime.* New York: Basic Books.

Kaufman, E. 1955. *Architecture in the Age of Reason.* Cambridge, MA: Harvard University Press.

Kenneally, C. 2011. "A Hero's Legend and a Stolen Skull Rustle Up a DNA Drama." *New York Times,* August 31, www.nytimes.com/2011/09/06/science/06kelly.html?_r = 0.

Key, A. 1973. *Beyond Four Walls.* Toronto: McClelland & Stewart.

Kirshenblatt-Gimblett, B. 1988. *Destination Culture.* Berkeley: University of California Press.

Knowles, D. 1963. *Monastic Orders in England.* Cambridge: Cambridge University Press.

Kratz, C. 2011. "Rhetorics of Value." *Visual Anthropology Review* 27 (1): 21–48.

Lacan, J. 1978. "What Is a Picture?" In *The Four Fundamental Concepts of Psychoanalysis,* edited by J. Miller, 79–90. New York: W. W. Norton.

Lake Snell Perry & Associates. 2001. *Americans Identify A Source of Information They Can Really Trust.* Washington, DC: American Association of Museums.

Lawrence, P. 2012. "History, Criminology and the 'Use' of the Past." *Theoretical Criminology* 16 (3): 313–28.

Leader, D. 2003. *Stealing the Mona Lisa.* New York: Counterpoint Press.

Lennon, J., and M. Foley. 2010. *Dark Tourism: The Attraction of Death and Disaster.* Andover, UK: Cengage Learning.

Levi-Strauss, C. 1955. *Tristes Tropiques.* New York: Penguin.

Lewis, O. F. 1967 (1922). *The Development of American Prison Customs, 1776–1845.* Montclair, NJ: Patterson Smith.

Lewis, W. D. 1965. *From Newgate to Dannemora.* Ithaca: Cornell University Press.

Lipton, D., R. M. Martinson, and J. Wilks. 1975. *The Effectiveness of Correctional Treatment.* New York: Praeger.

Loftus, E. 1995. "The Reality of Illusory Memories." In *Memory Distortions,* edited by D. L. Schacter, 47–68. Cambridge, MA: Harvard University Press.

Lombroso, C. 1911. "Il Mio Museo Criminale." *L'illustrazione Italiana* (Lombroso Archive).

———. 2006. *Criminal Man.* Translated by M. Gibson and N. H. Rafter. Durham: Duke University Press.

Lombroso, C., and G. Ferrero. 2004. *Criminal Woman, the Prostitute, and the Normal Woman.* Translated by N. H. Rafter and M. Gibson. Durham: Duke University Press.

Lonely Planet. 2005. *Argentina.* Oakland, CA: Lonely Planet.

Loo, T., and C. Strange. 2000. "'Rock Prison of Liberation': Alcatraz Island and the American Imagination." *Radical History Review* 78:27–56.

Lukes, S. 1975. *Emile Durkheim: His Life and Work.* New York: Peregrine.

Lukes, S., and A. Scull. 1983. *Durkheim and the Law.* London: Palgrave Macmillan.

Lynch, M. J. 2000. "The Power of Oppression." *Critical Criminology* 9 (1–2): 144–52.

Lyon, D. 1991. "Bentham's Panopticism: From Moral Architecture to Electronic Surveillance." *Queens Quarterly* 98 (3): 596–617.

Mabillon, D. J. 1724. *Reflexions sur les Prisons des Orders Religieux.* Vol. 2, *Overages posthumes.* Paris.

Macdonald, S. 1998. "Introduction." In *Theorizing Museum,* edited by S. Macdonald and G. Fyfe, 1–18. Oxford: Blackwell.

Macey, D. 1993. *The Lives of Michel Foucault.* New York: Vintage.

Malraux, A. 1967. *Museum without Walls.* Garden City, NY: Doubleday.

Mandela, N. 1994. *Long Walk to Freedom.* London: Little, Brown.

Mandeville, B. 1725. *An Inquiry into the Causes of the Frequent Executions at Tyburn.* London: J. Roberts.

Manfredo, T. 1976. *Architecture and Utopia: Design and Capitalist Development.* Cambridge, MA: MIT Press.

Marlow, L. 2009. *Mothers in Prison.* Saarbrucken, Germany: VDM Verlag.

Martini, J. 1990. *Fortress Alcatraz.* Kailua, HI: Pacific Monograph.

Martinson, R. 1974. "'What Works?' Questions and Answers about Prison Reform." *Public Interest* 35:22–54.

Mauss, M. 1979. "L'Oeuvre de Marcel Mauss par Lui-Meme." Reprinted in *Revue Francaise de Sociologie* 20:214–18.

Mbeki, G. 1991. *Learning from Robben Island.* Cape Town: David Philip.

McAtackney, L. 2013. "Dealing with Difficult Pasts: The Dark Heritage of Political Prisons in Transitional Northern Ireland and South Africa." *Prison Service Journal* 210:17–23.

———. 2014. *An Archaeology of the Troubles: The Dark Heritage of Long Kesh/Maze Prison.* Oxford: Oxford University Press.

McElwee, T. B. 1835. *A Concise History of the Eastern Penitentiary of Pennsylvania.* Philadelphia: Neall and Massey.

McHugh, P. 2007. *Alcatraz: The Official Guide.* San Francisco: Golden Gate National Parks Conservancy.

McLennan, R. 2008. *The Crisis of Imprisonment: Protest.* Cambridge: Cambridge University Press.

McLeod, S. 2005. *Reshaping Museum Space.* London: Routledge.

McManus, P. 1989. "Oh, Yes, They Do: How Museum Visitors Read Labels and Interact with Exhibit Texts." *Curator* 32 (3): 174–89.

Melossi, D. 2001. "The Cultural Embeddedness of Social Control." *Theoretical Criminology* 5 (4): 403–24.

Melossi, D., and M. Pavarani. 1981. *The Prison and the Factory.* Totowa, NJ: Barnes and Noble.

Melossi, D., M. Sozzo, and R. Sparks. 2011. *Travels of the Criminal Question: Cultural Embeddedness and Diffusion.* Oxford: Hart.

Meranze, M. 1996. *Laboratories of Virtue: Punishment, Revolution, and Authority in Philadelphia, 1760–1835.* Chapel Hill: University of North Carolina.

Miller, E. 1974. *That Noble Cabinet.* Athens: Ohio University Press.

Murray, David. 1904. *Museums: Their History and Their Use.* Glasgow: James MacLehose & Sons.

National Trust. n.d. *Old Melbourne Gaol: Crime & Justice Experience.* Visitors Guide. Melbourne: National Trust.

New York Times. 1989. "Pink Bracelets for Homosexuality Florida Jail Are Challenged." December 3, 35.

Nielson, M. 2000. "Stolen Lands, Stolen Lives: Native Americans in Criminal Justice." In *Investigating Differences: Human and Cultural Relations in Criminal*

Justice, edited by Criminal Justice Collective of Northern Arizona University, 47–58. Boston: Allyn and Bacon.

Nora, P. 1989. "Between Memory and History: Les Lieux de Memoire." *Representations,* 26:7–24.

———. 2002. "The Reasons for the Current Upsurge in Memory." *Tr@nsit-Virtuelles Forum* 22.

Norden, P. 2010. "Ned Kelly, John Barry and the Role of Social Activism on Criminal Justice Reform." John Barry Memorial Lecture. University of Melbourne. November 11.

Norris, R. 1985. "Prison Reformers and Penitential Publicists in France, England, and the United States." PhD diss., American University, Washington, DC.

Old Melbourne Gaol: Crime and Justice Experience. n.d. brochure.

Olsen, D. R., et al. 2006. "Prevalent Pain and Pain Level among Torture Survivors." *Danish Medical Bulletin* 53:210–14.

O'Malley, P. 1979. "Class Conflict, Land and Social Banditry: Bushranging in Nineteenth Century Australia." *Social Problems* 26 (3): 271–83.

Parenti, C. 2004. *The Soft Cage: Surveillance in America from Slavery to the War on Terror.* New York: Basic Books.

Pearson, N. 1982. *The State and the Visual Arts.* Milton Keys, UK: Open University Press.

Pecoil, V. 2004. "The Museum as Prison: Post Post-Scriptum on Control Societies." *Third Text* 18 (5): 435–47.

Pevsner, N. 1976. *A History of Building Types.* Princeton: Princeton University Press.

Physicians for Human Rights. 2009. *Aiding Torture.* Washington, DC: Physicians for Human Rights.

Piche, J., and K. Walby. 2010. "Problematizing Carceral Tours." *British Journal of Criminology* 50:570–81.

Pickering, W. S. F. 1984. *Durkheim's Sociology of Religion: Themes and Theories.* London: Routledge.

Plant, R. 1986. *The Pink Triangle: The Nazi War on Homosexuals.* New York: Henry Holt.

Pomian, K. 1990. *Collectors and Curiosities.* Cambridge: Polity.

Poultney, T. 2003. *Hangmen, Hunger and Hard Labour: Old Melbourne Gaol.* Melbourne: National Trust of Australia (Victoria).

Powers, G. 1826. *A Brief Account of the Construction, Management and Discipline of the New York State Prison at Auburn.* Auburn, NY: Henry Hall.

Pratt, J. 2002. *Punishment and Civilization.* London: Sage.

Presdee, M. 2001. *Cultural Criminology and the Carnival of Crime.* New York: Routledge.

Pretes, M. 2002. "Mining Mines and Mining Tourists." *Annals of Tourism Research* 29 (2): 439–56.

Preziosi, D. 2003. *Brain of the Earth's Body: Art, Museums and the Phantasms of Modernity.* Minneapolis: University of Minnesota Press.

Prior, N. 2002. *Museums & Modernity*. Oxford: Berg.

Pugh, R. B. 1970. *Imprisonment in Medieval England*. Cambridge: Cambridge University Press.

Rajchman, J. 1988. "Foucault's Art of Seeing." *October* 44:88–117.

Regener, S. 2003. "Criminological Museums and the Visualization of Evil." *Crime, History & Societies* 7 (1): 43–56.

Riley, A. T. 1999. "Whence Durkheim's Nietzschean Grandchildren? A Closer Look at Robert Hertz's Place in the Durkheimain Genealogy." *European Journal of Sociology/Archives Européennes de Sociologie* 40:302–30.

———. 2000. "In Pursuit of the Sacred: The Durkheimian Sociologists of Religion and Their Paths toward the Construction of the Modern Intellectual." PhD diss., University of California, San Diego.

———. 2005. "Renegade Durkheimianism." In *The Cambridge Companion to Durkheim*, edited by J. Alexander and P. Smith, 274–301. New York: Cambridge University Press.

Roberts, M. N. 1994. "Outside/Inside: The Space of Performance." In *In Exhibitionsim*, edited by M. N. Roberts, and S. Vogel, 78–92. New York: Museum for African Art.

Rochefoucauld-Liancourt, F. 1796. *On the Prisons in Philadelphia, by an European*. Philadelphia: Moreau de Saint Mery.

Rodriguez, J. 2004. "South Atlantic Crossings: Fingerprints, Science, and the State in Turn-of-the-Century Argentina." *American Historical Review* 109 (2): 387–416.

———. 2006. *Civilizing Argentina: Science, Medicine, and the Modern State*. Chapel Hill: University of North Carolina Press.

Rodriguez, S. 1944. *La Identificacion Humana: Historia, Sistemas y Legislacion*. La Plata, Argentina: Taller de Impresiones Oficiales.

Rojek, C. 1993. *Ways of Escape*. Basingstoke, UK: Macmillan.

Rosenblum, R. 1968. *Romantic Art in Britain*. Philadelphia: Philadelphia Museum of Art.

Roseneau, H. 1970. *Social Purpose in Architecture*. London: Studio Vista.

Ross, A. 1983. "The Alcatraz Effect: Belief and Postmodernity." *SubStance* 42:71–84.

Ross, J. I. 2012. "Touring Imprisonment: A Descriptive Statistical Analysis of Prison Museums." *Tourism Management Perspectives* 4:113–18.

Rothman, D. 1971. *The Discovery of the Asylum*. Boston: Little, Brown.

Ruggiero, K. 1992. "Honor, Maternity, and the Disciplining of Women: Infanticide in Late Nineteenth-Century Buenos Aires." *Hispanic American Historical Review* 72 (3): 353–73.

———. 2004. *Modernity in the Flesh: Medicine, Law, and Society in Turn-of-the-Century Argentina*. Stanford: Stanford University Press.

Ruibal, B. 1993. *Ideología del Control Social: Buenos Aires, 1880–1920*. Buenos Aires: Centro Editor de América Latina.

Rusche, G., and O. Kirchheimer. 1968 (1939). *Punishment and Social Structure*. New York: Russell and Russell.

Russell, K. 2002. "'Driving while Black': Corollary Phenomena and Collateral Consequences." In *Race, Class, Gender, and Justice in the United States,* edited by C. Reasons, D. Conley, and J. Debro, 191–200. Boston: Allyn & Bacon.

Sabatini, A. 2011. "Museums and New Aesthetic Practices." *Museums & Social Issues,* special issue, *Rethinking Incarceration* 6 (1): 71–79.

Salvatore, R. D. 1992. "Criminology, Prison Reform and the Buenos Aires Working Class, 1900–1920." *Journal of Interdisciplinary History* 23 (2): 279–99.

———. 1996. "Penitentiaries, Visions of Class, and Export Economies: Brazil and Argentina Compared." In *The Birth of the Penitentiary in Latin America,* edited by R. Salvatore and C. Aguirre, 194–223. Austin: University of Texas Press.

———. 2007. "Positivist Criminology and State Formation in Modern Argentina, 1890–1940." In *Criminals and Their Scientists,* edited by P. Becker and R. Wetzell, 253–80. New York: Cambridge University Press.

———. 2010. *Subalternos, Derechos y Justicia Penal.* Barcelona: Gedisa.

Salvatore, R. D., and C. Aguirre. 1996. *The Birth of the Penitentiary in Latin America.* Austin: University of Texas Press.

Salvatore, R. D., C. Aguirre, and G. Joseph, eds. 2001. *Crime and Punishment in Latin America.* Durham. Duke University Press.

Savelsberg, J. J. 2004. "Religion, Historical Contingencies, and Cultures of Punishment." *Law and Social Inquiry* 29 (2): 373–401.

Scarry, E. 1985. *The Body in Pain.* Oxford: Oxford University Press.

Schadeberg, J. 1994. *Voices from Robben Island.* Braamfontein, South Africa: Ravan.

Scicluna, S., and P. Knepper. 2008. "Prisoners of the Sun: The British Empire and Imprisonment in Malta in the Early Nineteenth Century." *British Journal of Criminology* 48:502–21.

Segal, L. 2006. *Number Four: The Making of Constitution Hill.* Johannesburg: Penguin.

Segal, L., and C. van den Berg. 2006. *Mapping Memory: Former Prisoners Tell Their Stories.* Parkwood, South Africa: David Krut.

Sellin, T. 1927. "Dom Jean Mabillon: A Prison Reformer of the Seventeenth Century." *Journal of the American Institute of Criminal Law and Criminology* 17 (4): 581–602.

Selznick, P. 1988. "The Moral Commonwealth." Unpublished manuscript.

Seodaemun Prison History Hall. 2010. *A Place of Independence and Democracy.* Seoul, South Korea: Seodaemun Prison History Hall.

———. n.d. English Version Brochure. Seoul, South Korea: Seodaemun Prison History Hall.

Sewell, W. H., Jr. 1999. "The Concept(s) of Culture." In *Beyond the Cultural Turn,* edited by V. E. Bonnell and L. Hunt, 35–61. Berkeley: University of California Press.

———. 2005. *Logics of History: Social Theory and Social Transformation.* Chicago: University of Chicago Press.

Sharpley, R. 2009. "Shedding Light on Dark Tourism." In *The Darker Side of Travel,* edited by R. Sharpley and P. Stone, 3–22. Bristol: Channel View.

Shearing, C., and M. Kempa. 2004. "A Museum of Hope: A Story of Robben Island." *Annals of the American Academy of Political and Social Science* 592 (1): 62–78.

Sibley, D. 1995. *Geographies of Exclusion: Society and Difference in the West*. London: Routledge.

Simon, J. 2007. *Governing through Crime*. New York: Oxford University Press.

Smeulers, A. 2011. "Editorial." *Newsletter: Criminology and International Crimes* 6 (2): 1–2.

Smith, C. 1997. *Robben Island*. Cape Town, South Africa: Struik.

Smith, G. 2011. *Opening the Black Box: The Everyday Life of Surveillance*. London: Routledge.

Smith, P. 2003a. "Culture and Punishment." Report on a Thematic Session at American Sociology Association Conference, Atlanta, August.

———. 2003b. "Narrating the Guillotine: Punishment Technology as Myth and Symbol." *Theory, Culture & Society* 20 (5): 27–51.

———. 2008. *Punishment and Culture*. Chicago: University of Chicago Press.

Smith, P., and J. Alexander. 2005. "The New Durkheim." In *The Cambridge Companion to Durkheim*, edited by J. Alexander and P. Smith, 1–37. New York: Cambridge University Press.

Sozzo, M. 1998. "Control Sociale e Interseccion Institutional Psiquiatria-Justicia Penal." In *Las Transformationes del Estado y del Derecho Contemporaneos*, edited by E. Bodelon and T.P. Novales, 47–76. Madrid: Aguilar.

———. 2009. *Historias Sobre la Cuestión Criminal*. Buenos Aires: Editores del Puerto.

State Library of Victoria. 2009. *The Changing Face of Victoria*. Melbourne: State Library of Victoria.

Stone, P. 2006. "A Dark Tourism Spectrum: Towards a Typology of Death and Macabre Related Tourist Sites, Attractions, and Exhibitions." *Tourism* 54 (2): 145–60.

Stone, P., and R. Sharpley. 2008. "Consuming Dark Tourism: A Thanatological Perspective." *Annals of Tourism Research* 35 (2): 574–95.

Strange, C., and M. Kempa. 2003. "Shades of Dark Tourism: Alcatraz and Robben Island." *Annals of Tourism Research* 30:386–405.

Stuller, J. 1998. *Alcatraz: The Prison*. San Francisco: Golden Gate National Parks Conservancy.

Sudjic, D. 2006. "Engineering Conflict." *New York Times Magazine*, May 21, 23–33.

Super, G. 2010. "The Spectacle of Crime in the 'New' South Africa: A Historical Perspective, 1976–2004." *British Journal of Criminology* 50:165–84.

———. 2011a. "Punishment and the Body in 'Old' and 'New' South Africa: A Story of Punitivist Humanism." *Theoretical Criminology* 15 (4): 427–44.

———. 2011b. "Like Some Rough Beast Slouching towards Bethlehem to Be Born: A Historical Perspective on the Institution of the Prison in South Africa, 1976–2004." *British Journal of Criminology* 51:201–21.

Sykes, G. 1958. *Society of Captives*. Princeton: Princeton University Press.

Szakolczai, A. 1998. *Max Weber and Michel Foucault: Parallel Life Works*. London: Routledge.

Taylor, A. 2000. "The Sun Always Shines on Perth: A Post-Colonial Geography of Identity, Memory, and Place." *Australian Geographical Studies* 38 (1): 27–35.

Teeters, N. 1970. "The Passing of Cherry Hill." *Prison Journal* 50 (1): 3–12.

Teeters, N., and J. Shearer. 1957. *The Prison at Philadelphia, Cherry Hill*. New York: Columbia University Press.

Tilly, C. 1994. *A Phenomenology of Landscape*. Oxford: Berg.

Turner, V. 1967. *The Forest of Symbols*. Ithaca: Cornell University Press.

Urry, J. 2002. *The Tourist Gaze*. London: Sage.

Vidler, A. 1978. *The Writing on the Walls*. Princeton: Princeton Architectural Press.

Violi, P. 2012. "Trauma Site Museums and Politics of Memory: Tuol Sleng, Villa Grimaldi and the Bologna Ustica Museum." *Theory, Culture & Society* 29 (1): 36–75.

Virilio, P. 1994. *The Vision Machine*. Bloomington: Indiana University Press.

Vogel, S. 1991. "Always True to the Object." In *Exhibiting Cultures: The Poetics and Politics of Museum Display*, edited by I. Karp and S. Lavine, 191–204. Washington, DC: Smithsonian Institution Press.

Walby, K., and J. Piche. 2011. "The Polysemy of Punishment Memorialization: Dark Tourism and Ontario's Penal History Museum." *Punishment & Society* 13 (4): 451–72.

Weber, M. 2002 (1904–5). *The Protestant Work Ethic and the Spirit of Capitalism*. Los Angeles, CA: Roxbury.

Weil, S. 1995. *Cabinet of Curiosities*. Washington, DC: Smithsonian Institution Press.

Welch, M. 2000. *Flag Burning: Moral Panic and the Criminalization of Protest*. New York: de Gruyter.

———. 2005. *Ironies of Imprisonment*. Thousand Oaks, CA: Sage.

———. 2006. *Scapegoats of September 11th: Hate Crimes and State Crimes in the War on Terror*. New Brunswick, NJ: Rutgers University Press.

———. 2007. "Fare l'Impensabile: Genealogia della Tortura Moderna" (Doing the unthinkable: A genealogy of modern torture). *Studi Sulla Questione Criminale* (Faculty of Law, University of Bologna, Italy) 2 (3): 41–64.

———. 2009a. *Crimes of Power & States of Impunity: The U.S. Response to Terror*. New Brunswick, NJ: Rutgers University Press.

———. 2009b. "American Pain-ology in the War on Terror: A Critique of 'Scientific' Torture." *Theoretical Criminology* 13 (4): 451–74.

———. 2009c. "Guantanamo Bay as a Foucauldian Phenomenon: An Analysis of Penal Discourse, Technologies, and Resistance." *Prison Journal* 89 (1): 3–20.

———. 2010a. Review of *The Culture of Punishment: Prison, Society and Spectacle* by Michelle Brown, New York: New York University Press, 2009. *Theoretical Criminology* 14 (2): 242–44.

———. 2010b. "Detained in Occupied Iraq: Deciphering the Narratives for Neocolonial Internment." *Punishment & Society: The International Journal of Penology* 12 (2): 123–46.

————. 2010c. "Pastoral Power as Penal Resistance: Foucault and the Groupe d'Information sur les Prisons." *Punishment & Society: The International Journal of Penology* 12 (1): 47–63.

————. 2011a. "Illusions in Truth Seeking: The Perils of Interrogation and Torture in the War on Terror." *Social Justice: A Journal of Crime, Conflict & World Order* 37 (2–3): 123–48.

————. 2011b. *Corrections: A Critical Approach*. 3rd ed. London: Routledge.

————. 2011c. "Penal Tourism: Exploring Prison Museums in Argentina and Australia." Featured Speaker to The Alpha Upsilon Chapter of Alpha Kappa Delta, Department of Sociology, State University of New York, Utica, March 31.

————. 2011d. "Counterveillance: How Foucault and the Groupe d'Information sur les Prisons Reversed the Optics." *Theoretical Criminology* 15 (3): 301–13.

————. 2012a. "Penal Tourism and the 'Dream of Order': Exhibiting Early Penology in Argentina and Australia." *Punishment & Society: The International Journal of Penology* 14 (5): 584–615.

————. 2012b. "Exploring Penal Tourism in Global Cities: Prison Museums, Culture and Punishment." Seminar at the Centre of Criminology, University of Cape Town, South Africa, July 20.

————. 2013. "Penal Tourism and a Tale of Four Cities: Reflecting on the Museum Effect in London, Sydney, Melbourne, and Buenos Aires." *Criminology and Criminal Justice: An International Journal* 13 (5): 479–505.

————. Forthcoming. *The Bastille Effect: Cultural Representations of Political Imprisonment.*

Welch, M., and M. Macuare. 2011. "Penal Tourism in Argentina: Bridging Foucauldian and Neo-Durkheimian Perspectives." *Theoretical Criminology* 15 (4): 401–25.

Weld, I. 1799. *Travels through the States of North America, and Provinces of Upper and Lower Canada, during Years 1795, 1796, 1797.* London: John Stockdale.

Wellman, G. L. 2008. *A History of Alcatraz Island, 1853–2008.* Charleston, SC: Arcadia.

Williams, P. 2007. *Memorial Museums: The Global Rush to Commemorate Atrocities.* Oxford: Berg.

Wilson, J. 2004. "Dark Tourism and the Celebrity Prisoner: Front and Back Regions in Representations of an Australian Historical Prison." *Journal of Australian Studies* 82 (1): 1–13.

————. 2008a. "Transgressive Deor: Narrative Glimpses in Australian Prisons, 1970s–1990s." *Crime, Media, Culture* 4 (3): 331–48.

————. 2008b. *Prison: Cultural Memory and Dark Tourism.* New York: Peter Lang.

Wilton-Ely, J. 1978. *The Mind and Art of Giovanni Battista Piranesi.* London: Thames & Hudson.

Wollan, M. 2012. "Antigovernment Graffiti Restored, Courtesy of Government," *New York Times,* December 24, www.nytimes.com/2012/12/25/us/alcatraz-american-indian-occupation-graffiti-preserved.html?hp.

Wright, P. 2000. "Cultural Commodification of Prisons." *Social Justice* 27 (3): 15–21.
Young, J. E. 1992. "The Counter-Monument." *Critical Inquiry* 18 (2): 267–96.
Zatz, M., C. C. Lujan, and Z. K. Synder-Joy. 1991. "American Indians and Criminal Justice." In *Race and Criminal Justice,* edited by M. J. Lynch and E. B. Patterson. New York: Harrow and Heston.

INDEX

Indians All Tribes, 212
Ingenieros, Jose, 182–183
Iron Maiden, 41

Jack the Ripper. *See* Deeming, Frederick
Jagger, Mick, 11–12,
Jameson Raid, 214
Jebb, Joshua, 105–106
Jesuits, 55, 58–59, 99, 119

Kelly, Ellen (Quinn), 73–74, 76, 77,
    235–236
Kelly, Ned, 5, 7, 11, 19, 49, 72–77, 134, 185,
    194, 231–235
Kennedy, Robert F., 187
"Kosher Mafia," 127
Kramat (Robben Island), 98–99
Kruger, Jimmy, 258
Kruger, Paul, 95
Kwan, Yoo Sun, 226–227, 230

laborterapia (labor therapy), 154
La Guma, Alex, 216
La Vuelta de Martin Fierro, 13–14, 61,
    241
Libeskind, Daniel, 237
Lily Law, 137
Lin, Maya, 237
Lincoln, Abraham, 94
Lombroso, Cesare 121–123, 168, 181–184
Lynds, Elam, 145

Mabillon, Jean, 99, 101, 116
Macquarie, Lachlan, 64, 195
Makana, Nxele, 86
manacles, 2, 170
Manana, Naphtali, 133
Mandela, Nelson, 30–31, 50, 95, 157–158,
    214–215, 223–226, 239
Mandela, Winnie (Madikizela), 104
Mandeville, Bernard de, 90
Mankiller, Wilma (Cherokee), 211
Marot, Daniel, 90
Martinson, Robert, 187–188
Marx, Karl, 63
Mauss, Michel, 131
Melbourne Gaol (Australia), 5–7, 16–19,
    49, 56, 65–78, 91, 106, 109, 134–135,

165–168, 173, 175–178, 185, 195, 231–235,
    251–253
Melker, Daisey de, 104, 249–250
Melville, George, 134–135
Meranze, Michael, 115, 144, 148
Mhlauli, Yvonne Ntonto, 220, 244–245
microeconomy of perpetual penal power,
    15, 241. *See also* Foucault, Michel
Miller, William, 161, 163–164, 248
"mind on legs," 5, 28, 92, 174, 178, 228, 244
mitzvah, 127
Mnisi, Assienah, 221
Molefe, Mmaguata, 219–220
Molesworth Commission, 13
Mona Lisa, 39
Montague, Chief Justice, 142
Morris, Frank, 30, 85. See also *Escape from
    Alcatraz*
Morris, John, 30, 85. See also *Escape from
    Alcatraz*
Moturu, Sayed (the Prince of Madura), 98
Mullane, Nancy, 135–136

National Penitentiary (Buenos Aires),
    53–54, 69, 70, 107, 120, 152, 160, 184,
    241
Newgate Prison (London), 87
Ngoma, Thoko, 219
Nietzsche, Friedrich, 131
Ninevites, 133
"nothing works." *See* Martinson, Robert
Ntamo, Nolundi, 219

Oakes, Richard (Mohawk), 210, 213
O'Connor, Juan, 159
Olver, Leigh, 234–235
ordeals (trials by), 169
organized touching, 172, 257
organized walking, 5, 171

panopticism, 32, 103–106, 255–256. *See also*
    Bentham, Jeremy
parti-coloured suit, 37, 69
Particulars of Execution, 17–18, 178
pass book, 218–219
Patrinado de Recluidas y Liberadas (PRL),
    123–124
Pearson, Nicholas, 27–28